MY BROTHER'S LETTERS

MY BROTHER'S LETTERS

Sergeant Robert LeRoy Watson USMCR
Combat Cinematographer
World War II

James J Watson

Twin View Publishing Company
Port Ludlow, WA

Dedication

This book is dedicated to all the combat photographers who served in the United States Marine Corps in the Pacific Theater during World War II and also to my mother Bertha Helen Watson who saved all of my brother's correspondence.

"On fame's eternal camping grounds,
Their silent tents are spread,
And glory guards with solemn rounds
The bivouac of the dead."

Theodore O'Hara (1820-1867)

TABLE OF CONTENTS

LIST OF MAPS

All maps are from History of U. S. Marine Corps Operations World War II. Volumes III through V

PHOTOGRAPHS

FORWARD

James Watson recounts with brotherly love and intriguing detail, the transition of a young man from the innocence of pre-WWII America to the violence and death of the war in the Pacific.

Trained by veterans of combat and of film at the Marine Corps Schools in Quantico, Virginia, Robert Watson became a skilled instructor himself, earning the respect and the friendship of his fellow Marines. When his time came to go overseas and into combat, he was well prepared and eager for the adventure ahead. Bob Watson was a tough Marine with the specialized skills of a combat cinematographer. He was one of the many who contributed to the victories in the amphibious landings on Guam, Peleliu, and Okinawa. As a combat cameraman, he was one of the chosen to contribute to the film history of those terrible conflicts that today, are our only visual record of the horrors of island warfare.

Bob and I were friends and Marine Corps buddies throughout training and into combat. I have come to know his brother Jim through his writing of this book and through our shared memories of Bob and his exploits. It has been a privilege to get to know Jim and to be able to contribute to this chronicle of Bob's life in this way. It is Jim's carefully documented tribute to his brother that this fine book so warmly and bravely reflects.

Grant Wolfkill
Shelton, WA

ACKNOWLEDGEMENTS

I am grateful to the following former Marine combat photographers: Grant Wolfkill, Norman Hatch, Glen Chittenden and Harold Palmer. Grant, my brother's best friend, shared some of his experiences and provided insight into the experience of photographers in combat. He edited an early manuscript and made significant suggestions. His encouragement and friendship are most appreciated. Norman Hatch provided helpful information, introduced me to an archivist, and enabled me to contact Harold Palmer, former Lieutenant. and commanding Officer of the Photo Section, Third Amphibious Corps. Glenn Chittenden provided a number of photographs and confirmed critical events. Ninety-four year old Harold Palmer related significant memories of my brother and verified key events.

Ned Steele, former Marine and friend of my brother, reviewed and edited information regarding his experiences in the Pacific theater and told me about the wake held after my brother was reburied in California.

Susan Strange, National Archives and Records Administrator, located significant records in the National and Marine Corps archives. More importantly she found and copied films shot by Robert, Grant Wolfkill and Hoyt Rhodes. I am grateful for her diligent effort that was most fruitful.

Col. Keith McConnell USMC (ret.) edited the manuscript and provided helpful suggestions and encouragement.

Peter B. Drysdale, National Archives and Records Administration, deserves special thanks for providing copies of ships' logs for LST 892 and 734, Fourth Marines' journal for the month of May 1945 recorded during the Okinawa campaign, and the Sixth Engineer Battalion Annex F to Sixth Marine Division Special Action Report for the month of May 1945.

Special thanks to Irma Turner in Team B, National Personnel Records Center, MO, who took extra effort to uncover the missing information in Robert's service record revealing the identity of the LST on which he sailed to Guam.

Bill Pierce, PR Chairman Sixth Marine Division Association, provided me copies of original film footage taken of the Sixth Marine Division in action during the Okinawa campaign.

I thank Peter Maslowski, author of Armed With Cameras, for his e-mail exchanges discussing his chapter on Marine Corps photographers, in particular the recapture of Guam. I also thank Peter for his incisive comments on the correct procedure for quoting and crediting other authors.

I must mention James H. Hallas, author of The Devil's Anvil, The Assault on Peleliu and Killing Ground on Okinawa "The Battle for Sugar Loaf Hill", for his insightful and helpful comments regarding writing history and his encouragement. He also made a digital copy of an Official Marine Corps photograph available to me.

I am indebted to my sister Zelda Harbison who made my brother's letters, pictures and our mother's diary available from her safe keeping all these years. Zelda also provided very helpful information regarding significant events and helped to jog my memory.

Above all I am indebted to Diane, my wife and life long love and companion who edited the manuscript several times and put up with my long hours researching important events and writing on the computer instead of spending time with her. Her editing was particularly profitable.

Of course any mistakes, errors or omissions are due to my ineptitude and not the fault of those loyal and helpful friends who reviewed the manuscript.

PREFACE

In 2008 my wife and I took a so-called World War II Cruise in which we visited many of the islands prominent during the Pacific Campaign. Passengers included large numbers of veterans reliving their experiences on islands such as Guadalcanal, Guam and Saipan. Stops were also made in New Caledonia, Okinawa and Nagasaki. Military historians described the major battles in detail. Discussions with the lecturers inspired me to write my brother's story based on letters saved by my Mother, along with boxes of photographs Robert had sent home.

Initially I intended to inform our children, nephews, nieces, and grandchildren about the uncle they never knew, but concluded the story could interest a wider audience. The narrative is written in chronological sequence driven by the letters. Because Robert revealed little of his combat experiences I have enmeshed his revelations within the backdrop of the campaigns he participated in based on the five volume Marine Corps Pacific History and an extensive bibliography.

Trivial comments in the letters that do not advance the narrative have been largely eliminated unless they contribute to an understanding of life during the war years. Parenthetical explanatory information has been italicized in lieu of footnotes. Endnotes identify all source material and in some cases provide additional information relative to the subject.

Many books about the war concentrate on battles and high level leaders, or tell stories of individuals who achieved great feats in battles. Little has been written about photographers who risked their lives to film the action. This book tells what it was like for one Marine Corps photographer during training and in combat. It is also intended to pay tribute to the men who served in the Marine Corps Photo Sections, many of whom were friends of Robert Watson.

James Watson
May 2013

PROLOGUE

The Great Depression years from 1930 to 1940 were difficult for most Americans, but in many cases people came together to help their less fortunate friends, neighbors and even strangers. As they struggled to survive the adverse economic conditions, the European war started by Adolph Hitler and the Nazi party threatened to envelop them in a war they did not want. Poland, Czechoslovakia, Belgium and France quickly fell to the Nazi onslaught. The battle for Britain raged threatening the very survival of the citizens of the English Islands. Participation of the United States in the European conflict seemed inevitable to many Americans. Then without warning, the Japanese Navy unleashed a devastating attack December 7, 1941 against the American Navy anchored at Pearl Harbor on the Hawaiian Island of Oahu. Just as suddenly the focus of the country changed when Congress declared war against Japan the next day. Germany declared war against the United States on the morning of 11 December; and immediately thereafter, congress declared that a state of war existed between the government of Germany and the United States.

In response to the Japanese attack, thousands of young men and boys volunteered to serve their country in the several branches of service. Those who were not yet eighteen years old could hardly wait for their chance to join up. Some really eager boys lied about their age to enlist in the Marine Corps or obtained their parents permission to join at seventeen. Robert LeRoy Watson, a seventeen-year-old senior at Vallejo Senior High School in Vallejo, California, anticipated that he too would become involved in the war effort.

Robert had only lived in Vallejo since the summer of 1941 when he moved with his family from Colusa in the Sacramento Valley. Although his father, an electrical contractor, had managed to support the family during the depression, it became more difficult when materials were in short supply as the United States began to build up its military capability. Reassessment of his meager earnings and the shortage of materials prompted him to seek employment at the Mare Island Navy ship yard where he installed temporary wiring in a submarine tender that was under construction.

Robert was born on June 24, 1924 at 9 A.M. in Colusa, California to Bertha and Earle Watson. Robert was the latest addition to the line of one of the early California pioneering families that had settled in the Sacramento Valley. One great-great grandfather, with his wife and

1

daughter, came to California in 1848 across the Donner Pass two years after the Donner party suffered its great ordeal[1]. Another great-great grandfather came to the gold country in 1853, then settled in Colusa County and began farming.

Colusa, a small farming town, was nestled against the Sacramento River protected by levees constructed to prevent flooding the town and the Eastside farmlands. The population was about 1,500 in the town proper with another 500 in two extensions. In the countryside tule marshes, sloughs, rice and barley fields gave forth a bounty of ducks, geese and ring neck pheasants. The river, languid in summer, vigorous in winter, teemed with steel head trout and Chinook salmon that rose to the bait of able fishermen during spawning season. This was the seemingly idyllic environment in which Robert learned the value of discipline, hard work, thrift, and charity, love of family, independence and self-reliance.

Robert, along with his siblings James and Zelda born two and three years later, was loved and supported by his maternal grandparents and paternal grandmother. His four uncles lived close by and were actively involved in his life imbuing him with their love of athletics, music and scouting skills. They also set a positive example of hard work and strong family values.

In high school Bob excelled in athletics as a hurdler in track and field events; and also played guard on the varsity football team. He sang in the mixed chorus and had a starring role in the junior class theatric production. Bob was very popular at school and well liked by his contemporaries. In addition to his school activities, Robert was certified as an advanced swimmer and earned the Junior Life Saving badge in the Red Cross swimming program. He also acquired an interest in photography and learned the art of developing film and making prints in a friend's darkroom.

Bob served as an acolyte in St. Stevens Episcopal Church and sang in the choir. He was elected president of the Young Peoples Fellowship at the church. Influenced by his parents who were active in the Masonic Lodge and the affiliate Eastern Star Lodge, he joined the Order of DeMolay, a Masonic youth organization, and served as chairman of publicity.

Robert participated in the Boy Scouts of America and became a Life Scout. The promulgated beliefs and Scout training became an important part of his persona. He tried to adhere to the motto: Be Prepared; and considered the pledge an important commitment.

PROLOGUE

"On my honor, I will do my best
To do my duty to God and my country and to obey the Scout Law;
To help other people at all times;
To keep myself physically strong, mentally awake and morally straight."

Consistent with his Scout training, Bob was quick to help people he believed to be in trouble whether it was his younger brother being attacked in the municipal swimming pool, a defenseless underclassman confronted by a bully, a thoughtless friend using foul language in his sister's presence, or defending his mother from a careless driver. He was quick to respond to a situation that troubled him without regard to his own well being. If he saw something that he believed to be wrong, he did not hesitate to respond as he deemed appropriate.

A relatively good student in high school, Robert seemed to enjoy history more than other subjects. He devoted exceptional energy to research and composition producing four essays concerned with military history: "Caesar and the Army", summarized Julius Caesar's exploits and the organization of his legions; "Sea History" discussed the invention of boats by early civilizations and then the period of exploration; "The Continental Navy" described the genesis of the United States Navy and its exploits; "The United States Infantry" provided "a generalized description of the Infantry including: Organization, the Squad, Training, Drill, the Uniform and Equipment, and weapons." In the preface to the third essay, Robert wrote, "As you probably know, I am interested in all things of a military nature."

Robert's interest in the military was stimulated by ominous events in other parts of the world. The Battle of Britain threatened the very existence of England and in response the United States on September 2, 1940 gave fifty obsolete destroyers from the U. S. Navy to the British and Canadian Navies, in exchange for the right to establish military bases on British possessions in Newfoundland and the Caribbean. Then on September 16 just after school had started, the U. S. Congress passed the Selective Training and Service Act[2] that required all men between the ages of 21 and 36 years of age to register for training for one year. The Act provided that not more than 900,000 men were to be in training at any one time and if drafted by a lottery system, their service was limited to the United States or its possessions and territories. All of these actions were an indication that the country was on the verge of a war and Robert recognized he might become involved, should the United States enter the conflict.

At the recommendation of his history teacher Bob was accepted as a delegate to the California Boys State where he learned the "rights and privileges[3], the duties and responsibilities of a franchised citizen." He participated in legislative sessions, court proceedings and law enforcement presentations.

When Bob returned from the weeklong session at the end of June, his father found a room to rent in Vallejo. Later his mother was able to rent an apartment, barely large enough to accommodate the entire family, just in time for the new school year.

The transition from a four-year high school with 250 students to a three-year school with nearly 1500 students went smoothly for Bob. Known for his smile and sincerity, he made many friends and was very popular with his classmates. He played baritone (a.k.a. Euphonium) in the school band and earned a Block V letter for football, making the first squad of the championship team. Bob was enjoying his senior year at Vallejo Senior High School with new friends and life in a bigger city, more exciting than the little town in the Sacramento Valley. Then on December 7, 1941 his life was forever changed.

The daily newspapers continually reported the status of the war, which was not good. Bob followed the reports closely and was very concerned about the seeming inability of our forces to stop the Japanese onslaught. While keeping tuned to the war, he continued his studies necessary for graduation and garnered a part in the senior play "You Can't Take it with You." He played the role, made famous by Edward Arnold in the movie version, of a rich over bearing banker who has a change of heart near the end of the story.

Extra-curricular activities included scouting as a member of Vallejo Sea Scout Ship 99. Bob learned basic seamanship and piloting of the open deck powerboat owned by the troop, and attained the rank of Second Mate. As he had done in Colusa, Robert earned a Block V running high and low hurdles on the Vallejo track team. He won several medals for his performance in dual meets against other schools in the North Bay League. Continuing to be active in the Order of DeMolay, Bob became Third Preceptor and was a member of the Attendance Committee. Although happy with his activities, he was anxious to finish school so that he could find a job and make some money.

Robert received his diploma on June 11, 1942, and then after a brief stint at temporary employment, was hired as an apprentice boilermaker in the Mare Island Navy Yard apprentice school.

PROLOGUE

He applied himself diligently for two months, and then persuaded those responsible for hiring electricians that he had learned enough working for his Dad to be able to carry out the responsibilities of an electrician's helper. Soon granted a transfer Bob was gainfully employed at almost twice the salary he had earned as an apprentice. He spent most of his time helping to wire World War I Destroyers that were being modified into Four-Stack All Purpose Destroyers (APD).

Robert had become more involved in his hobby of photography, and by this time the whole family was taking pictures. His mother found a job at a photo supply store and his father purchased an enlarger. Soon everyone was taking turns enlarging photos. Bob especially had been making 3x5, 4x6 and 5x7 inch prints from the 35 mm negatives and spent many hours in the dark room honing his skills. The budding photographer had his eye on a press camera manufactured by the Follmer Graflex Corporation in Rochester, New York. He chose to buy a Speed Graphic camera that used 3 ¼ by 4 ¼ plate film. Although similar to the standard 4 X 5 press camera, the version he selected featured a rear focal plane shutter with a speed of 1/1000 of a second that gave the camera a significant advantage for action shots. Bob spent much of his spare time learning the intricacies of the camera and enjoyed taking many pictures while he developed a fine sense for composition and the necessary exposure to obtain the best possible result.

The day after Bob bought his camera, the Marine Corps First Division landed on Guadalcanal August 7 in Operation Watch Tower. The ranks of the First Marine Division were filled mostly with recent enlistees under the age of twenty. The real strength of the division was made up of professionals who had fought in Haiti and Nicaragua, and had seen service in Shanghai, Manila, Tsingtao, Tientsin, and Peking. These tough marines who knew their weapons and tactics, known as the "Old Breed", inspired the young recruits with their combat skills and fighting spirit. Ned Steele, one of Bob's football teammate from Colusa, was among the under twenty year old green recruits assigned to the Division.

The invasion of Guadalcanal was the first offensive action by U. S. forces. Up until that time all American actions in the Pacific theater had been purely defensive. The Battle of the Coral Sea did stop Japanese efforts to invade Australia, and the Battle of Midway that prevented the Japanese from achieving a decisive victory set the stage for the Guadalcanal operation.

In October when the conflict on Guadalcanal was still in doubt, Secretary of War Henry Stimson urged the House Military Affairs Committee to expedite legislation for the drafting of 18 and 19 year old men. Stimson wrote in a letter to the Chairman that the urgency of building up the best army in the world "cannot be overemphasized." "Our own survival is in the balance. Its accomplishment demands the substitution of current necessity for our peace time preferences."

A news article headline declared, "U. S. to Raise Army of 7,500,000 Men by '43. New Draft Bill Due to Pass By Next Week." This news was disturbing to many 18 and 19 year old young men as well as their parents. Although Bob was probably safe from being drafted because of his employment at Mare Island Navy Yard, he could not be sure. All young men would be subject to the draft as soon as they graduated from high school and attained the age of 18. Bob began to think seriously about leaving Mare Island and enlisting in a military service. Aware that his friend from Colusa had joined the Marine Corps that had a reputation as an exceptional fighting force, Robert began to focus on becoming a Marine. The news from Guadalcanal was always in his mind and no doubt had further influence on his thinking. For certain, Bob did not wish to be drafted into the Army if he could find an alternative.

World War II, a conflagration of immense proportions, required great sacrifices of the peace loving people of the United States. Virtually the entire American population rose to the challenge; whether it was the more than eleven million that served in the armed forces or the millions that toiled long hours in the shipyards and factories to provide the ships, tanks, aircraft weapons and munitions that helped to overwhelm the Axis powers of Japan, Germany and Italy. Everyone sacrificed in one way or another to bring an end to the conflict and return peace to the world. It wasn't someone else's war; it was everyone's war.

What follows is the story of Robert Watson's contribution to that effort, and his life as a Marine combat photographer, told through 150 letters he wrote to his parents and siblings. Information gained primarily from the official five volumes History of Marine Corps Operations in World War II provides the backdrop for Robert's climatic adventure and ultimate sacrifice.

1

THE NEW RECRUIT

Aware of the potential dangers but with the bravado of youth Bob was determined to enlist in the Marine Corps and do his part to help defeat Japan in defense of freedom. With great sense of purpose, he took the Greyhound Bus on December 13, 1942, from the Vallejo station to San Francisco and went immediately to the Marine Corps recruiting office. He applied for enlistment, and after a physical examination was accepted as a private (pvt.). The term of the enlistment was "for the duration" of the war. He came home and gave his parents the good news. They were happy for him, but were filled with trepidation fearing for his future participation in the war effort. Bob resigned from his job at Mare Island Navy Yard and began preparation for departure to the Marine Corps Recruit Depot in San Diego, California. He returned to the recruiting office a week later to be photographed.

Bob spent the first five days of the New Year enjoying himself: three days boating with his friend Lee Setterquist, visiting and being visited by relatives and many friends, attending the Sea Scout Troop meeting one last time, and eating dinner each evening with his family. The demands of the shipyard forced his father to work New Year's Day and Sunday the 3rd, so they were only able to be together a few short hours in the evening. Bob packed his suitcase on the 5th, addressed twenty post cards to be mailed to friends and relatives from San Diego, and after an early family dinner, went to bed at 8:05 followed shortly thereafter by the rest of the family.[4]

Awakened at 5 A. M. by the incessant buzzing of the alarm the entire family dressed and hurriedly escorted Bob to the Greyhound Bus station. Everyone hugged Bob, wished him good luck and reluctantly said goodbye. Following one last hug and a tearful goodbye from his mother, Bob boarded the six o'clock bus for San Francisco.

Private Robert LeRoy Watson arrived in San Francisco, reported to the Marine Corps for a final physical examination, last minute instructions, and finally boarded the diesel powered Sante Fe streamliner in the afternoon. Pleased to discover that he had been

1. **High School Graduation Photo**

2. Recruit Photo

assigned to a Pullman Car Bob stashed his suitcase, settled into his assigned seat and looked forward to a good night's sleep when the chairs were converted to beds. As the Streamliner crept out of the station and gathered speed heading south, Bob explored the other passenger cars before entering the dining car for dinner. When he climbed into his bunk that night Bob contemplated his future as a boot marine and his transition as a full-fledged member of the toughest and best fighting organization in the United States Military. He was anxious to become a marine and was determined to be the best he could.

At some time during the overnight journey Bob reviewed the pamphlet that he had received in San Francisco that explained the process he was to follow as a new recruit arriving at the San Diego Recruit Depot.[5] It said in part:

"After you have taken the oath of enlistment at the Recruiting Station you are escorted by one of the recruiting party to the railroad depot and put safely aboard the train for San Diego. Prior to your departure from the Recruiting Station you are provided with ten cents for carfare for use on arrival in San Diego. When you arrive at the Union Depot in San Diego, board a streetcar opposite the railroad station. Take any car which bears the number 14 or 16 or 'L' Bus and ask the conductor to let you off at the Marine Corps Base."

The next day Bob enjoyed watching the scenery roll by in an unfamiliar part of California. After a stop in Los Angeles the train proceeded south and eventually rolled along near the Pacific Ocean. He was quick to view the Mission in San Juan Capistrano and scanned the area to see as much of San Diego as he could. When the stream liner braked to a stop at the station in the afternoon of the seventh Bob stepped out of his car and took the recommended ground transportation to the Recruit Depot where he checked in and was assigned to Platoon Eight of the Third Recruit Battalion.

The new arrival sent a post card addressed to Earle & Bertha Watson from Pvt. Robert L. Watson, Plt. 8 Recruit Depot, Marine Corp Base, San Diego, Calif.

"Dear Mom and Dad, Had a good trip down, Pullman, streamliner, everything. Saw Mission San Juan Capistrano. Got here 4:30 PM, Jan. 7. Got sheets, pillow, blankets. Good chow. Sante Fe better than S.P. (Southern Pacific Railroad) Training 7 wks. long. 3 wks. here, 3 wks on rifle pistol range. 1 wk breaking up to go advanced training.

Love, Bob

The small town boy was impressed with the size and beauty of the depot and the number of airplanes flying overhead, more than he had ever seen before. He took the time to write about his experience in a

10

card to his brother and sister, setting a trend of constant communication with his family, often describing the scenery and other points of interest.

"Dear Jim & Zel,

Saw P-38, B-24 & Lockheed Hudson. One whole hill covered with red flowers. Get shot in the arm tomorrow, I guess. Airplanes galore. Receiving base real pretty. Nice big parade ground for <u>marching</u>. Have open-air theatre. Got a swell temporary Corporal so far as I can tell. I think he is from the South. Love, Bob"

Bob was immediately assigned to the receiving barracks then transferred to a tent compound and finally to huts that held twenty recruits. The huts had an oil-burning heater, which occasionally ran out of fuel, usually when there was inclement weather. Each man had his own bunk complete with mattress, pillow, sheets and two blankets. Along with his new hut mates he was issued a "tooth brush, (tooth) powder, 4 cakes soap, 2 towels, 1 bucket, 2 cans (of shoe) polish, mirror, shaving cream, (and razor) blades, uniform dungaree, lots more."[6] "They took $10 out of our pay for paper, toilet articles except razor."[7]

Each recruit was issued standard Marine green dress uniform with an overseas cap, also known as fore and aft cap and dress oxfords. Normal duty clothes included light green dungaree trousers, jacket and field shoes. They were also issued green overcoats. His civilian clothes were sent home cash on delivery much to his chagrin. "That was a heck of a thing to do (sending the clothes home C.O.D.), but they wouldn't let us do it any other way. I suppose they got there OK?"[8]

Every new recruit had heard stories about the non-commissioned officer, usually called a drill instructor or D.I., who would be in charge of his platoon. Bob was no exception and soon developed a strong opinion about the corporal that would rule his life for the next few weeks. "We got a pretty tough corporal[9]. We all thought he was a big a__, but he's a pretty good guy and sure knows his stuff. If we don't try, he said that he'd kick our ass until our nose bled and if that doesn't work, he'll shake us until our freckles rattle."

The recruit pamphlet mentioned previously gave the official version of the non com in charge of the platoon:

"…the recruit is sent to a filling platoon, which has experienced non-commissioned officers in charge and who pilot the recruits through their training period along recognized lines. You should from the beginning bear in mind that this platoon to which you are assigned is to be the family of which you are a member during your entire recruit instruction. Remember that the men in charge are striving to make of you the kind of Marine you are really desirous of becoming and that to accomplish that object you must give them your undivided support and cooperation. "

"If you are in trouble, desire advice or information, go to your platoon leader with the assurance that he will cheerfully do everything in his power to assist you. Your platoon instructors are interested in you and your work and they are constantly striving to build up in their men military discipline and habits of cleanliness, study and efficiency which will hold you in good stead, not only in your military life but in your future life after leaving the service. To accomplish this you must aid them by paying close attention to all they tell you and must put forth your best efforts at all times."

Whether coerced or not the eighth platoon paid tribute to its Corporal in words[10] sung to the tune of the Notre Dame Victory March.

> "Our Corporal Thompson is really the tops,
> He is well nourished from ale and hops,
> We do nothing on the sly,
> Because he is a swell D. I.
> Thompson is quite a jolly old bean,
> He was named after a sub-machine,
> He's a pretty damned good corporal
> And he stands tops with us."

The platoon song also included a verse about the second in command, Corporal Tiner.

> "Then we have Corporal Tiner too,
> He's just a Texas Buckaroo,
> We won't give him stars and dents,
> If he gives us back our 80 cents,
> Tiner don't mind the card games and noise,
> He really stands A-1 with the boys,
> On his loyal boys are playing -----
> Poker for Victory."

Lyrics applied to popular songs were used to build esprit de corps. One sung by the eighth platoon was set to the "Beer Barrel Polka:"

THE NEW RECRUIT

"Down in Dago, Down in Dago,
  You will never find no gloom there,
  You go in each saloon there,
  You will find the 8th platoon there.
  We don't trifle, with our rifle,
  We're the best shots in the nation,
  When we hear the signal,
  We all will hit the deck."

"All the Dago women want a date,
  With the expert shots from Platoon 8,
  And all the coaches we will please,
  When they look at our trigger squeeze."

"Roll up the targets
  We'll have them all heaving sighs,
  Roll up the targets
  We'll get our share of bull's eyes.
  We're full of action
  From early morning 'till taps,
  We will sure avenge Pearl Harbor,
  So look out you Japs!"

Avenging Pearl Harbor was a major motivation for many enlistments during World War II. Bob was certainly no exception.

Another important issue in the life of a new recruit was the question about the quality of the food and what would be on the menu.

The recruits were all used to their mother's home cooking so that a comparison was inevitable. "What's cookin'?" I'll tell you about chow."[11]

"We have had beans but twice. (*We had*) beans and sausage one breakfast and brown beans for one lunch. All the other meals (*were*) good. First Sunday chicken lunch. Second Sunday turkey lunch."

Bob provided a sketch of the mess hall.

Growing up in a small town in the Sacramento Valley, and living in Vallejo for only one and a half years, Bob was unsophisticated and had no experience with celebrities or movie stars. When he learned that Tyrone Power, a popular movie star, was also at the Recruit Depot he immediately informed his family.

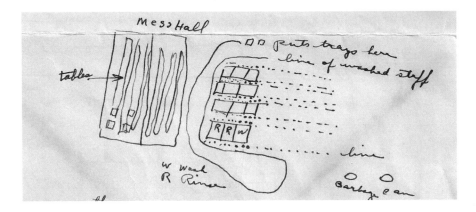

Bob's sketch of Mess Hall

"Zelda, Tyrone Power is here in Plt. 3. I've seen him over a doz. times.[12] Just about ran into him once. He's about 5' 11 ½ ". Looks practically the same as in the show."

" I saw Victor Moore at the LARR (*Los Angeles Railroad*) station. Didn't stop at San Juan Capistrano. Just went by in the train."

Bob had never been out of California and although he may have met some people from other states when he worked at Mare Island Navy Yard, it was a happy experience for him to become acquainted with young men from other locales and states. "Harry Wilson a kid from Yuba City is in the bunk under mine. A real nice kid. Lived on the Colusa Highway. Kids here in our hut are from everywhere. Some from Texas, Montana, New York, & California. There is a kid in my hut, Walt Travis from Vallejo. (I) didn't know him before." He continued, "Been sunny every day. Last 2 days rain. Airplanes galore."

"Have a new kind of pack."

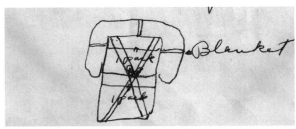

Bob's Sketch of Pack

Robert seemed to have an obsession with sweets, especially candy. He added, "Send down about 20 candy bars. Cheap ones, (costing) 1 cent. Can't get candy here."

Five days later Bob wrote, "I got the check from Mare Island.[13] I got the money belt. I got a 21 Jewel Waltham pocket watch, 14 carat case."

All new recruits regardless of service are soon subjected to vaccinations and inoculations; and are always impressed by the experience because it is usually their first exposure to so many "shots". Bob wrote about his reaction: "I got 2 shots in the left arm, one for tetanus & another for typhoid.[14] Didn't get too sore and (got) a vaccination for small pox in the right arm. Then a week later got a second typhoid. It was so sore the 1st night I couldn't sleep on it."

"My cold was practically gone and then the other guys got colds and then mine got a little worse, but it's almost gone now. I got the tobacco too."

"Don't wear yourself out hunting for candy and don't use all the sugar making it either." Bob was mindful of sugar rationing on the "home front". That was followed by a post card in which he wrote, "This is to ask you not to send candy. A kid got some today and the corporals ate about all of it."

Bob had started smoking a pipe when he worked at Mare Island, but had left his tobacco burner home and thoughtfully informed his father, "Dad you can have my pipe if you want it."

In response to a question from his brother, Bob added, "Jim, I like it here okay and it isn't as tough as I thought it would be. Reveille 5:30 wash, shave, make up bunk special way (*no doubt with hospital corners and taut sheets from which a tossed coin would bounce*) swab deck, cleanup stuff, then go to chow. Take rifles & cartridge belts, go out on the parade ground, do exercises with rifle."

"Each of these things done 8 times, many can't draw. They are like those in 'The Shores of Tripoli'. We do it to '3 o'clock in the Morning.' (*Three O'clock in the Morning, copyright 1922*) Same as show."

Bob's Sketch of Exercises

"Then we go out in sand and simulate warfare conditions. Noon chow. Go to movie usually on warfare. Wash clothes and shower every day. Cold water. Two mail calls a day. 1 in morning & afternoon. Evening chow. Movies or study manual and learn parts (of rifle) by heart. After 5 PM is the only time for writing so you see I don't have much time for writing. Bed 9:30."

"We saw the Shores of Tripoli[15] the other night. It is exactly the same as what we're going through. I stayed in the same tents as they did in the show, same parade ground, everything, except blue uniforms. We wear greens & overseas cap for dress (uniform); wear light green dungaree trousers & jacket, field shoes. We have dress oxfords, but haven't worn them yet. Our dress (uniforms) are the same as they (*Marines stationed on Mare Island*) wear in Vallejo. We have green overcoats. We have bunks, mattresses, pillows, sheets, and two blankets. 'I'm not sorry I joined. We go to the rifle range next week."

The Recruit pamphlet described the training regimen: "For three weeks the new platoon is schooled in the evolutions of an infantryman: facings, manual of arms, bayonet exercises, close and extended order drills. The first part of your training is a trying one for both you and your instructors, because everything is new to you and you will find yourself very awkward in executing the movements described to you. Only weaklings fail to derive the benefits and to attain the physical perfection which this training develops. The man who works hard and obeys cheerfully never experiences any trouble during his early training and he will find his instructors glad to help him overcome any difficulties he may encounter."

The reality of the experience was no doubt not as pleasant as the pamphlet described, but Bob seemed to enjoy the life and accepted what ever challenges there were with good humor.

"It's raining here just as hard as up there (*Vallejo*). Though it's only the 2nd or 3rd day since I've been here. It's just as cold here as it was in Vallejo before I left. But no frost. We have an oil heater but we ran out of oil this morning."

"Sunday I said that we've only had beans twice. Well since then we've had beans about once a day and stew once a day They give us real butter every meal. We have to eat all of it because you have such a hard time getting it. All the sugar we want too. We have scrambled eggs 3 or four times a wk., but it's scrambled with flour & milk & doesn't taste too good. Have oatmeal once in a while but isn't cooked enough."

"Thanks for the letters, clippings, pictures and magazines. But don't send me any magazines except my own, because I don't have time. Well so long." Love, Bob P.S. Chow now. Sending pictures of platoon."

A few days later[16], "We marched an hour and one half today with pack and rifle. The doggoned corporal left us at left shoulder arms for 20 min. Boy were our arms & shoulders tired."

Then obsessed with candy, "Forget what I said concerning the candy. The corporals haven't been taking so much. They only took a few pieces that you sent."

Bob related some of the difficulties of recruit life.[17] "We had a 45 mile gale here and 3 inches of rain in 3 days. Power out in parts of town Bakershop had electrical beater for dough. No power. Couldn't beat bread. Began to rise. Rose and broke plate glass window in front.."

"We have no radio here so don't hear news or new music. Just read newspapers. We were going to have inspection with packs & rifle but it rained us out. There we were out on the parade ground & no coats. We double timed back. About 1/3 of a mile."

"We live out of sea bags. Not too convenient. I have to clean my rifle.

Will close now. Love, Bob"

3. Eighth Platoon San Diego Recruit Depot, Private Robert Watson 2nd from right fourth row

2

RIFLE RANGE

"Today we moved to Camp Mathews about 15 miles north of San Diego in the hills[18]. Colder here, so they gave us another blanket. Have same kind of huts & oil heaters. We have asphalt walkways here. But didn't in S.D. Camp Mathews is a large rifle training center. Five ranges of about 25 targets each."

The Marine rifle range at La Jolla, California was established in late 1918. The name was changed March 23, 1942 to Camp Matthews in honor of Lieutenant Colonel Calvin B. Matthews, who was a distinguished marksman in the 1930s. The original rifle range had eight targets built by the Marine recruits; five more targets were added in 1925, and the first buildings were constructed in 1927. In March 1942 a new administrative building was completed as well as a large mess hall, swimming pool, outdoor theater and post office. During the peak of World War II as many as 9,000 men were processed through the range every three weeks.[19]

Marines were typically transported to Camp Mathews by grey Navy busses unless their drill instructor chose to march them.[20] Trainees lived out of duffel bags for the duration of their stay at the range as mentioned by Bob along with a description of living conditions, "Did I ever tell you we live out of sea bags? Well whatever you want, hardly without exception, is on the bottom. Mess hall is real close. Same with toilet and washbasins and showers. Can get coke but no candy. Don't send gum. Can't have it."

"Had noon chow. Eat out of mess gear. Food better, but they throw it in. Had first real beef yet. Not so bad so far."

"We snap in here for 2 weeks. That is practice aiming & such. Shoot for one week. "

"We've been getting into position on the range the last couple of days[21]. It seems the harder the position to get into the steadier it is.

"We hardly have time to go to the toilet let alone write letters."

"Last night we had a lecture on barb wire entanglements. Part of us went under it and part over just as we would in night battle."

"Those positions look pretty doggone easy, but try it. Boy do your muscles get sore. I didn't know I had so many. We fired 22 caliber rifles today. I didn't do so exceptional. I wouldn't own one of the rifles although they're very high priced. They're all worn out. They won't eject shells or fire half the shells."

In his next communiqué[22] Bob wrote, "Target practice is ok, but the positions are very tough, you have to stretch your left triceps a heck of a lot."

Marksmanship has been emphasized since the founding of the Corps November 10, 1775. During the revolutionary war marines were posted in the riggings of sailing vessels to fire down on the crews of enemy ships during naval battles. All marine recruits had to qualify as marksman, sharpshooter or expert in order to complete recruit training. Today the Marine Corps is the only service that requires all of its uniformed personnel to be trained to fire a rifle accurately. No matter what rank or job a marine holds, he or she must go to the rifle range each year to qualify.

During World War II, as well as today, marines were required to fire from four positions: standing, kneeling, sitting and prone (lying flat on the stomach). The kneeling position was considered most useful in combat because there typically is not enough time to get down in the prone position. However the prone position was considered the steadiest. They had to fire at targets 200, 300 and 500 yards away. Safety was of paramount concern. Consequently recruits were under constant surveillance by marksmanship instructors, coaches and drill instructors to avoid accidents and to assure safe weapons handling.

While at the rifle range the marines lived in rows of tents that accommodated a squad of eight men each. These were erected over a plywood floor with an outside frame of two by fours, with the heavy five-inch octagon pole in the middle for the principle support. The sides of the tent could be rolled up on hot days when authorized. The sides were kept down and secured at night. There were eight canvas cots in each tent around the outside edge.

Marine recruits were taught early in boot camp the importance of their rifle and that they were expected to maintain it clean oiled and in good firing condition at all times. They were admonished to refer to it always as my rifle and not a gun. For a marine, his gun was in his pants. The marines were also compelled to memorize "This is my Rifle" the creed of a U S Marine that begins: "This is my rifle. There are many like it, but this one is mine. My rifle is my best friend. It is my life. I must master it as I must master my life." See Appendix 1 for full Creed.

Bob continued to describe conditions and events at the range. "Everything here is OK.[23] It sure is a lot more rugged here at Camp Mathews than at the Base. You really go through the paces, from 7:00 A.M. until 5:00 P.M. with just time to eat."

"Don't send the towel until I get out of Boot Camp or somebody will probably appropriate it."

"I got a letter from Bill Pillsbury[24]. It was written after he broke his leg. Too bad."

Then Bob followed with some advice to Zelda who had not done as well as she thought she should have in some high school classes, "Zelda, if you want to take over those courses, it's ok, but do better the second time than the 1st."

And always attentive to his parents and special days, he added, "I'll get you a present for your birthday[25] & anniversary after Boot Camp Mom & Dad."

"It has been very sunny[26] here, in the 70's." "Gum-It's against B. C. rules to have gum. Don't miss slippers & bathrobe."

"We'll get paid in a few days. After the 7 wks are up I'll go to a line camp to get combat practice or go to school."

"This is the 4th letter I've written tonight. Twenty guys make a lot of noise and they're doing it now."

Describing his fellow trainees Bob wrote: "Onc guy worked in a shell loading factory in Texas. A guy from a copper smelter in Montana, a cabbie from Miami, an electrician from Western Pipe, San Francisco, a farmer from South Dakota, and ambulance driver from Van Nuys, a butcher from South Dakota, a grocery clerk from Texas, a shrinker, shrunk metal in a shipyard, from San Francisco originally and then New York, a machinist from a Richmond ship yard, truck driver from Texas, and in another hut a bartender. Quite a variety, huh?"

Bob described a typical day[27], "It rained here yesterday. Pretty bad at that. We went out on the range early and it started to drizzle. The coach not wanting to work had us sit on benches out on the range while it sprinkled. Then it began to rain and we marched back to the huts. During the night it rained and wherever we went, we slipped along. The corporal said, 'March at ease', and some kid says, 'Slip at ease."

"Our rifles were all wet, so we had to dry & oil them. Stayed in huts until lunch. Went back on range & had lecture in a shed. No rain.

Then at the end of the lecture a squall of rain got our rifles wet again. Rain over, we went out and practiced standing position. Another squall came up and before we could get to a shed we were soaked. As soon as it stopped, we marched back to the huts."

"The wind was from the NNE. It would clear in that direction, 5 min. more there'd be clouds, 20 more min. a squall of rain would hit us. That's how hard the wind was blowing. We wouldn't feel it until it was right on us. The wind was at a high altitude so we didn't feel it."

"We changed clothes, dried rifles. Then we were supposed to wash clothes, but I washed Sunday. So I didn't wash again. They asked if we had hung ours on the line already: the others said, 'Yes.' So I got away OK."

"It rained again during part of the evening and night. Clear today. Coffey, Ashton & I painted (the walls) in the Armory School building. Got through about 10:30."

"Knowledge gained: There are appr. 100 parts in a Springfield bolt action rifle. Best are those that have a serial number of 1,275,000 & higher. They have nickel chromium barrels. This afternoon we'll snap some more."

The next day Bob wrote[28], "Today we fired the 22's, 100 rounds. We fire at about 50 feet. We fire from 10 to 15 rounds at each target. I get so now I fire so many shots in the same place I knock out a hole about 5/8 inches in diameter."

Then on February 12th, "Everything is hunky dory here. Yesterday we fired the .30 caliber rifle for the first time. We fired 12 rounds each, four on each target. Four fired on the 200 yd. line at a 10 inch bull's eye. The first two shots were just out of the black then the coach changed the sights and I got two bull's eyes. We then fired at a silhouette target 26 inches wide by 19 inches high. I got all four bulls. Moved to 300 yds. raised sights got 4 bulls."

The Bull's eye was ten inches in diameter when at the 200 to 300 yard range, and twenty inches in diameter at the 500-yard range. See Bob's sketches below.

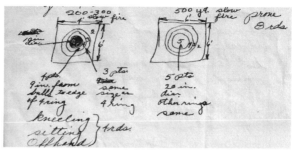

Bob's Sketch of Bulls Eyes

Bob's Sketch of Rapid Fire Bulls Eye

"Today we snapped in. Tomorrow we sight in some more. Today some platoons fired for record. Ty Power didn't qualify because they rushed him to be on the radio and because so many were staring at him, so they say. They're giving him another week.[29] He is staying in the corporal's hut to keep everyone from bothering him."

Bob had a subscription to some photography magazines keeping him up to date on the latest camera and photo news. He added in the same letter, "I got No. 46 Complete Photographer, thanks, also paper."

"Rained a couple of days sun shined a couple of days. Ground all dry. Wind blew, dust flew. Got our hut covered with dust inside and out."

Two days later Bob wrote: "Got your letter and card yesterday; thanks a lot Mom, I used some of the stamps to send you two Chevrons (a M. C. paper) and one Leatherneck (a M.C. magazine)."

"We had a baby snow here the other morning."

"I get $50 a month and 20% more for duty outside the Continental United States. They take out $10 for toilet articles, Post Exchange credit tickets, and miscellaneous articles. They take out $6.50 a month for $10,000 insurance."

In response to a question from his parents: "Combat-the way I used it was combat training. I meant I will be trained for combat duty in a camp in the U. S. or the Hawaiian Islands, unless I go to a school."

"This morning we had extended order drill in the hills around the range. The grass is green and (*there were*) small tricklets of water in the gullies. It was very pretty and then we did double time and boy, were we pooped. We wore leggings, cartridge belts, and carried rifles."

Always with a sweet tooth Bob added a note in a subsequent post card. "Please send me some of that 10 cent store candy those little red peppermint hearts & maybe some caramels. 25 cents worth. I don't like to ask for it, but it's nice. Love, Bob"

Two days later, "Dear Folks, Everything is fair here[30]. We fire for record Thursday and of course I won't get Expert. My cold is almost well all I have left is a very slight sniffle."

"I got a valentine and the chocolate one you sent me plus the U. S. Camera (*magazine*). You should be getting the U. S. Camera Annual in a very short time."

"Tonight I read that the Chicago was sunk. I saw that at M. I. (*Mare Island*) quite a few times."

"I did fairly well in firing today except in kneeling position. I don't know what the heck to write. So with Love, Bob"

The USS Chicago, a Northampton-class heavy cruiser, was launched at Mare Island Naval shipyard in April 1930 and commissioned March 9, 1931. She supported the initial landings on Guadalcanal and continued in action during 1942. The cruiser was hit by a Japanese destroyer's torpedo during the battle of Savo Island on August 9, 1942. It was repaired at Noumea, New Caledonia, and Sydney, Australia and at Mare Island shipyard after arriving in San Francisco in October. Bob would have seen the ship during this time when he was employed at the shipyard.

After repairs the Chicago (CA29) sailed from San Francisco in early January 1943. Upon reaching Noumea, she escorted a convoy headed for Guadalcanal on January 27th. Japanese aircraft attacked the convoy on the night of the 29th between Guadalcanal and Rennell Island. Chicago was hit twice by torpedoes, which caused severe flooding and loss of power. While under tow, the next afternoon nine Betty torpedo airplanes attacked again and succeeded in hitting the disabled cruiser with four torpedoes that sank her. Six Officers and fifty-six men went down with the ship. There were 1,069 survivors.

Meanwhile at Camp Matthews training to join in the fight, Bob reported, "I made Sharpshooter in rifle qualification today.[31] When you get all bull's eyes you get a score of 340. Expert is from 306 to 340. Sharpshooter from 292 to 305. Marksman from 268 to 291. Below that you don't qualify. I got 300 points even. I'm sorry I didn't get higher. I was shooting lousy all week with the Garand, then, today I got a better score all around. What I made better in was kneeling (I usually drop 25 pts. And today I dropped 15 pts.), in 500 yard prone slow fire I usually drop 6 pts. And I only dropped 2 pts. In prone rapid fire 6 rounds, I dropped 8 pts. When I usually drop from 1 to 3. On sitting position I dropped 6 pts. when I usually drop 3. I did better in all the slow fire, off-hand, kneeling and fair in sitting slow fire. I get $3 more per month for shooting Sharpshooter. If I had of made Expert I would have gotten $5 more per month."

Then as an aside (probably in response to a question about the possibility of being assigned to Mare Island Naval Yard), "Most of the Marines around Vallejo are fellows that are reserves called back into service, or fellows not qualified for overseas service". And then Bob commented about shaving lotion on the stationery and the shenanigans of young recruits, "One of the fellows had a little hair on his chest so the fellows shaved it off using no water. The after shave lotion was from what they poured on him. They really raised hell."

Then back to the serious side, "We got 18 Experts in our platoon and only 3 didn't qualify. Our plt. had the highest rating of all that fired today. Usually about 6 make Expert and 6 don't qualify."

"We move back to the base Saturday.

3

WAITING ORDERS

Bob returned to the Recruit Depot in San Diego where he awaited orders for his next assignment not knowing if he would stay there for a few weeks or be immediately assigned to a school or infantry training. In the military there is always uncertainty about future assignments including the location.

He wrote to Jim, [32]"I didn't realize basketball season was so near being over or that track was so near. Your grades are very good, but what is the matter with Chemistry?

"I hope Norma isn't as bad as her sister, smoking a pipe and eating gold fish, ugh." It was OK for Bob to smoke a pipe, but not a female his same age. Eating gold fish was the latest fad among college students.

"Today we moved back from the rifle range in transport buses carrying fifty or over. The first three weeks the food was lousy. We went to the range and the food was good. We moved back here and our first meal was grand. I hope all the rest are equal."

"They passed out the Corps medallions that we wear on our overseas caps and blouse lapels. They also passed out Expert medals, but beings I'm a Sharpshooter I didn't get one. I'll have to buy one at the Post Exchange. It's cheaper there than in town."

"We were supposed to have gotten paid today but I guess we'll have to wait another week."

"I met the youngest Ullory kid here. I guess that's the way to spell it. He was at Scout Camp when we went. He has been here 4 weeks but has to go home because he broke his collar bone once and the doctors say it won't stand up under the gaff, too bad."

In response to his mother's concern for Bob's diet, he wrote[33], "First to answer your questions. Up at the range the only time we had milk was for breakfast with cereal. Here at the base we get milk quite often. I haven't weighed lately."

"This evening's meal was fair. We had baloney, creamed celery, cheese, milk & cake. Noon we had spare-ribs, creamed celery, rudabacres or rudabakers, (*rutabagas*) coffee, tomatoes and potatoes, dessert was ice cream."

"Tonight we have to go to an incendiary bomb lecture, a waste of time."

"Up at the range there was a shortage of water so we couldn't wash clothes for 3 or 4 days. Now it's raining and I washed clothes today."

"Tomorrow we loaf most of the day. Sometime we'll get a couple of shots. We'll drill, have lectures, get identification tags, and prepare to breakup. We might get a month on mess duty at one of the camps near here. If we don't we'll go to a camp for appr. another month's training or go to school. It looks like I'll be here awhile."

Bob continued to describe his activities while in a holding situation,[34] "Raining here. We have guard duty tonight starting at 6:00 for 24 hours. I was to be an M.P. (*Military Policeman*) at the open air theatre but it's raining so they called the show off. Now I'm back at the hut where it's dry and fairly warm. The others had to carry their mattresses and blankets to the guardhouse and they dropped them all the way. Boy! Was it funny, but the sad part of it was, because I could come back to the hut after the show I didn't have to carry any, I ended up carrying 30 lbs. of rifles and 5 or 10 blankets"

"Zelda get rid of that cold. All that's left of mine is a slight sniffle."

"Jim, Good luck with Lee Scott." (*Lee Scott was a bandleader who asked Jim to audition playing trumpet during a performance at a public dance.*)

Three days later: "Yesterday[35] we were going to have a pack & equipment inspection but it rained and they called it off. We had it today. Tomorrow we have a very stiff rifle inspection at 8 A. M."

"I'm glad Jim is getting to play with Lee Scott[36] once in a while. Get over that cold Zel. Good going Mom, making $30."

"Tomorrow we'll know where we are going. I'll stop for now and as soon as I know I'll finish the letter."

The next page started with, "Feb. 28. That was a mistake sending the check home. I'm glad you sent it back"

"The reason I didn't give you any details (*about his assignment after returning from Camp Matthews*) before is because I didn't know any."

"Friday we had a pack inspection in which we had to have certain articles and then display them on the parade ground in a certain manner. Saturday we had a speech from Colonel Hall the C.O. (*Commanding Officer*) and then a pack and uniform inspection. It didn't matter what was in the pack, but it had to be square. Sat. was our break up day. About 20 guys went to schools. The rest of us got mess duty."

"I'll be here for 30 days. I check the plts. (*Platoons*) in at one of the doors & sweep up around. It's pretty easy. Every night from 6 until 10 we get base liberty. We can go anywhere around in the base. On Wednesday, Sat. Sun. we get liberty from 6 P.M. until 1 A.M. I doubt very much if I can get special liberty to go up home."

"We get up at 4:30 A.M. eat at 5:15 A.M., 10:15 A.M., & 4:15 P.M. M.S.M.-N means Men Serving Mess; the N is the mess hall."

In the next letter[37] Bob wrote, "I didn't write (*before*) because our platoon broke up and we were changing (*our*) address.

"I see Jim is getting along very well. I hope he gets the tux." (*The tux was needed to play in Lee Scott's band. Jim bought one for the princely sum of twenty-nine dollars.*)

"Dear Zelda just now got off work, it is about 9:40 A.M. now.[38] I'm doorman, checking platoons, plus caretaker of huts, and commissary worker. About four of us work cleaning the huts, and two of us take charge of unloading a truck half full of vegetables meat and such. We pass it down to others and help load it. This takes place 5 days a week and 3 of us doing it, 2 each day."

"If I don't write it's because I'm changing address like the other day or I'm too damn busy. There is always a good reason."

"We could leave the base last night from 6 'til one. It had been raining but a kid & and I decided we'd try to go in. Some others had already gone in. We left the hut & got about 200 yds. away, and down it poured. We ran back to the huts, fast. We then decided we'd just go to the base theatre. It was 'Crystal Ball' with Ray Milland & Paulette Goddard. It is a good show. I guess I'll go to town Sat. night. It will be the 1st time in town."

"Jim go to the Photography studio, the one I got my graduation pictures, and see if you can get a couple of prints of my football picture. Maybe he still has the negative. Tell me how much it comes to."

"Did I ever tell you that I got paid? Well I did about a week ago Sunday, $45. I think we get paid again Sat. or Sun. Not as much of course. I'm going to close now. I'm due back to work in about 10 min. Love, Bob"

In response to a misperception on the part of his parents, Bob wrote[39] <u>Attention!</u> I did not get mess duty because I was bad. I got fed by someone and now it's my turn to feed some of the 'boots'. About forty fellows out of each platoon (of which there were about twenty) got mess duty. I don't think that large a percentage could have gone wrong."

"If I get time (*to*) go home I will be surprised. The kids have to talk like politicians to even get to L.A. when that is their home."

"By the figures you gave me I can see that you have a damn good job, Dad. I hope you get some more good ones."

"I get to sleep by 10:30 at the latest unless I go to town, which tonight will be my first time. I could have gone Wed. but it rained too hard."

Bob had to file an income tax return for his earnings accumulated from the time of high school graduation until the end of 1942. "I was going to ask you to send me a list of the pay I got, but if you're going to take care of it, why go ahead. If you can why not pay it all at once and get it over with." Bob had a joint savings account with his mother, so she could write a check to cover the tax.

"Send me the book I bought, the 'Handbook of Photography' and my sheath knife, the Finnish knife."

"I think when I go to town I'll have my uniform tailored & pressed. It will only cost about three dollars.

In the next letter[40] Bob reported, "I went into San Diego last night with Harry Wilson from Marysville, and Herb Piper from L.A. We got our uniforms altered and pressed. I had to have my trouser legs shortened in the front, and belt loops put on my blouse and both ironed. It only cost $1.00. I bought a barracks cap, the one with the black visor and a medal to go on it. I also bought a basic training medal."

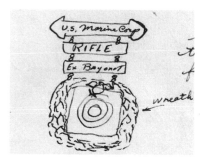 

Sketch of Basic Training Medal　　　**Sketch of Sharpshooter Medal**

"Maybe I'm entitled to have a chemical warfare bar on it too. There are a great many bars you can buy"

"I bought a sharpshooter medal too."

"I got a milkshake, chocolate, $.20 that was thin as milk. Chocolate was all they had."

"I thought Vallejo was a military town, but here it is 4X as bad. You see very few civilians in comparison. We got back about 9:30 although we could have stayed 'til 5 A.M."

"Today at noon we had chicken stew on toast, asparagus, milk, ice cream, salad. Another day we had chili-beans, Spanish spaghetti, creamed celery, & water." Aware of sugar rationing, Bob added, "We can buy all the chocolate candy bars we want here, now; so keep what you can get for yourselves."

"Dad, Remember the picture they made at M. I. (*Mare Island*) at the finger piers? Well, I saw it, 'Stand by for Action.' I think that's the name[41]. Maybe I told you before. Be sure to see it. The 4 stacker[42] is the kind I worked on most."

Bob's comment that San Diego was four times worse than Vallejo because of its military presence no doubt came from his experience growing up in a small farm town with a population of about 2,500 made up of farmers, small town merchants and craftsmen and then moving to Vallejo with a population of about 25,000. Vallejo had always been a navy yard town, but had grown substantially to support the war effort. Sailors from the many ships being repaired in the Yard roamed the streets, especially lower Georgia Street that was lined with bars and saloons. Although Bob was now in the Marine Corps he remembered the pre war reputation of sailors as hard drinking carousing young men with a girl in every port. From his perspective Vallejo paled in comparison to San Diego, which was inundated with soldiers, marines and sailors as well as Army Air Corp activities at nearby airfields. Early in the war the Pacific Fleet headquarters were transferred from Honolulu to San Diego. There was fear of invasion and aerial attacks in San Diego and all of the California coast the first year of the war. The only air defense available was from ships in the harbor until the army moved in an air defense unit.

By 1943 there were numerous military activities in the San Diego area.[43] In June the Navy acquired land located on the Silver Strand between the Pacific Ocean and San Diego Bay just south of Coronado and established an Amphibious Training Base. The Navy Seals

Special Forces train there now. The base was used for amphibious warfare training. Three miles north of La Jolla on Torrey Pines Mesa the Army built Camp Callan to train coast artillerymen and anti-aircraft gunners, where as many as 7500 army personnel occupied the facility at its peak. A training facility for paratroopers was established on the north edge of El Cajon named Camp Gillespie where trainees jumped from three 256 high towers.

The Marine Corps leased 26,000 acres of land located east of Kearney Mesa, where the Navy's Top Gun School is now located at Miramar Naval Air Station, and established Camp Elliott. It was used as a training base for large military units. The Army's Camp Kearney located west of Camp Elliott was transferred to the Navy at the beginning of the war. The Marines built the Marine Corps Air Depot, Miramar on the north end and the Navy built the U. S. Navy Auxiliary Air Station, Camp Kearney, attached to NAS San Diego. The Navy also had auxiliary airfields at Del Mar for blimps, Brown Field southeast of Otay near the Mexican border and Ream field just south of Imperial Beach. Because Camp Elliott could not be expanded the Marine Corps, in 1942, acquired a much larger base further north near Oceanside and named it Camp Joseph H. Pendleton.

The main Navy air facility was located on the extreme northern end of the Silver Strand Peninsula on North Island designated Naval Air Station, San Diego. Glenn Curtiss an early air pioneer had a flying camp there. The main mission of NAS San Diego was to train pilots and aircraft mechanics. During the war as the Navy acquired more aircraft carriers the station was expanded and deep water docking facilities were constructed. Shortly after the attack on Pearl Harbor, Army combat-ready fighter squadrons were rushed to the station to bolster the area's air defenses. The station had nine auxiliary fields during World War II within a radius of less than 90 miles.

San Diego Municipal Airport was an auxiliary field to the San Bernardino Army Air Field and was also used by the Navy and Coast Guard. Ryan Aeronautical Company,[44] that built the Spirit of St. Louis flown across the Atlantic Ocean by Charles Lindberg, was located there. The company produced the PT-22 primary trainer used to train thousands of Navy and Army pilots at the Ryan School of Aeronautics, one of the first schools selected by the Army Air Corps to train fledgling pilots.

Consolidated-Vultee Corp. the largest aircraft manufacturer in the area produced the B-24 four-engine bomber and also the PBY Catalina seaplane. The PBY was a long-range patrol plane that could land on water or land and was also used for air sea rescue and anti submarine patrol.

Fort Rosecrans located on the Eastside of the Point Loma Peninsula, built on the site of a Spanish fort from the 1700s, was the headquarters of the Army's coastal defenses for the San Diego area. The 155mm battery from the northwest part of Fort Rosecrans was moved to Fort Emory located on the Coronado Heights. The new, at the time, Anti-Motor Torpedo Boat armament and anti-aircraft machine guns were manned at Fort Emory.

The Navy trained raw recruits in 16 weeks of "Boot Camp" at the Naval Training Center located at the north end of San Diego Bay. During the war the center could train 25,000 recruits at a time as well as other personnel in special schools.

Even though Bob had worked at the Navy Mare Island Ship Yard where many navy ships were built and repaired and where there was a small Marine contingent he had never seen as much military activity as there was in San Diego. He wrote about an exciting aerial display and accident that was his first experience as an observer of the perils of war even in training circumstances. It would prove to be a prelude to the personal dangers he would be exposed to later.

"Something a little exciting happened today.[45] P-38s, B-24s and many other planes take-off and land and dogfight and play follow the leader over the base all the time. Today a group of 5 P-38s were dog fighting over the base and two rammed. One's wing clipped the tail off the other. All of the elevator piece of the tail came off. The wing of the other came off. Both pilots were able to bail out, but one parachute had a big split in it and he came down a lot faster than the other fellow. Scuttlebutt says that the one with the rip had his arm and head cut off. I'm certain he had his head, 'cause I saw it on him as he came down. It must have been the other one because some say that he was limp in the harness."

"Both planes came down in a flat spin and then one slithered down nose first in a flat dive for about 100 ft. A prop hit the eaves of a mess hall and a piece of metal went through a two story building down into the basement. One of the kids from our hut just stepped into a room there, the one it went through, and wham! Some guy hollers, 'A bomb.'"

"The planes crashed together about a mile up and about 300 yds over from our hut. They hit the parade ground about 500 & 550 yds.

from our hut. They both pancaked and made holes about 10-14 ins. thru the asphalt where the engines hit. They both burst into flames. I hear now that the one with the intact parachute is the one that lost his head & arm. I guess the other is OK. I hear that the one that had the ripped parachute was caught in a fire net. If I find out the truth about the injuries, I'll let you know. I saw everything else except the collision and the holes in the building where the piece went clear through. Machine gun bullets went off in the fires.

Returning to more mundane issues, Bob continued, "I'm glad you were able to get a tux, Jim."

"That $10 they took out (of my pay) for the Post Exchange (canteen coupon) only came out once."

"I got the candy you sent with the picture and I got a box from Edna (*Uncle Raymond's wife*). I now can get all the chocolate bars I want. We all liked what you sent."

The next day Bob was still writing[46] about candy, "I got Jim's picture and the candy. They both were very good. Is it OK if I keep the picture, or do you want it back?"

"Jim, I'm glad you got a permanent seat in the dance band. It must have been quite a thrill playing for that acrobatic team."

"Don't send me a jigsaw puzzle; I wouldn't have time to use it and neither would the others."

Bob touted the good fortune he had regarding the food he was served. "Whenever we have pork for dinner we get the tenderloin and the boots get the chops. We get all the left over ice cream and cake-whenever we have it. So it isn't too bad. We have potatoes every meal. We can always count on that; sometimes it's candied sweet potatoes and that's good. We've only had beef once since we've been here. Our meat is almost always pork, if we have it, once in awhile chicken or bacon. We can drink all the milk we want and we have coffee often so I have learned to drink it; although I don't like it too good."

Then he gave news about a possible future assignment: "I've signed up for photography 1st choice and infantry 2nd. If there is room I will go to Quantico, Virginia to school of photog. Otherwise I will go in the infantry."

The Marine Corps had never had a photo section for filming Corps activities in peace or war until it established a photo section at the Marine Base in Quantico, VA in late 1941. Captain Wallace Nelson was the officer in charge of the Photo Section in October 1941.

Nelson, an Annapolis graduate, was put in charge because he had recommended that the Corps have a photo section. Karl T. Soule, age 24 an experienced travel photographer who had worked for Burton Holmes, the world leader in travelogues, received a direct commission as a Second Lt. without the benefit of boot camp or any military training. Upon reporting for duty in early February he was assigned to the Photo Section as Officer in charge of the Editorial Department. Other members of the newly formed section were: First Lt. William Halpern, who had a background in motion pictures; Captain Bert Cunningham, recently employed by Pathe News in New York; Master Sergeant Dean C. Barnum a career enlisted man; and Master Tech Sgt. Morris Abrams who had spent fifteen years in major Hollywood studios.[47]

Still waiting for the knife to come from home he wrote[48], "The knife I meant was the longer of the two & the oldest."

"I could have gone into town tonight, but there is nothing there to interest me; so I didn't go. Instead I went to the base theater at 5:30 & saw 'George W. Slept Here' with J. Benny & Ann Sheridan. It was funny at the last."

Two days later, still trying to get his knife from home, Bob wrote,[49] "The knife I want is the one I got from the sailor, the longer of the two. It is the Finnish knife."

Sketch of Finnish Knife

"Thanks for telling me how much I made, but don't I have to sign the paper you send into the revenue department?" Bob had earned $1,228.11 at the Yard. His total income for 1942 was $1,252.61, for which he was required to pay income tax of $123.00.to the Federal Government and $1.75 to the State of California. [50]

Bob's family liked the idea of Photography School because Bob had been interested in photography for some time and they also believed he would be safer than in the infantry. Attendance at photo school would also delay his transfer to overseas' combat.

At home in Vallejo, Bertha had also become interested in

photography and had applied for a job at Corbin's Photo Supply. Earle had been interested also ever since he bought a Kodak bellows camera that is now a classic antique. He had renewed his interest at the same time Bob and Jim became interested in developing 35 mm film. Bob also had the Speed Graphic camera that he had left at home.

The next day Bob wrote,[51] "We ran a bayonet course without any practice and we all qualified, so you can see how hard it must have been. All that go to line camps learn bayonet fighting and they're really good."

"I hope you get the phone and the job at Corbin's, if you'll like it." (*The family had been without a telephone, which was hard to get during the war.*)

"I can go to town tonight but there is nothing to do there, so I'm going to stay in and read that book; I got it today."

"Did you give Leta Clifford (*a friend of his mother*) my address?"

"Paris Island, the Recruit Depot for the East is overflowing and so they're sending them out here. We have a lot of easterners here now."

Right on schedule, Bob wrote two days later,[52] "I'm OK and it isn't so bad here. I still have a slight sniffle."

"Last night I went to a dance in S.D. One of the best halls in town. Admission $1.00. Horace Heidt[53] and orchestra were there. It was broadcast over the radio, too, for about one-half hour. A blind guy whistled[54] and was he good. He whistled like a canary, a thrush, and a loon, plus some songs. Boy! He was good. Three fellows came out in strapless formals with wigs on and pantomimed while they played Andrew Sisters' songs. It looked just exactly like they were singing the songs. They went through many antics so forceful that one of the fellows dress came down. He threw away his padding and had a heck of a time keeping his dress up. I almost split. Heidt said that he didn't know he had a burlesque show. Three girls & three fellows sang. Altogether it was very good."

Then a follow up comment about the mid air collision he wrote about previously: "The fellow with the good parachute was killed. That article in the paper referred to the same accident."

Again after a two day respite, Bob wrote,[55] "Everything here is going along smoothly. We got paid yesterday. I drew thirty-five dollars."

"Tonight is liberty night but I'm staying in. There isn't too much to do in town anyhow.

"I got the camera annual, Complete Photographer, and a (*Vallejo*)

Times Herald in the last couple of days."

"It has been fairly nice weather here the last few days. It was clear & crisp this morning"

"I wonder how come Raymond (*his uncle*) got in the medical outfit." Raymond had lost the sight in one eye as a result of an automobile accident, but miraculously regained it just before the war started. Even though he was married and thirty-one years old, he felt compelled to do his part and enlisted in the army.

"Harry Wilson, the kid from Marysville, has a girl friend in Nevada. One of her brothers was killed in the war, another one was wounded in a submarine, and another has malaria down in S. America. (*That is*) hitting pretty hard, all at once too."

"It is cloudy tonight. I doubt if it will rain, because it has rained about four inches more than usual so far."

"Keith Jensen a kid from Williams heard that I was here and came over & visited awhile. I knew him before. Neither he nor I have been able to find John Ramos." (*John Ramos was a classmate of Bob's in Colusa.*)

Bob continued to enjoy his adventure away from home, on his own except under the discipline of the Marine Corp. Although he was essentially a small town boy, he was not enamored with celebrities.

"Tonight[56] a Red Cross benefit is to be here, starring Maureen O'Hara, Tyrone Power, Leo Carrillo, & many others. I am not going. A show that they're in is better than seeing them in person. Sat. Night, I think I'll go to Mission Beach a few miles away by bus. It has an amusement park. Sunday night I am going to a Philharmonic Concert. Some say it is to be Stokowsky or Tchailowsky." (*Leopold Stokowsky, a famous symphony conductor. A number of people not too familiar with the names of conductors and composers were confused between the names of the conductor and the famous Russian composer, Tchaikovsky.*)

And finally the issue of the knife was resolved. "I got the knife & candy & (*the magazine*) Outdoorsman. Thanks."

"I hope you get another (*Gantry*) crane (*to wire*) Dad. It certainly sounds interesting."

Earle worked at Mare Island Navy Yard, as an electrician, initially installing temporary wiring in submarine tenders under construction. Temporary wiring provided lighting and power for the work on board the ships. In March of 1943 Earle was assigned to install electrical wiring on gantry cranes. Gantry cranes built at Mare Island were mounted on rails along the dock where the ships were being built. A structural beam was designed to extend over the ship so that heavy objects could be lifted and placed onboard, facilitating the construction process.

"We have a week or 1 1/2 to go. There seems to be some question. If we won't get any leave, but if we break up on a Wed. I might get a 72 hr. leave. I can then come home."

Still uncertain about his next assignment, three days later Bob wrote, "I believe that we will break up Sat. I'll either go to Vir (*ginia*). Or a line camp here in California.

"Go ahead and give Leta Clifford my address, it won't hurt anything, I guess. It might be a good experience.

"I danced at the dance hall the other night. This Sat. and Sun. night I went to Mission Beach, an amusement park about four miles from S. D. I rode on the roller coaster, merry go-round, and many other rides."

"I couldn't have a camera even if I wanted one yet."

Then, revealing his true feelings about his future, "I sure hope I can go to that school."

"I went to the show last night here at the base. The picture was 'Silvery Skates'. There was a Walt Disney picture too. The name of it was 'Saludos Amigos'. I didn't like the movie but Saludos Amigos was good. It portrayed a trip that Disney's artists took to S. America and the ideas they got made into a continuous run of short comedies."

Still on his two to three day schedule for writing letters, Bob speculated about his future[57], "Everything here is going along OK. I still don't know what I'm to be placed in, yet. A captain, from Camp Pendleton about 50 miles up the coast from here, offered me and several others a chance to play in a military & dance band that is being formed there. I turned it down because I may still get in photography school. It sounds very good and I would have taken it except for the chance in school. "

"I drew $35 because they pay us approximately every two weeks. They also pay us in fives and tens, no change. I have enough money to go home if I get the chance."

"There is a kid from Marysville in Keith Jensen's plt. who knows Harry Wilson. Harry found out where Keith was from and told him that I was here; so over he came. I doubt very much that Bowen will go across without more training. They do send some to camps over, but very few."

"Don't count too much on me coming home because I doubt if I can get enough leave."

4. Amusement Park Photo c/w Lawson, Lindsey, Waddill, and Watson

Describing his first experience with a photo booth at an amusement park, Bob added, "I am enclosing a picture that four of us had taken at the amusement park that I was telling you about. With the type of film they used they don't need a negative; and so I should be on the left side instead of on the right. It is reversed like a mirror. The medals go on the left of the coat instead of the right as they appear."

Taking advantage of the movies available at the base, Bob stated, "Mon. nite I saw Silvery Skates, Tues. nite Lucky Jordan, & Wed. night American Empire. I liked them all except the first, but it did have pretty figure skating in it."

"Gen. Platoff's Don Cossack Chorus is going to be here Fri. night, but I have to get ready for inspection & I doubt if I'll have time. This is the original, the same ones that were in Vallejo."

"I have never told you but we have two identical brass identification tags." They were worn around the neck and were engraved with his name, serial number (490975), blood type (O), and date of month of active duty: 1/43, then his service (USMC).

Bob visited the "Star of India", ship built in 1863 that had been turned into a museum. He was interested because the local Sea Scout unit used the ship for meetings. After sending more post cards with no news, he finally sent the message the family had hoped for, "We'll I'm going to Photographic School. I don't know where, but I'll let you know when I get there. It may be here or it may be back East. I'll give you my address as soon as I get it."

Although the Marine Corps had established a Photo Section in late 1941 at the Marine Base in Quantico, VA, men selected to become photographers were trained at several locations including: Quantico, Hollywood Studios' photo school, MGM movie school in Culver City, CA, March of Time newsreel course, Life Magazine School in N. Y., and a Navy school at Pensacola, Florida.

Everyone in the family was relieved when they learned of Bob's hoped for assignment. Celebrations were in order that included Jimmie and Rita Turner, the owners of their rental flat at 642 Louisiana Street in Vallejo. They waited anxiously for more news of the school location.

Although it was written on April Fools Day, the message[58] was no joke. "It looks as though I may be here for a week or so. I'm to be sent back to Quantico[59] for schooling."

"I am sleeping in a tent surrounded by officer candidates. I'm sleeping in the same tent with one. A few are going to Quantico officers' school Sat, my tent partner too."

"There are two other photographers here. They did live in L.A. and are to be sent to Hollywood for moving picture schooling, near home. They went to a Hi School[60] that has the best course on photo (*graphy*) of any hi school of the state and it is better than the course the L. A. City College has. I wish I could have gone there. I've seen some of one kid's pictures and they could go in a photo magazine. They are really good and he's only 18. I wish I had of had their opportunities. They tell me that the Art Center School, I was so hot on, is no good."

"Last night I went into S.D. had a fried chicken dinner, shave, face massage, shine, and went to a show of Dot Lamour & Bob Hope."

"I went to the base library tonight & read photo books. I get up at 7 A.M., eat at the P. EX (*Post Exchange*) & loaf, & read all day & write letters."

Four days later, Bob notified his parents of his new address verifying his assignment to the Photo detachment of the Head Quarters Marine Corps Base in San Diego.

4

EXPLORING SOUTHERN CALIFORNIA

Taking advantage of relative freedom made possible by his assignment in limbo, Bob expanded his horizons by exploring the Los Angeles basin including Santa Monica, enjoying female company and discovering how other people lived. Although subjected to the disciplined routine of the Corps and its training regimen the experience since leaving home had been an adventure that he eagerly shared with his family.

"Starting in Sat. 12 noon I had a 36 hr. pass allowing me to go to L.A[61]. Taking advantage of this, I saw the Clifford family and ate duck dinner there. I got there about 4:30. He is a butcher and because of meat shortage he is looking for a job in case he loses the one he has. They live in a not too rich part of Bell Gardens; which is a suburb of Bell, Calif. They own their home but she isn't what you'd call a good housekeeper. It seems everyone does as they please. When she wants to work she does. When she doesn't things get sloppy. They were very nice to me. Were they that way before? You are a much better housekeeper."

"They then took me to the Avery's and dumped me off. That was about 8:40. I had intended talking a little while and then go up town to a hotel. But they said all were filled and persuaded me to stay all night. She had to go to work early so I didn't see her the next morning. Mr. & I had breakfast and he showed me their garden and part of the town, his school, the Rose Bowl & golf course (really beautiful and a swell course, Dad), millionaire street (where the rich used to live, but are moving into the hills because of traffic), and then he and I had dinner at a house where they serve meals. He had turkey & I had chicken, 75 cents each. It was served farmhouse style although we had individual tables for 2, 4 or 6 as the case demanded. It was very nice. He then let me off at a blvd. and I caught a ride. I only had to wait 2 or 3 minutes between rides all of the way back."

"Everybody is very nice to servicemen. I got to the base about 5 or 6."

"Mrs. Avery is working in a place where they put up frozen foods. Mr. said she got nervous from worrying about the son that was captured. One of the sons that is in his 30s got released from the Army and is working in Richmond. Cecil is his name. He is sending for a lady from Indiana and is to be married."

The United States had now been in the war for fourteen months and by this time thousands in the military services had been killed or wounded and many were in Japanese or German prisons. Many families were greatly affected and there was constant concern about the safety of loved ones.

"I got two cards from Ray[62]. Everything seems to be OK with him."

"That girl[63] you wrote me about, the friend of the Clifford's, is rather wild & not my type at all."

"This is rather belated, but if Grandma is there, this is wishing her a happy birthday."

Leta Clifford was impressed with Bob and wrote to Bertha the same day,[64] "Evidently you haven't heard from Bob recently? Well I wanted him to tell you first but I'll tell you also. He surprised me Sat. afternoon April 3rd. Was I glad to see him. We had a duck dinner & his favorite lemon pie & all the trimmings & around 7:30 P.M. we took him over to Pasadena to his Aunt's. On the way he got out to ask a direction & he came back with a great big fish bowl full of beautiful flowers & moss & beautiful rocks. They're growing in this big fish bowl. I felt bad to think he wasted his money on me because the boys don't get so much. And what they get they need for their enjoyments. Bless his heart. He's sure a lovely boy & no wonder you're so proud of him. I'm proud of him also. We went wild over him. I just can't begin to sing his praises & I suppose if I did, he'd think I was silly. Kids generally do. Such a beautiful smile as he had. I had Colleen over to help entertain him. And she was thrilled over it. They got along swell. We had a nice ride to Pasadena. We took him through Coyote Pass & Mexican Hollywood & Alhambra also. But did he like Pasadena & how. He says after the war he thinks he would like to live there. Well I hope he gets what he likes. I know he will go far in his course as he looks like the type that likes to study."

"Gee kid I wish my boy could be home for a week. Boy would I be happy. But guess that's not for me yet. But I keep hoping & praying. Well so long & best of everything. Love & kisses, Leta."

After his exploration of Pasadena, Bob sent post cards with

pictures of three grizzly and two polar bears that he saw in Balboa Park, and the San Diego Zoo, his first sighting of live species. Always thoughtful and caring about other people, he penned, "Dear Mom, I'm sending you a little present for Mother's Day a little ahead of time. Love, Bob"

Bob received a telegram from his mother asking him to call her after the duty officer had rejected her call to him. On 31 March Bob telephoned Rita Turner and asked if she would mind going next door to ask his family to come to the telephone. When Mrs. Turner came to the flat Bertha was in the kitchen, Earle on the back porch, Zelda had just gotten out of the bathtub, and Jim was in bed. Bertha recorded in her diary that she was thrilled and dashed out "followed by Earle, next Jim losing a slipper and carrying it the rest of the way, then Zel putting bathrobe on-on the way.[65] We were all so terribly excited. Mrs. Turner was very thrilled and excited too."

"It must have been a sight: all of you running over to Turner's house in all stages of dress.[66] It was certainly nice to hear all of you that night."

"Everyone that enlists in or is drafted in takes tests to find out his capabilities and adaptabilities. One of the tests I took was like the Mare Island Apprentice Test."

"That letter that you found with the dates on it so far apart must have been misplaced in the post office and found on the date of the postmark. I wrote Dick Hutsell a letter but it looks as though he hasn't gotten it. I wrote it about three weeks ago." Lost, misplaced, and delayed mail would plague Bob and all servicemen and their families throughout the war.

"I weigh about the same as when I joined up. I may have gained a few pounds."

"As I told you in my last letter, I was able to go up to L.A. & see the Clifford's & Avery's. Pasadena certainly is a very pretty city. I didn't know that it was so large. It is about the same as Sacramento."

"I was supposed to get a pass for this weekend but someone bungled the deal and it was never made out. The damn fools."

"Here is a typical day that I'm spending and you'll see how soft I'm getting.[67] I sleep through reveille and morning chow, get up about 6:45 roll my tent sides, make down my bunk, sweep the deck, pick up papers around the tent if there are any and wash up. I then do any chores I may have to do like sorting my clothes or ironing or washing clothes. I then go to the Post Exchange or PX as I shall call it, and get milk, sandwiches, and doughnuts. I then stall around until after inspection which is anywhere from 9:30 until 11:00. In the meantime I go over to the mail window to hear the man say no, up until yesterday. I then go back to the tent and fiddle around until chow. I then do any washing or other chores that I may have. I can then go to the Base Library or can sleep all afternoon, then evening chow. I can then go to the Library as I did last night or go to a show or anything else within reason. Pretty soft."

"How is your work coming Dad ? How are all the kids doing in school, Jim & Zel?"

"I just got through mailing a letter to you and now I go over to the postal window and ask for my mail and now I have to answer another.[68] I don't have anything new to add except that it looks like I'll be here another week."

"Leta C. cooked the meal very well and cleaned up the dining room a little, so the meal was alright. Maybe I painted the picture, too dark. I enjoyed both visits immensely. She didn't say anything about her daughter getting her teeth pulled."

"Dad, I thought all Jepson's and Watson's made good choices of wives."

"Well here it is 2:45, after a slight interval. I've been over to the Base Library. I finished a storybook called 'Captain Blood' by Raphael Sabatini. It has taken me 6 to 8 hrs. to read it. Not all today as you can see."

"The chow was very good. I am now eating in a base mess hall, instead of a R. D. (*Recruit Depot*) mess hall and I get better fed."

"I haven't received your telegram yet. It doesn't pay to send them. It took two days to get the last one. This time it is longer."

"I think I'll go to a show tonight."

Bob's parents were finally able to get a telephone and after informing Bob, he wrote[69] "I've received two letters with the phone number in them, but I have never gotten the telegram."

Mom---I'm glad that you got to go up home (*Colusa*). It must have been nice to see all of those people again. That sounds like a pretty dress of yours."

"It rained a couple of days ago and then cleared up very sunny. Then yesterday the wind blew practically all day. This evening there is a breeze blowing in clouds off the ocean, but I doubt if it will rain."

"Last night I went to the show 'Dr. Gillespie's New Assistant.' I saw it in town once before. It is very good. I bought a book of tickets,

20 for $1.00. Very cheap, isn't it? That is for the base theater."

The next day,[70] "I don't know how long I'm going to be here, probably until the 1st of the month and then they may tell me tonight to get ready to leave early tomorrow. That's the way they do things around here. They never tell you anything until the last minute."

"Four movie photographers left this morning to go to Camp Elliott for combat training before they go to school. They weren't notified until yesterday morning and then the actual orders hadn't shown up yet."

"Yesterday I had a headache and threw up so I went to sick call. They made me stay in a ward over night, but they let me out early this morning, there wasn't anything wrong. Something in the food must not have agreed with me. The letter that I wrote the 13th was written in the ward but I didn't tell you because I wanted to wait until it was all over so you wouldn't have any cause to worry."

"I got a card today notifying me that the Western Union had a telegram for me. It was the one that you sent me."

Then he wrote to Jim,[71]"I was very pleased to get your letter. I like to read Zel's & your letters including the mistakes. For instance, people usually spell seconed, second. Don't mind me, I'm just kidding."

"I'm glad to hear that you're doing well in track but don't let that guy beat you all the time. I'm glad that you got your block. (*Block V for successful participation on the varsity football team and track*)

"The schools you speak of sound fairly good. But are their scholastic standards as high as Wash.? Don't go to some middle rate school. "Be sure and stay in school until June. Don't graduate early like I was planning, to become a mechanic learner. I'm certainly glad Mom talked me out of it."

"Don't feel guilty or funny because you're not in a service. Here I am sitting on my fanny just waiting. Get in the reserve. That's your best bet."

Two days later,[72] "This morning I slept until seven. I washed and then took my sheets & pillowcase over to the warehouse to turn them in for clean ones. I can do this twice a week, both sheets. I then made down my bunk and cleaned up the tent. I have a tent to myself. I then went over to the PX and got some breakfast. Now I'm back at the tent answering your letter, Mom."

"Go ahead and send the U.S. Camera & Comp. Photos (*magazines*). I guess I'll be here another week. A bunch of Officer

Candidates are going back to Vir. this weekend, but as far as I know, no photogs will go. Maybe next weekend. That will give a week to travel in so we could get there by the 1st and start to school then. This is just supposition. I don't know anymore about it than you. I'm just guessing."

In his next epistle,[73] Bob revealed a new assignment, "I've just gotten orders that while I'm waiting to go back east, I shall be on police duty. I shall be under a Sergeant and most likely have very green recruits under me to do the dirt. These recruits will be fellows that have just come into 'Boot Camp' but haven't gone on schedule yet. My working hours are: 6:45 A.M. to 11:30 & 12:45 P.M. till about 4:00 P.M. I start tomorrow morning. I'll tell you all about it as soon as I've had a taste."

While waiting Bob took advantage of a forty-four hour pass to explore more of Southern California and become acquainted with more civilians of the opposite sex. He also experienced the uncertainties of hitchhiking to return to the Base as related in his mini saga[74]:

"My pass started at 10 A.M. but a fellow was going that had a car and he didn't get off work until 11:30 so we didn't leave until 12:00. He had a Ford Model B Coupe. 3 went in it. He is an officer candidate; and another photog went. He took me right to Wilbert's home, one of the movie photogs that went to Elliott. He had fixed it up thru his girl to get a date for me and I was to stay all night there at the house. When I got out of the car I left the little leather case that you gave me. It will hold shaving gear, toothbrush & paste, and a towel. It surely is nice. I went inside and met his mom and two brothers and a boy friend that was waiting to see him. He had been home but had gone over to see a kid that he knew. We, this kid & I, decided to go over & see him."

"We met them, Wilbert, friend & friend's girl, on the way. Wil told 1st kid we were going out. So we went to see girls. This kid that I met first got a girl, so that he didn't go to grave yard shift (midnight until 8 am) at Douglas, 1 less plane. (*Reference to Douglas Aircraft production line.*) Then (we) went to the house of the girl that I was to take out. Will's girl entered the group somewhere I forget and went into my girl's house. She had just gotten out of the tub so I couldn't see her, but she saw me thru the front window. Went back & ate. Picked up girls. Mine: 5'4", lovely long blonde hair, blue eyes, very pretty face and swell figure. Woo, woo I'm a wolf. The first real blonde that I have ever thought was OK."

5. Bob with First OK Blonde

"Three couples went in one car & another couple in a coupe. We went to Ocean Park, an amusement center (big) on a pier at Santa Monica. We rode practically everything, didn't get in until 3:30. It was about 18 to 20 miles from where we started or more. Slept until 9:30 or there abouts, had ham & eggs for breakfast. (Oh I forgot. This kid that brought me up brought back the case while the first kid & I went to see if we could find Wilbert (last name)."

"Mr. Wilbert killed 3 rabbits and dressed them for dinner. 11:00 Wil went & got his girl (going to get married after war). 1:30 got my girl. Came back, fooled around took girls home at 7:00, came back to house."

"His Dad took us out to Manchester Blvd. at 8:00 to get a ride. Got one with a lady. Took us to Santa Ana. We waited there for an hour. Finally took a ride for about 3 miles to a town where the truck cut off hit the highway we were on. There were about 30 Marines waiting there, so we walked about 2 miles out of town, Tustin. Finally some guy & gal picked us up took us to San Juan Capistrano. We waited there about 20 min. & decided to walk. We got into the country about a mile and a guy picked us up and took us to San Clemente. We waited there about 15 min. & I began to want coffee to get warm so I went in to get some (first time I ever wanted coffee, would rather have had tea.) We had an understanding that if a single ride came he was to take it because he had to go to San Diego & there catch a bus to Elliott. He got a ride I guess anyhow he was gone when I got back."

"Finally some sailors came by in a Ford (*Model*) A coupe and a sailor and I got in the turtle back with a gob (*slang for sailor*) that was already there. We had to hold up the shell with our heads & shoulders until I got a jack handle to prop it up. After about 5 miles the sailor that was orig. there got out & we had some room. We then went on, saw a wreck, and finally the driver stopped out in the middle of nowhere & says, 'Here's where we stop.' We then had to walk about 2 miles into Oceanside. Finally we decided that we couldn't beat the bus out of any more money. It cost me $0.65 into Diego. In all of the places that I said we waited or we walked cars were passing all of the time. They just wouldn't stop that late at night. My pass was good until 6:00 A.M. and I got in about 3:30."

"I got up this morning about 8:30, washed clothes, showered, and then we had to carry locker boxes, that O. (*Officer*) C. (*Candidates*) had left, to a warehouse. I didn't eat breakfast because it was 11 by then."

"I sent those post cards, 6 or so on purpose. I just got the letter that you wrote the 13th today. (Six days in transit) I got the U.S. Camera & C. Photos OK. The pictures are very good."

"I got the letter of the 15th under the pillow at 3:30 this morning. All of the photo mail (*mail for the photo school candidates*) is in one pigeon hole & whoever goes over 1st brings it all back."

"I'm not going to get a good picture taken until I get back east so I'll know how long I'm to be in one place. I might get a picture taken on a Sat. and leave the next day, then I'll be out that much money."

"I'm going to answer Jim's & Zel's letter (direct to them) themselves.

I'm going to address (*this*) letter to Mr. & Mrs. So if Jim & Zel want me to write them, they better write me."

"Enough now. Do you think so? I think I'll apply for a copy write." (*He may have meant the spelling of Copyright as a joke.*)

"P.S. I forgot to say that we danced at this amusement park. I learned to do a couple of jitterbug steps with Ruby Atwood my date. I don't like her first name very much. The hall is the Aragon, nicely decorated & large, but no ventilation just like all public halls. Herb

Miller played trumpet. He is supposed to be Glenn[75] Miller's brother. A pretty good orchestra."

Then in a letter[76] addressed to Dear Dad, "You sure had a swell job on that crane (*wiring a gantry crane*). That's sure good only one mistake on that big a job. It sure must have been an interesting job. I hope you get some more that are just as interesting."

"There is nothing that I want now. I don't sleep in pajamas. No one does that I know of."

"I wish I did have that new convertible that Jim dreamt about. Boy! Could I have a time."

"That little blonde that I was telling you about, umm, ummmmm."

"I've written myself out in that 10 page letter, so I'm going to close now. Tell me about your new job, Dad.

As promised, Bob wrote to Jim and Zelda.[77] "Today I got up at 5:30, cleaned up my tent, washed & shaved, and ate breakfast. That is one of 3 or 4 times that I have gotten up that early in two weeks. This morning we had scrambled eggs with bacon chopped up in it, milk, toast and butter, and potatoes, all I could eat. At 6:45 I started out on my new duties."

"I'm in charge of 'boots' that are assigned to work for a gardener who is a Sergeant. We transplanted shrubs and trees around the swimming pool and raked and smoothed out the dirt for planting lawn. A couple of 'boots' had a hard time getting one of the shrubs out of a five gal. sq. gas can with all of the dirt still on the roots. For my troubles I cut my knuckle to the bone of my middle finger of my left hand: the big knuckle that sticks up when you close your hand to a fist. I also cut the big knuckles on my first & ring finger, but not as bad. I had it fixed up so it will heal alright. I have to get it redressed at 6:00 and it is now about 5:30. Quit work at 11:00; got ready for chow; ate at 11:30: went back to being a straw boss at 12:45 and quit at 3:30; ate chow at 4:30; and now I'm writing you two."

"Jim, It sounds as though the kids at school are full of mischief. I hope those pictures turn out good. Send me some prints about 2 ½ by 2 ½. I hope you do well in the (*track*) meets. Tell me all about them. After the war we will take that canoe trip. It would be swell."

Bob and Jim had several summer vacations on the Russian River near Guerneville, California where they worked to become proficient at paddling in rapids. They also practiced over turning and righting the canoe, bailing and clambering back in to resume paddling. During that time the novice canoeists talked about paddling a canoe down the

Sacramento River camping along the way. Jim reminded Bob of their plan and expressed the hope that they could do that some day.

"I'm glad that you oiled the <u>rifles, not guns.</u>"

"Zelda—I'm sorry to hear about your glasses. Three of us kids bought an iron when we were in mess duty and I bought their share when we broke up. We paid $6 for it and rented it to other kids. I only paid them about $1 a piece because they couldn't very well take it with them or didn't want to be bothered, mostly."

"I'm going over and get my hand fixed. Well I'm back. The navy corpsman put a whole roll of gauze on my hand, wow. It was cut a little on the side of the knuckle, so it didn't cut any of the tendons on top. Have a good trip, or should I make that a question now? Good typing; better do better."

"Both of you--------I'm not addressing any more letters to the whole family; so if you want a letter you had better answer mine."

"P.S. Jim don't know what to get you for a (*birthday*) present except moccasins. If you want them send size-otherwise, I'll give you money."

Bob described another adventure exploring Southern California.[78] "An officer candidate and I decided we would hitch hike to L.A. This is the same guy that gave me a ride up last week. He left his car there. He was going to get off at Santa Ana. We walked about a mile along the highway towards L.A. and got a ride on a truck to Oceanside. There we saw about fifty or more Marines trying to get rides, so we decided to walk a little and get away from the crowd. We walked about a mile out of town and there we were at the South entrance to Camp Pendleton with about 30 Marines waiting. I wanted to get a ride back and get a bus but he was stubborn. So we kept walking. After an hour we didn't see any more fellows ahead of us so we took it easy. Finally a car stopped. Wowie! Were we relieved?"

"It was an elderly couple. Then we picked up two more. She then made it clear she preferred that we didn't smoke. It seems a car they had before burnt because someone was careless. And then she said smoke made her sick although her husband, driving, was smoking a cigar. She said it was cigarettes that made her ill. We then went inland through San Juan Capistrano to Santa Ana and let the O. (*Officer*) C. (*Candidate*) off."

"We then took a cut-off to Long Beach instead of going to L.A. I got a bus in Long Beach to L.A. Got to Wilbert's house about 8. He was with his girl friend taking her to a show. I ate a little bit and Earl's

Mom called a taxi and I went over to the girl I had taken out a wk. before. You see I had a date. We took a street car into town and saw a show."

"The next morning we went to church (Baptist, I don't appreciate their services) that is she, sister, Mom & Dad. I had lunch with them. Then she and I went over to Earl's house (he & girl were there). Took girl home."

"Got a ride about 6:30. Picked up sailor that was on truck coming up. He and I came back all of the way together. We got dropped off at a little town just 16 miles north of S. J. Cap. Two Marines there had waited 2 hrs. So we decided to walk. Got a little ways and had a blackout. Of course no cars. Kept walking 4 mi. altogether. Finally cars came. No luck. Pickup stopped, one sailor in, my friend in front because of no coat. I got in back, road 40 mi. to Oceanside. Picked up 2 sailors. Rode 40 more mi. to S.D. froze all of the 80 miles. Brrrrrrrrr. The 5 mi. walking with the O. C. gave me a sunburnt nose and froze for 80 mi. Some change, huh? I got in about 12:00. I had until 6 A.M."

"I'm going to phone you Fri. night. I've heard about fellows that had furloughs home and they say that it's worse than pulling teeth to leave. Everyone cries and the dogs whine. If it's that way, maybe it's just as good that I don't go up home, because I would have to leave."

"I hitch hiked to save money so I'd have more to spend on non-essentials. I have plenty of money. You don't need to send me any."

Bob wrote to Zelda the same day.[79] "Well hello, Zel. Have you broken your glasses a 3rd time? I'm sorry that I spelled there, their. It was very careless of me."

"Don't call me a wolf. A wolf, technically, is a guy who hollers and whistles at every 'bag' on two feet. I hope I'm not that bad. Jitterbugging is kind of strenuous. Conventional dancing to smooth music is more to my liking."

"I don't know of anything else to write beings that I just wrote five pages to Mom& Dad."

"I shall try to be more correct in my spelling after this.

5

PHOTO SCHOOL QUANTICO VIRGINIA

Private Robert Watson received orders transferring him to Photo School in Quantico, Virginia along with five other candidates. The original plan included ten, reduced to seven and finally only five were allowed. Bob made a surprise telephone call home with the good news and the next day packed his gear, checked out of the base and boarded a train in San Diego at three o'clock on Wednesday April 28, 1943. The train loaded with other military personnel being transferred to new duty stations and the five future photo students soon rolled out of the station headed east across the southern part of the United States with short sojourns into Mexico. During the trip Bob became acquainted with Grant Wolfkill, from Washington State, a fellow student who would become one of his best friends.

When the train finally approached the Quantico station, Bob eagerly peered out a window into the dark night searching for a glimpse of his new surroundings. Arriving about midnight on 3 May he immediately sent a telegram, in the early morning hours with the following message:

"ARRIVED OK MARINE CORP PHOTOGRAPHIC SECTION MARINE CORPS SCHOOL QUANTICO VA CARE STILL PHOTO SCHOOL LOVE=
BOB"

A letter followed the wire later in the day, "May 4 at 1:12 E.W.T. (*Eastern War Time*),[80] "Well, I've arrived safe and sound. We boarded the train at S.D. at 3 P.M. Wed. We went through Arizona, Tex., N. Mex., Okla., Kans., Missouri, Ill., Ind., Ohio, W. Vir., and Vir. Went in and out of Tex. And N. Mex. Several times. The parts of Ariz., N. Mex., & Tex. that we went through were hell. It was hot; dusty, and hot, & dusty. Okla. & Tex. weren't too bad. It was night when we went through Missouri. Vir. mts. are very pretty. Many people live in them. Just starting Spring here. Snow is gone. Not cold."

"I met the Abreu boy of Colusa, (who) worked at Zumwalt's (*Farm Implement Company*), in Arizona. I met a soldier from Howard

51

Co. Missouri on the train. He knows Uncle Floyd[81]. He says that Floyd does a good business, but doesn't make any money."

"Everything here is coal, no oil."

"I start to school Mon. – 8 wks. longer if they put me on mess duty as they can again."

"Send me my Speed Graphic, case, and holders with all unexposed film that is there. Holders are full. Send me any 3 ¼ x 4 ¼ film that you can send. <u>Panchromatic 100 Weston preferred.</u> Otherwise ask them for next best film. Send me the leather binder that I bought when I was going to nite-school. <u>Pack carefully, insure, and take money from bank to do this.</u>"

"We don't start school (*Still Photography School*) until Mon. but we sat in on a class and I made 16 exposures with a Kodak 35 mm camera. It is very neat. The only other camera that the Marines use for combat photo is the 4x5 Speed Graphic."[82]

"I was on the train when I was to be paid, and I won't be paid for over 2 weeks. So I'm sending a telegram for you to send me $15. I spent too much on that blond and I spent some on the way out so I'm down pretty low."

"We live in steam heated barracks very close to the school and the mess hall is on the ground floor of our barracks."

"Everything here is Okiedoaks I hear. Especially liberty. There are 8 women to every man in Washington, D.C."

"I got the telegram OK.[83] It certainly was fast service. I sent the telegram last night and got the answer this morning about 10:30. I'm going to send $15 to you next pay. I want to keep up what little I have in the bank. I shall send some more to pay for those telegrams; too. Thanks a lot."

"I made some shots with a Kodak 35 the day before yesterday. Almost all were over exposed. I need a lot of practice."

"I hope everything is OK there. Some mail almost beat me here that was forwarded from S.D."

"I had better mail this or I shall keep on adding stuff to it."

Bob then wrote to Jim.[84] "I understand that Wash., D.C. is a good deal. They have a bunch of tents with bunks, clean linen, and blankets all for $0.50 a night. There is a Pepsi Cola place where you can drink all you want free. And the Red Cross has a free coffee & sandwich place. These are for servicemen only. I've also heard that there are eight girls to every boy there, too. It hadn't ought to be so hard to meet a very nice girl."

"Later we shall take pictures under actual battle conditions of exploding shells, firing guns, etc."

In a letter to Zelda,[85] "Well, here is where I try and answer your 3 letters. That bond (*war bond that Zelda purchased*) was a fitting present for Hitler[86] on his birthday."

"I haven't gotten those cookies yet. That is unless you only sent one box, because I did get one, but I was thinking that was before the 26th."

"That (Marine that you met) must have been placed on inactive duty or was sick in boot camp quite awhile if he was in Plt. 120, because they go in numerical order and 8 was broken up long before 120. I'm closing now because a fellow is going to take this to the mail box."

Bob wrote another letter the same day to his parents,[87] "The letter that you began April 27th surely has a strange start. That was quite a coincidence for you to be starting and have me phone you. We can get practically all of the candy and gum that we want. Maybe I shall send some more to you."

"I shall now tell you about my trip. As said before we left S.D. at 3 P.M., went to El Centro, down into Mex. a couple times and then into Ariz. Mexico was green and there were some very pretty horses. The people live in the same type of houses as they do in Zumwalt's (*orchards*)[88] and far worse."

"Ariz., the part that we went through, was a desert. Cactus, sage brush, and desert bushes. Along dried creek beds were cottonwood trees. New Mex. & Tex. were practically the same except there wasn't any cactus and there were a few cattle wandering around. We went through the outskirts of Tijuana, Yuma, and El Paso. Those were the main cities. Okla. was green and the wheat was about 5 in. tall. Kansas was very green and wheat was shorter as we moved north. In the Northern part of Kansas we got in foothills. Tex., Okla., & Kan. as far as you can see no hills or mts., just rolling plains. West Va. and Va. are kind of pretty. I said that it was sultry here, but we had a small shower last evening, and now it is clear and there is a nice breeze blowing."

"The class going now had a test just awhile ago. They take notes during the week and take a test on Sat. Just by listening during the week I could answer all questions fairly accurately, I believe."
"I'm going to Wash., D.C. this evening. It seems that I am getting to see quite a bit of the Country and being paid, too. That's alright."

Four days later,[89] "I got the money quite alright and I shall get paid $52 a week from tomorrow. I shall send $20 to put back in the bank and pay for the telegrams and part of the film if you can buy any. Here they pay to the dollar; back West paid to the $5.

"It takes but three days to get your letters by airmail. This is in answer to your letters of the 5th and seventh. I got the Vallejo papers but not the magazines yet. Mosquitoes haven't bothered me. There are gnats here too."

"Talking about not having to light the stove in the morning. Here we sweat all day long and don't use any heat at night. Sometimes I sleep all night with only a sheet. Last night it cooled off because it rained. It rained hard again this morning. It has rained 3 or 4 days out of the last 7."

"I went to Wash. over the weekend. We (some photo. guys) went to a show, and slept in 'tent city', an Army camp where service men can get clean linen, blankets, bunks, coffee, and doughnuts, all free. The Army furnishes the lodging and the Red Cross the eats. Very nice. 'Tent city is at Arlington, Va., next to the famous cemetery where the Unknown Soldier is buried. It is about 2 ½ miles from the center of Wash."

"Sunday we saw the Lincoln, Washington, and Jefferson memorials. We went through part of the Smithsonian Institute & saw part of the Capitol City. We went to the Zoological Park, too."

"I believe that I shall stay here this weekend. Nothing more to add, except I am enclosing pictures; most show the wrong way. A couple show the right (*way*)."

Bob had an assignment to take pictures showing the right and wrong way for a marine to be dressed. Unshined shoes, necktie hanging loose and brown belt over shoulder were examples of unsatisfactory dress.

6. Unshined and Shined Shoes

7. Proper Dress, Watson and unknown

8. Improper Dress L-R Watson Unknown and Wolfkill

FICIAL PHOTOGRAPH — Marine Corps Photographic Section
Marine Corps Schools, Quantico, Va.

9. Improper Dress Pvt. Watson with jacket off, hat back and smoking

Only a day later Bob wrote,[90] Everything here is going along OK. I just got your letter of the 9th this morning. I'm glad to get it."

"That is a very good picture of Zelda, although you can but barely make out her glasses."

"What are you doing now, Dad? Are you through with the cafeteria? (*Earle had an assignment wiring a cafeteria at the Navy Yard*) Have you played much golf since I left?

"Those fellows that are getting 10 day furloughs are draftees. They surely have it soft compared with what we had to go through. We didn't have to join so they made it a little tough. Now because these fellows were made to go in they get it soft."

Bob's conclusion may have overlooked the possibility that the Marine Corps basic training and attitude about limiting early furloughs when he enlisted was simply a belief in a more arduous training regimen coupled with the need to get trained marines to the Pacific Theater as soon as possible

"Why didn't you use the toaster (*a gift from Bob when he was still in San Diego*) before? I didn't give it to you to look at."[91]

"I had thought of sending you a pillow slip; but I thought it looked too much like a carnival pillow, so I didn't. They are pretty though."

"Some of those pictures that I sent you are Official Marine Photographs showing how a Marine shouldn't appear. Whenever you are out in the public you have to keep neat. Many times you see fellows that aren't; but if an M.P. (*Military Police*) catches them they are S.O.L." (S—t Out of Luck)

"We made some flash pictures, indoors, and out, today. I certainly hope that they turn out OK. You see, if I make very good here, maybe I shall be sent to the MGM movie school in Culver City very near to Hollywood. They have a school here too, but I'm hoping that I can go there. There is a life (*Life Magazine*) school in N.Y. too. If I don't go on to school, I shall go to a line camp (infantry)."

Although Bob did not mention it, some of the students were destined to be still photographers assigned to combat units while others were selected to become cinematographers.

"We got some more clothes yesterday. Mon. we started wearing summer service uniform. It is made up of shirt, field scarf (tie), trousers (light tan like Jim & I had once; we called it army cloth), and overseas cap made of same material as trousers. We call the cap, garrison cap. We can wear barracks cap with tan cover. It has a beak same as Marines wear in Vallejo, only with tan cover."

"It's now 5:45 P.M. here, 2:45 P.M. there. At 7 I have to be at a lecture on syncro-photography. Last night I made a couple of enlargements of Mother's Day negatives some fellow made."

Bob further described the school and the course he was taking to Jim.[92] "We have a pretty good course. It is a brand new school even though it is in an old wooden building. I'm in its 7th class. It (*the school*) just started in Sept. (*1942*).[93] There are but approximately 15 in my class.[94] As each class starts they add new improvements to it. It still isn't as good as it could be."

"I don't think that I shall reveal any secret by telling you the types of pictures that we are to take. Here are a few:

Enemy personnel-dead or alive (preferably alive with equipment as they use it.) Enemy equipment, roads, landscape, bridges, etc. New improvements (*and*) improvisations."

"These pictures are to be taken from every conceivable angle and in utmost detail. They say don't worry about film they'll supply it, if possible. This is overseas, not here. We have to conserve here."

In his naivety Bob added, "The above is strictly confidential. It may be secret."

"I hate to see you join the Army, but the opportunities for flying are better, I think. It will be awful having two dog-faces in the family, Raymond and you."

"That summer school sounds good, but you only go to school once. Go the regular time and get as much out of it as you can and have a lot of fun too. Or, go to summer school and go on to J. (*Junior*) C. (*College*); get as much education as you can, but don't slight the fun of school because this may be your last chance to go to school. High School days and those immediately following are the most enjoyable and they shape your following life. Get the most from them. I didn't realize it before; now I do. Just ask Dad."

"If it is legal, practice this spring; but if it isn't, be careful. We want a championship (*football*) team this year."

"Look into the R.O.C. (*Reserve Officer Course*) course at Berkeley. It sounds like a good deal. Let me know all the details, whatever you do.

Don't think I'm preaching; but, it may help you."

Still concerned about money and his Speed Graphic camera, Bob informed his parents,[95] "I am enclosing $20 in a Postal Money Order. Put fifteen in the bank and keep $5 to pay for the telegrams. If you bought any film take money out of the $15 and tell me so that I shall know how much more to send. I've started a letter and will send it a short time later. I hope that you didn't send my camera unless you could insure it for at least $200."

The promised letter started on May 20 was mailed two days later,[96] "I've been so busy lately that I hardly have time to go to a show during the week. Last night I had a class."

"1st call is at 5:20 A.M.; Reveille 5:25; roll call; chow, 6:00; clean barracks; 7:00 clean heads, showers, halls; 7:45 roll call; 8:00 class; 8:30 or 9:00 roll call; 11:45 class dismissed; 12:00 chow; 1:00 P.M. class (usually take and develop pictures); 4:45, class over; 5:30 chow; at least one night a week we have a class, 6:30; 10:00 taps. Chow is lousy. San Diego chow is much better."

"You know how it gets sultry sometimes just before a spring or fall shower, well the weather here is like that quite often. It is very sultry and humid but it isn't relieved by rain. Although, it does rain here quite frequently during the summer."

"Quantico is 42 mi. south of Wash. D.C. and 20 mi. N. of Fredericksburg, Va. We are on the very edge of the river. In fact there is no levee. My barracks is about 800 yds. from the water. Others are within 100 yds. We are about 20 mi. south of Alexandria, Va."

"The girls in Wash. are extremely friendly. I've taken out 3 girls in 2 weekends. They are nice and very good looking. We, the 4 of us Marines, were walking along a street one Sun. and 5 girls were in a bus; they hollered at the driver to slow down they then hollered at us to find out if we wanted to go along. See how friendly they are? The funny part of it is that a lot of them are good looking and nice girls, not bad ones."

"Two of the five[97] of us that came out here from S.D. are leaving this weekend to go to school in Culver City, Calif. M.G.M. (*Metro Golden Mayer*) studio. It is at least a 2 month course. I stay here and study. One lives in Glendale and the other in Mich."

"The two clippings that you sent me about the crash at S.D., I was glad to get. The plane crashed into the same building that a piece of one of the props from the P-38's, which I had mentioned before, but this is about 100 yds. from where the P-38's hit. I've been expecting a plane to miss its take-off there. Many a plane has but barely missed the fence between the base & airport. Some planes flew over marching platoons as close as 30 ft. and I think some were closer. One plane just barely made it once. He overshot the field and had to zoom up. His landing gear cleared the fence not over 5 ft."

"I just got your letter of the 15th. I think the camera will be alright, at least I hope so. I just sent you $20. Let me know if you don't get it."

"Someone appropriated a shirt of mine, so I had to buy a new one. It cost $2.35. Another kid and I ate at the PX restaurant. We had roast beef sirloin. It only cost me $0.75. Beef, carrots, peas, milk and apple pie alamode. Doggone good I say and cheap."

"Four of us just finished making some portraits of each other. Some day when I get a chance I'll make some prints. It is very hard though to get permission. .

10. Smiling Bob with Pipe   **11. Bob with Pipe**

12. Bob in Garrison Hat, aka Pisscutter

"The picture that you sent me before of Zel surely resembles you, Mom. Send more small pictures. I enjoy them. I shall try & do the same whenever possible."

"What are you doing Dad? Do you still play golf?"

May 26, 1943: "Boy! Am I kept busy (?). I don't have time to answer your letters even. We don't work hard but we don't have much time for ourselves. We have class in the evenings, twice a week, I wash clothes 1 or 2 nites, and shower & shave. I go to D.C., to relieve the monotony, over the weekend. I was lucky and found time to see the show 'Casablanca' one night."

"I shall try and write a little every night and mail my notes of my doings twice a week. I haven't had time to answer any letters other than yours except B. Pillsbury's and Craig Wilson's."

"I got the camera OK as far as I have been able to tell. You certainly packed it well and boy did it cost to send it. I shall send you some more money the first time it is available. I took the camera to Wash. over the weekend, but I didn't take any pictures. It is very heavy to carry around. I am going to take it next weekend; and this time I shall try & take some pictures and send some to you. Don't count too heavily on it though."

Bobs camera was a Speed Graphic that used 3 ¼ x 4 ¼ film similar to the standard press camera that used 4x5 film. The Marine Corps used the 4x5 camera in combat because it had proven its worth as a press camera and was very rugged. There were three viewfinders: wire frame, optical; and ground glass. A distance scale and rangefinder supplemented the ground glass to aid focusing. Combat photographers would not use the ground glass viewing and focusing capability. It was best suited for formal portrait or landscape photography.

"I'm pretty sure I shall have to have another month of mess duty starting Monday. If that happens I won't be able to be in Wash. during the day, just at night. Next weekend looks to be my last. There is a ruling in the U.S.M.C. that each man shall serve 30 days mess a year, but apparently it doesn't hold true during war time."

"The 2 fellows, that I told you of, left for L.A. today, the lucky bums. I don't mind it here though."

"Those pictures I sent you were an assignment to show how a Marine shouldn't look. That cigarette was for affect. They take out about $6.50 a month for insurance and I still get, and will for 10 more months, $3 a mon. for sharpshooter. I haven't noticed how long it takes to get the papers. I think it takes about a week. I got your cookies. Only half were crumbs; but they were all dried up. The fellow in the picture with the hickies, I met in S.D., the other kid I met here. My ring got bent in boot camp, so I don't wear it anymore."

"It is very humid and it rains very often. We had a thunder and lighting storm Fri. Some of the bolts were but ½ mile away. I timed the interval between lightning and sound. It rained last night too."

"I have taken action shots, flash shots (portrait, auxiliary, & indoor), and portraits under flood lighting. I have also taken panorama shots under good and bad conditions. I have developed negatives and enlarged. My experience is increasing as the days pass. I have also used the Kodak 35, a 35 mm camera."

"We have seen training film (movie) on all types of subjects &

types of photography. I go to class tonight."

Bob congratulated Zelda for her achievement in the Rainbow affiliate of the Eastern Star Lodge.[98] "Dear Zel, Congratulations on acquiring a new office.."

"You should see the show 'My Friend Flicka'. A couple of kids saw it and they really enjoyed it. I saw the show 'More the Merrier'; and it is true to Wash. D.C. in more ways than one. Some of us went cycling near the Lincoln, Jefferson, & Washington memorials & monuments. Washington is really a pretty town. We are in school from 8 until 4:45 and we have 2 classes a week in the evening. I don't even have time to answer your letters. I go to Wash. over the weekend to relieve the monotony and then spend the rest of the week catching up on sleep."

"The school started in Sept. This class that I'm in is the 7th since the school started. In other words the Marines didn't have a photo school until Sept. and I am in the 7th class."

Bob clarified the nicknames given men in the different services and assured Zelda that his training would keep him safe. "A soldier is a 'dogface' the same as a sailor is a 'swab jockey' or 'gob' and a Marine is a 'leatherneck', 'sea going bell hop' or 'devil dog'. So don't get all hot and bothered. Don't you worry! They teach us to take care of ourselves. I have another class tonight."

"Don't write more than twice a week and I could answer your letters better if you wrote but 1 a week. We don't have much time to ourselves."

1 3. **Still Photography Class 7: Front row Walavich, Unknown, Bill Genaust; Straneiri standing ; Second Row Martin McEvilly, Robert Watson**

6

MESS DUTY AND FURLOUGH

Marines have to be fed, so as Bob predicted he received the assignment once more,[99] "Well! I got mess duty. They told us the same this time as they told us at S.D. 'So many have to do it and you're it.' Five fellows in the class already had mess duty here at school and there are about 4 cpls. and 6 of us were eligible. Three of us got mess and 1 got orderly (duty) in the barracks; two didn't get anything, they continue to school."

"I got the camera May 20th. When you had that heat wave it must have been pretty bad. We had a thunder & lightning storm yesterday evening. It was a regular cloud burst for the first 15 or 20 min."

"It looks as though Jim has a few dances lined up (*playing in Lew Scott's band*). I can hear Jim snoring now."

"I guess I didn't tell you but when I was waiting to come here to school, I was eating in a mess hall for permanent personnel and the food was very, very good. Here the food doesn't compare. We don't get strawberries here although I had some in S.D. There are wild strawberries here though. I've seen some small ones; and out in the woods where they go for combat maneuvers there are large ones."

"I travel by train (*to Washington D.C.*). About 200 or 300 (people) get on the train on Sat. nite. They stand everywhere, even in the baggage cars. I never did get the cookies & eggs."

"There are a couple of radios in the barracks; but they are so far away it is hard to listen with all of the noise. Besides, I'm usually busy."

"No Zelda, I don't have to clean the head." *The Navy and Marine Corps called a bathroom, "The Head" and the Army called it a "Latrine".*

"For chow—breakfast, mush cooked or prepared, hard boiled eggs, coffee, milk (refrigerator on the bum, not low enough temperature milk beginning to sour), toast. Noon-filet de sole, milk, canned peas, macaroni with cheese, and pumpkin pie. This was a very good meal in comparison."

"Hey! How does Jim rate going out with Betty Shaw?" (*Betty Shaw was a very pretty girl in Vallejo High School whose father was a successful boxing promoter, who made more money than most men.*)

63

"They don't sell papers at the PX. We have to go into the business part of Quantico at civilian stores, but still are on the base. I have never bought one. When I go to the barbershop, I read the paper. There is a shop in each barracks."

Bob's family was surprised and pleased to receive a telegram from Bob that said,

"VA: EXPECT FURLOUGH SEND $65 START JULY 3RD="

Then he described his new duties,[100] "I now have time to answer your letter Dad I have some good news; I'm in for another month of mess duty. My job won't be so easy this time. I don't know what it is yet, but I shall in the morning. I shall have to work everyday, of course, that means that I shan't have any more weekends. That is alright, though; I won't spend so much money."

"I'm doing mess in the barracks that I'm bunking in so I only had to move my gear down one deck. Here are some diagrams:

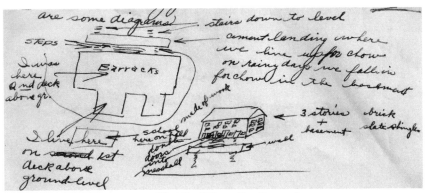

Sketch of Quantico Barracks

"I don't know whether you can make any sense of the scratching or not. Ask questions."

"When I find about my job, I put it in. I'm to cut & take care of bread and wait on tables."

Then a note to Jim followed: "I was only kidding you about joining the Air Force. We have some good planes, too. The Corsair is a very good one and besides they aren't always cracking up like the P-38s."

"That sounded like a good trip to Palo Alto. I'll bet that was a good trip to Fresno, also." (*Jim was on a relay team in which each*

*member ran 220 yards. The team won the North Coast Championship
and qualified to run in the West Coast Relays conducted in Fresno, CA.
The East Coast had a similar event called the "Drake Relays".)*

"What is this I hear about you dating B. Shaw? Man O man you
are stepping."

One day after the anniversary of Earle moving to Vallejo to work
at the Navy Yard, Bob wrote,[101] "I see that you don't have a very good
opinion of that Marine from Wisconsin. You see the Marines have
such a reputation for being rugged individualists and still being able to
fight together in a well knit team, fellows that have joined since P
(*earl*) H (*arbo*r) and especially fellows that have joined within the last
year try to make themselves appear as heroes in their own eyes and
especially the public. They try to make believe that they are 'old salts'.
Those that have been overseas or have been in for sometime brag very,
very little, especially those that have seen action." Bob's parents had
invited the Marine from Wisconsin to their home and he stayed and
talked for several hours. Bertha recorded in her diary that "he was
certainly homesick."

"In mess hall we get awakened at 4:30, but we manage to sleep in
until 4:45 or 4:50. Cooks get up earlier and get food prepared. Tables
are set from night before so fellows (mess men) bring out our breakfast
while I make toast or cut bread. We eat; clean tables, cut bread, put out
food for chow at 6:00. Wait on tables, clear tables; reset them for noon
chow, swab decks; have 1 ½ hour rest. Today I took a sunbath for ¼
hr. I slept total time. Boy! Do I perspire when I sleep? Had to fix
mess hall for inspection. 10:00 went back to work. Cut more bread,
set tables, ate, and served chow. 11:00 same procedure; 12:00 chow
same procedure. 3:00 went back to work, cut bread, chow 4:30, chow
5:30 same procedure except while fellows swabbed I cut bread for
toast for tomorrow's breakfast. We feed 400 fellows each meal
divided between each (2) chow."

"I perspired so much that I have taken two showers today. I could
stand many more."

"I'm sitting in a little library here in the barracks. We have books,
magazines, a radio, card tables, chess, checkers, and a telephone. This
is on the first deck in the front of the building."

Then in a letter to Jim, Bob wrote,[102] "Say, I've been wondering
ever since I heard you were going around with Lee Monroe if he ever
tried preaching to you? That time we (Sea Scouts) went to San Rafael,
a drunk was standing on the street corner and Lee tries to convert him.

The fellow keeps asking Lee if he would care for a drink. The drunk finally got rid of him and Lee goes tearing down the street after a girl he had met at the skating rink. He had a date to go to church with her the next morning; but, he never kept it."

"You certainly must have had fun at that meet (*West Coast Relays in Fresno*). I have heard much about Grover Klemmer and Harold Davis. (*sprinters*) They are both very good. It was very worthwhile to see them. Was Warmerdam (*World record for pole vaulting with bamboo* pole) at the meet?"[103]

"I'm glad to hear that Kilby is going to coach, although he has eccentricities. Tell him hello. I bet that you and Betty made a good looking couple, especially you in your tux. Send me a picture. I hope the baseball team gets the gold balls." (*Small gold balls that hung on a chain were often rewards for players on championship teams.*)

"What Granddad said about girls is very true. You whisper sweet nothings in their ears and sugar comes dribbling out their noses."

Responding to parental concern, Bob wrote,[104] "Mess duty doesn't cut me out of finishing school. I asked for the camera to use personally."

"Hitch hiking isn't bad here at all. I've hitch hiked to D.C. twice. I get a taxi and ride to Triangle, VA., approximately 3 mi. (from here) and (it) is on the highway. From there it is fairly easy to catch a ride. When you go by train it is so hot & the cars are so crowded most of us stand at the doors with them open. The cinders come in and it is very, very dirty. The chow has gotten better lately."

"I'm glad that you like your job, Mom. I'm glad that you were lucky enough to get in with such nice people." (*No doubt this was the Corbin Photo Supply Store.*)

"That balloon going to Colorado was really something, wasn't it?" (*This may have been a reference to the balloon that sailed on the wind from Japan to Colorado. Although the Japanese balloon campaign started in earnest in November 1944.*)

"It is very nice also, that Ray is so close to home. I got a letter from him, one of those 'longest letters that you've ever received', things."

"I'm glad that Kilby is getting back into the harness again.

"I'm glad to hear that Jim is Student Body Pres."

"I went swimming today between the time that I got off noon work and afternoon work. This is the first time since 'boot camp'. I was in for an hour and my shoulders are slightly red, not a real sunburn."

"Last night I saw the show Edge of Darkness, the second time. I saw it in L.A. with Ruby At. (*wood*)"

To let his parents know "what is cooking", Bob wrote,[105] "Every Tues. we have 'field day' in the mess hall to be ready for inspection on Wed. (field day is cleaning everything & going over it all with a fine tooth comb & I'm not exaggerating one 'eentsy bit.) We still washed all dishes, bon ammied windows (*using Bon Ami, a commercial cleaning product*), scrubbed decks, washed tables, and innumerable other things had to be done. I started work at 4:00 and got through at 6:45. All together I did about 12 hours solid work, although some of it was cutting bread which is fairly easy although I was on my feet all of the day except when eating."

"I don't want anything for a present. Send me my bathing suit. I have a GI suit, but it is nothing much more than a G string. I went swimming again today. There were girls there today and yesterday and so I stayed in the water all of the time. The suit is white cotton and when you get away from me it looks as though I'm nude. I went swimming from 7 'til 7:30 tonight. It was swell."

Supplementing the letter on June 18 at 9 PM, Bob added, "Last night I went to the show 'He Married his Boss'. When I got out it was beginning to rain and was thundering and lightning to beat hell. The drops were as big as hail stones. Tonight I went swimming. The water was very nice. It was nice all day with pretty cloud formations."

"'My Friend Flicka' is on at the show tonight; but I hope to go to N.Y. City tomorrow so I stayed and spit shined my shoes. You can use the toes to powder your nose by. I'm not exaggerating either."

"When you tell me about some ship, either put in more details or don't tell me about them, because you stir my curiosity."

"About your dream—I cut two of my fingers on the bread knife very small cuts. Strange"

"If I go to N.Y., I shall tell you all about it."

In a note to Zel written June 15, "I shall be able to finish school."

"I have asked for this week end off. If I get it, I shall go to N.Y.-Long Island. A kid here lives there and has invited me up. Very nice of him, wasn't it?"

"Let me know what your grades are, Zelda. In three tests on Photo I got 100% in all. Let me see you get to work."

Zelda and Bertha were visiting her parents in Colusa when Bob reported good news in his next missive,[106] "This is for all, Gr-ma-pa,

Mom, Jim, & Zel. I went to NY over the weekend and now I have a chance to get a 15 day furlough home. I wrote Dad. I shall leave the nite of the 2nd or the 6th. It will take me 4 days to get home. I have applied for furlough but won't know until Wed. Remember because of the distance and time required I may not get it. So Mom you stay there until I telegraph Dad telling him all and he can phone you. Dad will have to get some money from the bank to send me so that I can get home & back. I shall be able to save enough afterwards to pay income tax."

"I'm writing to Dad and having him look into getting ration stamps from the board while I'm home, if I get there. Please do not count on me coming home too heavily because of reasons stated before. I'm not writing anything more, because I don't know anything def. I shall let you all know the details."

"Dear Dad,[107] I went to N.Y. over the weekend. I stayed at this fellow's house. He was very kind to invite me to his place. It took us from 6 to 7 hours to make the trip one way, and it cost about $8 to go there round trip. Altogether I spent $15. Sat. night we got some girls and went to a little nightclub on Long Island. The name of it was Seville's. Two bros. own it. One just came back from N. Africa (infantry) and the other is a ballroom dancer. The latter and his partner toured Europe and the States dancing. Now he & his brother own this nite club. Since I've been in the service I have found out how much I can hold and how much is too much (liquor)."

"Sunday we went swimming. Mac, the fellow that I was with told me that we were going to a lake; so, I naturally supposed it to be like those in Calif. Was I surprised? It was fenced in, we had to pay for the girls, and they had diving boards, water slides and floats out in the middle. There were about 5000+ people there. My gosh, it was awful. They had a filtering system also. I was told that it wasn't crowded that day. The lake was about 100 yds by 880."

"After mess duty we are getting furloughs and I stand a good chance of getting 15 days. So be prepared to send me some money from my account. I shall either leave the 3rd or the 6th or 7th. If I leave the 6th or 7th I shall get a pay, and shall need $60 if I can't wait and have to leave the 3rd I shall need $85. I didn't think I would get a furlough so I went to N.Y. and I didn't raise your hopes, if you were hoping. Now I stand a pretty good chance. I shall be able to save enough to send back afterwards in time to pay the 3rd quarter of my income tax. It will take 4 days to get there. Mom can get some of her teeth fixed before I get there anyhow."

"I don't like to come home like this, but if I don't grab the chance I might not get another. I will send you a telegram telling when I leave & when I will arrive. If I get the furlough. Remember I have not got this in the bag. I have submitted an application but haven't an answer. Tell Mom to stay in Colusa until I tell you definitely. Or maybe don't tell her because then she will come back home without getting her teeth fixed. I don't know whether you have all gone to Colusa or not. I shall tell Mom & Jim & Zel in a letter."

"P.S. Find out from the ration board about stamps for extra food for me, also gas."

As promised Bob wrote,[108] "I got the money Mon. OK. You didn't need to send $70; but in a way, I'm glad. I got your package of stationery today. Did you think that I'd run out or needed a reminder?"

"I'm through mess now and I shall have more time to myself. I shall be able to write more often, too."

"I shall send you a telegram telling you when I shall arrive. I will go through Chicago on the way; so, I shall see some more of the country. I shall either catch the 5:10, 6:50, or 10:00 train from Wash., Fri. night."

"I (hope) that you got everything straightened out in Colusa. I wrote a letter to Grandma telling you about my chance in getting a furlough, but you got home I guess before it arrived. They haven't turned it down yet so I guess that I shall get it."

"9:30 July 1, I'm packing my stuff. I shall leave here tomorrow night; I should be in S.F. Tues. morning or Tues. night. I'll send a telegram telling you when I shall arrive. I will catch a bus to Vallejo."

In a telegram sent from Omaha, Nebraska, Bob wrote,

"ARRIVE VALLEJO PM TUESDAY=BOB"

Bob arrived home on Tuesday July 6th tired and dirty from his long train ride. Everyone was very happy to see him; Bertha struggled to keep from crying. After eating dinner, hurriedly prepared by Bertha for her hungry Marine, Bob visited Doc Pierce, the Sea Scout Master and then went to a Sea Scout meeting with Bill Pillsbury, and later to a movie. Bob spent the next day loafing around and visiting friends in town.

About nine o'clock a day later everyone piled into the Studebaker and drove out Highway 80 towards Sacramento and then took the

Winters cut-off, a two lane country road (now freeway 505), and headed for Highway 99 to Williams and finally into Colusa. The family enjoyed seeing the old familiar roads and the panoramic view of the flat valley land with foothills in the distance. The rice and stubble barley fields were a welcome sight on Highway 20 as the travelers entered town.

Two nights stay at Bertha's parents' house provided an opportunity for everyone to catch up on recent activities and for Bob to tell his grandparents about life as a Marine. Old friends were visited, the car received minor repairs, and Bob and Jim swam for hours in the municipal swimming pool where they both had earned Red Cross Life Saving badges.

Saturday morning goodbyes were followed by a stop at the local butcher to purchase meat hard to find in Vallejo. Following a three-hour drive back to the Navy town the family spent the rest of the day lounging around and "enjoying each others' company."[109] With no duties to perform Bob and his family slept late Sunday morning and after a leisurely breakfast were hosts to a relay of visits from relatives and friends.

A high school girl friend cancelled a date with Bob in order to spend time with another girl. Knowing the girls in Washington D. C. were more reliable, Bob went to a movie with his boating friend Lee Setterquist. His penultimate day was spent quietly but capped off with a visit from Doc Pierce who showed home movies of Sea Scout activities that included Bob in many of the scenes. Photographs were taken during the day to memorialize his all too short time at home.

Bob spent the next day quietly at home while his mother ironed his clothes and prepared a fried chicken lunch for his return to Quantico. In the evening the family enjoyed a quiet but special dinner ever mindful of Bob's imminent departure. When the dishes were washed and dried everyone got into the car and drove through Vallejo, across the Carquinez Bridge and to the train station in Crocket. The tearful goodbyes of six months before were repeated as Bob climbed the steps up into his car "at 9:30 P.M." Bertha recorded in her diary, "We came home and when we went to bed I had to cry."

14. Watson Family: James, Earle, Bertha, Robert, and Zelda

Five days later Bob sent a telegram from Quantico,
"1943 JUL 18 AM 12 15 ARRIVED ALL RIGHT TRIP UNEVENTFUL=BOB"

7

BACK IN STILL PHOTO SCHOOL

Robert wrote a more detailed report about his return to Quantico,[110] "I'm back to dear ole Quantico where the temperature is nice and cool (94 degrees). As soon as I got in I shaved and took a shower. I then ate chow and came back upstairs and slept all afternoon. I ate evening chow, sent you the telegram and then saw the show. I saw Saludos Amigos for the second time and Bambi. I enjoyed them both."

"My trip was uneventful. The car from Crockett to Chicago was a little better. The car was the same kind only it had electric lights and the windows fit better, so it was cleaner. At Chicago I had a stop of one hour and caught the Capitol Limited. It is all Pullman but lately they have put on a chair car to take care of the overflow. It is a good streamliner train, clean and nice soft seats with pillows available at $0.15 a piece."

"On this train I went by one of the Great Lakes and through the town Harpers Ferry, W. VA. Look in a history book for H-F-."[111]

"The weather is hot & so of course we eat hot food although we have milk and watermelon. All afternoon I slept. This morning I washed clothes."

Bob continued to describe his return trip to Quantico,[112] "I was certainly thankful for the food you packed. It lasted until Thurs. night. I threw away two peanut butter sandwiches; they were squashed. I didn't see the WAC (*Women's Army Corps*)[113] Lt. on the train; but between Chicago and Wash. I met 2 Waves (*Women Accepted for Volunteer Emergency Service in the Navy*)[114]; they wanted to know if I had any dice. I said, 'no'. I then asked an army nurse a Lt. if she had any dice. Of course she said, 'no'. Later she asked me if I had found any dice. I hadn't."

"I got paid today; and I'm sending $10 to you. You can pay for the watch & postage and keep the rest. Next pay I shall get paid ration money for my furlough and I shall be able to send that home plus some more. I didn't know we got ration money on a furlough. I think it is $0.55 a day. It isn't much but it helps."

"Yesterday I took some outdoor flash pictures. The flash is used to fill in shadows. I developed them yesterday and printed them today. Tonight I made some enlargements of some pictures that a kid took of me. Maybe I can send some home. Tomorrow I shall work in the identification part of photo."

Bob provided further descriptions of his assignments,[115] "Saturday I have the watch and so I can't go anywhere so last night I went to D.C. with a kid and he got me a date with a girl friend of his girl. She wasn't beautiful and she wasn't homely, but I might say she is slightly better than average." We will learn later that Bob had his eye on his friend's girl friend and she was attracted to him.

"I go on watch at 6:45 A.M. Sat. and get relieved 7:45 Sun. I'm on watch 25 hrs. so that the fellow relieving me can eat. Chow (breakfast) is one hour later on Sunday."

"I have to go out on a job this afternoon as a helper. We are to take pictures of officers. I shall have to be on my toes. I shall close now and find out what my job shall be." (Later) My job isn't to be what I thought it was. I go out and get the names of O. Cs (*Officer Candidates*) & R. O. C's. (*Reserve Officer Candidates*) that are to graduate, and find out the days that they go on maneuvers, and the equipment that photographers shall take on it."

And furthermore,[116] "Here I am sitting at a desk in the Photo School writing this letter. You see I'm on watch and this is the noon hour. I have to answer the phone calls and see that everything is secure. I went on watch at 0745 this morning, was relieved for chow at 10:45 & came back at 11: 35. I will be relieved again at 4:15 (1645) and I'm on after chow until 0730 tomorrow morning."

"Tomorrow I'm going to D.C. about noon. You see I get to sleep during the night. A girl and I are going to a show and ride bicycles when it gets cool."

"A few minutes ago I had to hang some negatives up to dry that a fellow left washing."

Bob described his latest trip to D.C.,[117] "When I went to D.C. Sunday, I went to a sunset concert on the bank of the Potomac (*River*). The Wash. Symphony Orch. played and Frank Sinatra sang. I got just as much pleasure listening to the girls around me as I did hearing him sing. Every time he would announce a song or come back on the stage the girls would scream and sigh as though the world were about to end. Two cops guarded Frank and an ambulance was parked near. The stage was on a barge moored to the bank. It was a nice setting."

"Sat. the Corps is giving the Marine Corps Schools here in Quantico a picnic and a beer bust. Cold cuts, hot dogs and I don't know what else. It surely is nice of them."

"Tonight we have a class on military courtesy in which we have a test on the General Orders. I suppose those that don't know them won't be able to attend the picnic. This morning we are to attend a movie, 'We are the Marines.'"

"I have another month of still (*photography*) work ahead of me.

"It is 8:30 and we leave for the movie in 15 min. (Later) I just got back from the movie. A great deal of it was taken at the Base in S.D., Camp Elliott, and Camp Pendleton. If you ever see it remember this: digging fox holes in the sand was taken on the 'boon-docks' (a maneuver area on the base), boots marching on parade ground I saw them take, and destroyers 222 (*USS Bulmer*) & 213 (*USS Barker*) I worked on at M. I. (*Destroyers Barker and Bulmer were assigned convoy duty between San Francisco and Pearl Harbor at that time and were repaired at Mare island Navy Yard*.) The picture was made by March of Time."[118]

A few days later Bob described his photo training activities,[119] "Starting in last Mon. of this week, the fellows in my class were paired off. Each pair chooses a different subject on which to work. We then make a number of shots on this subject doing all the work ourselves. They then are mounted on a card. From five to twelve or even fifteen can be mounted depending on size."

"A fellow named Besser from Topeka, Kansas and I are working together. Our subject this week is Post Recreation. We made shots of the swimming pool, dance band in the theater, beer bar down stairs under the theater, Pvt's & NCO's clubs, Gym-boxers, and the pool room & the library in my barracks. I shall try to send you some prints."

The next morning Bob added, "For 2 nights Besser & I worked until after 9:15 P.M. on our sequence and last night, & every Thurs. night, we had a lecture by a Chief Marine Gunner (*equal to a Chief Warrant in the Navy*.) We finished our sequence shots this morning. They aren't anything to boast over, though. In fact they're crummy."

15. Post Swimming Pool   **16. Boxers**

17. Pool Room by Watson

18. Barracks Library

After another trip to Washington Bob wrote,[120] "Sunday I went up into the Washington monument. It is a very good view from there. One can see the whole city and more from there. Most of the city is very well laid out."

"Sat. nite I went to Uline's Icc Arena with a girl Marine. The Coca Cola Spotlights of Bands was broadcast from there. Gracie Barry's band was playing. It is a little ways from the center of town and so it wasn't crowded at all. It was very nice dancing. We had free cokes and saw the broadcast. I was in there yelling with the rest. It was very nice at that concert."

"This week my partner and I are making a sequence on a sequence. We are following a pair thru' on theirs to show future students the methods and order of operation."

"Friday. We improved our sequence this week.[121] At least our negatives and print quality are better. We are almost finished."

"I'm sure glad that Ray got his PFC chevron. It was nice for him to get home again, too."

"I have some pictures but no envelope large enough. I've come back from the building next door with an 8x10 box-which will hold the pictures. I'm sending some of myself and some that I took. Those that have Besser's (name) written on them were printed by him. I took part & he took the rest. I've written on the back of them." Added on the 14th, "We finished our sequence early this morning and they were judged about 11:15. We didn't win, but our pictures are a heck of a lot better. I have the watch today. I get relieved at 0800 tomorrow.

"Monday 2000 (8:00 P.M.)[122] I just got back from visiting my sweetheart. I think that you've heard of her. Lorraine Day is her name. She was in a show with Cary Grant; Mr. Lucky was the title. It is one of her best pictures."

"We are now making individual sequences with the Kodak 35. I'm making one on the Post Band."

"Sunday I went to the Knights of Columbus USO in D.C. I had a good time dancing and had a damn good meal, all free. Sat. I had the watch as I told you before."

"I met Mitchell, one of the kids I came from S.D. with, at the Pepsi Cola Center at noon. We went to see the show Dixie & then went to the K of C."

Four days later, Bob wrote,[123] "Tues. afternoon I went out and made some 35 mm shots of the 105mm cannon. Wed. I had laundry detail. Yesterday a lieutenant back from Guadalcanal gave a talk about photography as it was there."

First Lieutenant Karl Soule had returned from a year in the Pacific theater where he had been assigned as Assistant Intelligence Officer for Photography, Division Intelligence Section, D-2 of the First Marine Division. In April 1942 2nd Lt. Soule outlined his idea of his duties:

Make "a record of significant phases of training and of all operations against the enemy,[124] providing visual aids in intelligence: panoramas, aerial photographs, whatever photography could do to aid in the job ahead." His superior added a requirement to make maps using lithographic equipment.

Lt. Soule landed on Guadalcanal with the First Division in August 1942, where he and the men of his unit distinguished themselves by producing maps and providing photographic coverage of the campaign.

The work was often interrupted by enemy attacks, but the darkroom and map department were never hit. His unoccupied living tent was blown up twice and his office tent once. He lost 30 percent of his men and narrowly escaped rifle fire and survived shelling from two Japanese battleships. Soule's unit shipped 35mm movie film to the States including extensive coverage of the battle of the Tenaru River, the first land battle. The Tenaru film that included scenes of enemy dead, was released to the newsreels and shown uncut in theaters in the States.

Karl Soule had worked for Burton Holmes, a well known travelogue producer, before the war and had graduated from Harvard at the age of 18 Cum Laude. When he arrived back at Quantico Soule was pleased to learn that a "still-picture section had been added, along with an animation department and production facilities."[125] Major Franklin P. Adreon Jr., the officer in charge took Soule to the Cine school, which he had recommended be established in reports of a year earlier. There he "spoke to the men briefly about the importance of combat photography."[126] Soule was informed that he was to take over the cine school and was promoted to Captain.

Bob added to his letter, "Aug. 26, 1943. I got off from noon Sat. until 0600 Mon. I went to New York. I went up with a kid that lives (there). His house was full of relatives, so I got a hotel room on 42nd St. next to Times Square. I went down to Greenwich Village to the Cobra Club owned by Zorita[127]. She is the great burlesque dancer that some Army officer paid $1,000 to stay with. Maybe you remember it. I don't. On the whole I had a good time there."

"All day yesterday I worked on laundry detail. I checked in dirty laundry & money, took clothes to laundry, picked up clean laundry, and checked it out to the fellows. I'm the lead man on that detail & two fellows helped."

"Last night the Marine Corps Schools had a beer bust. The 1st Sgt., Chief Clerk, & Chief Gunner (Chief W.O.) were all rather high. They mixed right in with the fellows."

"I'm out of class now. All I have to do is take a final test. I made prints off about 100 negatives. Fri. I went out with the Captain (Soule), a Master Tech. Sgt. and three other fellows. We went out to the demolition area. I got fairly good pictures of a huge flame. It was made with Graflex camera. It is the first time that I ever handled one. I'm sending it to you. <u>Do Not</u> show it to anyone else. I'm not just asking you; <u>I'm telling you.</u>"

Bob described a trip to Washington D. C.,[128] "Last night I went to D.C. with four other fellows. We visited the skating rink. It had been so long since I had skated that I wasn't able to skate as freely as the others. Toward the close of the evening I was going very good. I told a girl that it was the first time that I was ever in a rink. I don't think she believed me. I certainly had a swell time."

"There certainly were some graceful skaters there. They did waltzes, tangos, & fox trots. Of course it looks very much different on skates than the actual ballroom stuff. If it wasn't for the music you wouldn't be able to tell what kind of dance it was. There are three classes of dancing: Bronze Skates, Silver Skates, and Gold Skates. Each classification is harder to execute than the one preceding it. In each classification are three or four dances. They certainly are graceful on skates."

"Now comes the best part WOMEN. While skating, it was just like swimming in a pool of females. Of course all types were represented. Many lovelies were present along with others. It is almost like comparing gold fish to catfish. Of course there weren't any bull cats. I'm only kidding. There were many nice looking girls present and more girls than boys.

"Today (afternoon) I had charge of the equipment at school. Monday I start attending movie school. My new address will be: M.C.S. Motion Picture Section, Quantico, VA."

Official photographs were taken of graduates of the Still Photo School.

OFFICIAL PHOTOGRAPH — Marine Corps Photographic Section

19. Graduation Publicity Photo, Official Marine Corps Photographic   Section, Photo School

78

8

CINEMATOGRAPHY SCHOOL

Now assigned to the Cinematography School, Bob was immediately subjected to more military training. "This afternoon[129] and evening I've been getting my equipment ready for three days of war maneuvers. Here is my equipment pack, cartridge belt, first-aid kit, mess gear, canteen, change of underwear and socks, toilet paper, toilet gear (articles), poncho, tent half, blanket, and steel helmet."

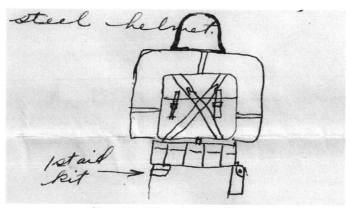

Sketch of Equipment Pack

"I leave tomorrow noon and get back sometime Sat. On the offensive side is a regiment and on the defensive will be a group of men that will man machine guns with live ammunition which they fire over our heads; and set-off booby traps and land mines near us to give a realistic (experience). All of this is under the direction of safety officers. Everything is safe and under the direction of competent men. I'll tell you all about it afterwards."

Before Captain Soule took over the cine school the students did no fieldwork much less military operations. The single instructor from Hollywood had no experience with military operations and the photo gear was heavy professional equipment mounted on tripods. Soule returned the tripods and light meters to the quartermaster. He was determined that the men would learn to shoot movie film "as we would in combat, with cameras and film, no gadgets."[130]   After some difficulty, Soule arranged for his students to participate in Officer Candidate School war maneuvers that gave his men a suggestion of life in combat.

20. Grant Wolfkill with Heavy Camera on Tripod

"Sunday.[131]

Yesterday morning I got back from the maneuvers and found your letters waiting for me. Eight of us left in a group about 5:30 for the maneuvers with some communications men and officer candidates. The eight of us and 20 O. C's. were assigned to the Hdqtrs. Co. of the Regimental Command Post. We did guard duty out there. We guarded cross roads and allowed no one to pass without the password. I had a post at which I was required to challenge all persons coming or going and enforce blackout regulations. Chow trucks would come along and be held up because they didn't have the password. I bet that we were cussed a good many times during those days. The eight of us had the two main points to guard. We did guard duty singly, 4 hrs. on and 8 off. The O. C's. had intermediate points along the road at night and other places during the day and night. At night they went in pairs."

"Thursday afternoon and night it tried to rain, but could only sprinkle. Fri, A.M. & P.M. it rained like hell. We had ponchos and shelter halves. My poncho needed a waterproofing job. We didn't use the shelter halves Thurs.; we slept in foxholes. Fri. we put up the tents. My partner and I slept dry. One pair didn't."

"The country we were in was a lot like the approach to Fort Bragg (*in Northern California*). We were in a wooded area, the roads were dirt, and it was very foggy and wet when it didn't rain. The woods are

80

very thick; the tree trunks are small, and there are more oaks than pines. The ground is rolling hills (red dirt)."

"We were given field rations morning noon and hot food at night. Thurs. night I was on watch while chow was served. By the time I got relieved for chow, I only got one weenie and a cup of black coffee. I brought along some oranges though and ate one of those. Fri. morning we had one can of meat and beans about 3 in. high and 2 in. in diameter, cold and a can the same size of no good crackers. I threw half away. We also had little candies (orange, lemon, butterscotch) and a little can of coffee powder. I didn't drink the coffee. I also ate an orange. For lunch we had a chocolate bar with concentrated vitamins and meal mixed that was two inches wide by four inches long. I also ate another orange. That night I helped serve chow. Had two big helpings. We had lamb stew, hot peas, and of course the coffee was straight. We had a lot more chow to go around that night."

"I got back to the barracks just before colors at 8 A.M. A fellow and I went down to the mess Sgt. to see about chow. We had scrambled eggs, bacon, cold cereal & fruit. This noon we had fried chicken the first time here at Quantico."

"We were issued helmets and cartridge belts also. We wore those plus the pack containing: change of underwear & socks, mess gear, oranges, poncho and toilet paper, one blanket and shelter half was made into a roll on outside of pack. Canteen and cup and first aid kit are on cartridge belt."

"In the final test at still school I missed one question and forgot to answer one I knew, so only got 98%. About 7 fellows went to Rochester to a school at the Folmer Graflex Corp. there. Out of those left, I got the highest % right."

"At movie school we have taken notes, viewed pictures and loaded the cameras with dummy film plus 1/2 hr. of calisthenics."

As soon as I get some stamps I will send those pictures to you. One is of me in combat gear. A copy is going to the papers."

Bob explained the new order requiring attendance at Cine School and his current activities,[132] "Movie school lasts 8 wks. Every combat photographer has to attend it before he is shipped out. This is a new order and was made because some still photographers at Guadalcanal were given movie cameras and wrecked the film. This doesn't mean I'm to be cine (*photographer*). It all depends upon my ability, what they need at the time and what I want. Another fellow, named Genaust[133], and I have started to make a little movie. It is on the care of shoes. The fellow starts out on liberty. He goes through dust and then stumbles; scuffing his shoe. He goes back to quarters; wipes off dust; puts dye on scuff; polishes shoe; spit shines it; goes on to liberty; scuffs shoe again, and starts pulling hair.

21. **Official Marine Corps Photo of Robert L. Watson**

All during this we show close ups, expressions on his face, and different angles. We made the script yesterday and today. Tomorrow we shoot it. It is silent; so script is just diagrams of scenes, descriptions, etc."

"About four fellows from here went to S.D. The name of a very nice kid is Loren F. Dillon. I told him that if he ever got a 72 hr. pass and didn't have anything planned to go see you. I doubt if he will ever get a chance, but if he should, maybe Jim can get him a date. He is a very clean cut kid. He is 18 or 19 years of age."

"The fellow that sleeps below me is writing a letter; two fellows are playing Gin-Rummy on the bottom bunk next to me; several other fellows around are writing letters; one is shining shoes, and another fellow is trying to play a harmonica. I sold mine. I don't get any time to practice, and the kid I sold it to can play fairly good; so, I sold it to him. It is German made and one of the best makes. Because of the war no more are available so I figured he might as well get some enjoyment from it."

"In the mornings we have lectures and afternoons we view pictures. Most everyday this happens. Our class was the first to have pictures in home town papers. I sent you a copy."

Two days later,[134] "In the Oct. issue of Popular Photography there is an article of the still school here at Quantico. My back is in one of the pictures. It is made in the big enlarging and printing room."

"Today we finished our short picture. Afterwards the whole class except those who had the afternoon off ran through the obstacle course."

Here are the directions for the obstacle course: Run and jump on dummy boat over other side, pull up weight, climb rope (just hands), climb up ladder, go down rope ladder, just hands, jump off boat, run stepping between logs, climb over wall, climb along ladder hanging from arms, go through tunnel, over dummy boat."

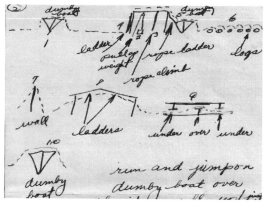

Bob's Sketch of Obstacle Course

Captain Soule was very concerned that the men in photo school were given no physical preparation for combat. Typically photographers were assigned to units at the last minute and would go into combat within days of leaving Quantico.

He also discerned that the men were in poor shape not having exercised since their physical conditioning at boot camp. Soule "set aside one hour at the end of each day for exercise: calisthenics, obstacle courses, swimming and conditioning runs." [135] Soule even cancelled orders for deployment of the current class to give him more time to improve their physical condition.

22. Hand Grenade Course, Wolfkill on Left

Captain Soule also made sure the photographers under his charge were skilled in other aspects of combat. They were trained in an area identified as "Guadalcanal" where they utilized the hand grenade course.

"I'm staying in this weekend. On that short (movie) I shot 100 feet and the other fellow shot the same. Every week we hand in notebooks, get grades. I got 6th highest in class. Fourteen are in the class. All but 3 of us were in the class for a month before we got there

23. Carothers hugging Ground in Live Fire Range

"Less than 50 yds. from our barracks, the O. Cs. are having a dance. The post dance band is playing. Most all of them played with name bands. They are very good. The O. Cs. have invited girl marines and other girls as their guests. The music sure sounds good."

The following Sunday, Bob wrote to his siblings,[136] "I'm very glad that you both wrote to me. I sent you an 8x10 copy of the picture that appeared in the paper. It was made while I was in still school. My class was the first to have pictures made of its members and then sent out to their hometown papers.

After a several day hiatus, Bob described another maneuver exercise,[137] "Thurs. & Fri. I went on another 3 day war. We left 3:00 P.M. Thurs. in trucks; marched about a mi. with packs like the last time, plus camera & case, film, canned rations, and tripod. Two of us went together divided load. Bedded down for night, went out and looked over area we were to fight on. Slept until 4:00 A.M. Marched to jumping off place. While waiting for artillery barrage to lift, a shell fell short and a spent piece of shrapnel hit a Lt. in the shoulder. He said it felt like someone hit him with an apple."

"My partner and I followed the infantry, (leaving packs behind; they were to follow in a truck) taking pictures all of the time. About the time we would get set up they would move out. We shot 300 feet apiece. It was 35mm size."

"After our attack started some tear gas bombs were let loose in the woods about 300 yds. away from where I was. Later on some smoke bombs were let loose. We were in the very center then."

"On Fri. we took pictures of infantry advancing and firing, machine gun firing and mortar and artillery fire. In the evening we made some shots of fellows in the captured woods."

"Later we ate and hooked a ride on a chow truck back to the post. We couldn't take any pictures after dark and the maneuvers were to be secured at 6 A.M. Sat. Besides that, instead of bringing our packs along in trucks they brought them to the post. We didn't want to stay out there without any blankets if we didn't have to. Everyone else had to stay. They were to make a night attack at 1 A.M. We got back at the base about 9:45, cleaned up and hit our sacks (bed)."

"Sat. morning we turned in our equipment, made out our reports, and returned to the barracks to get ready for liberty. Last weekend I didn't have liberty. This weekend a fellow from Seattle and I went to Coney Island out on Long Island N. Y. I had a date with a girl and in the six hrs. that we were there, I didn't spend over $5 (Coney Is. I mean.)"

"One Section, the Steeplechase, you buy a ticket for $1 and get 35 rides, etc. A person can go there and have a h---uva good time for very little. Of course I wouldn't have enjoyed it so much if I had been alone. It is human nature to like company."

"We have peaches every once in awhile, but they are the little ones that people grow in their back yards at home."

"Still School sent the picture to the paper. I didn't have anything to say about it. There is a slim chance that I will get what I want when I get out of school. I'm glad to hear that you can make gravy, Zel."

"Dear Jim,[138] I got your letter today after being out on a boat landing party. Wolfkill[139], a fellow from Bremerton, and I worked together. We used Kodachrome, 16mm. We made shots of men and equipment going over the side, climbing down the landing net, and getting into the Higgins boats and drop front boats like the tank lighters made at M. I. only smaller. I got scenes of them going to the beach, the landing, advance, and consolidation of captured positions. Wolfkill went in the first boat and jumped into the water up to his waist. I went in the Staff and Command boat, came in last and only got wet up to my knees."

"Last night Spangler[140], and a few other fellows; and I did acrobatics on mattresses that we took off of some empty sacks. I felt it a little today."

"I'm glad to hear that Ted[141] is a good coach. I'm glad to hear that you are using the old formation. Will you send me the list of all Conference men, first and second strings? Spangler says that I was second string on the list in the paper and I wish to prove that he is wrong."

"They held the senior class, in school back a month so that 3 of us could be with them. I'm in the same class as Spangler now."

In his next letter, Bob explained the rules about weekend liberty to Zelda,[142] "I'm staying in again this weekend. You see we only get every other weekend off now. They had a fire here, which caused the ammo dump to blow. Fifty percent of all personnel are supposed to be on the post at all times. An officer came around to get men to fight the fire and could only get about 40 men from our barracks, which is about 10%. Now that can't happen again."

"Last night the M.C.S. (*Marine Corps School*) Detachment had a beer bust. Afterwards Walavich and I went to the show. He went to sleep during the picture, ha! Ha! Today we were divided into 4's and we then laid out compass courses for the new class coming in. Most of the new class is made up of fellows that went to Rochester a month ago. In case I didn't tell you, we ran a similar course laid out by the Captain."

"The weather is very nice here now. The air is crisp and the sun shines. The woods are very pretty especially along a small stream. On some trees all of the leaves have turned red. It has been clear all day and the cloud formations have been very pretty. Some black clouds are passing over now, so it may rain tonight."

"My weekly grades have an average of 84% and I'm about 6th from the top. The tests are much more difficult than in still school, although the grades aren't made up of test grades alone. If that were so my percentage would go up. I shall cut now and give you another scene later."

Captain Soule also made sure his photographers knew how to descend a cargo net and abandon ship, using scaffolding for the drill.

24. Watson Climbing Down Cargo Net   **25. Watson in Abandon Ship Drill**

Five days later Bob related further activities,[143] "Yesterday a fellow and I made a picture on tanks. We used the wrong film speed on the exposure meter; so it will be over exposed one (f) stop. We made some swell scenes. We are both hoping and praying."

"We still get only 2 out of 4 weekends off. Today it rained. It has stopped; but it is cloudy and may rain some more."

"Mon. & Tues. nights we ran the compass courses instead of Mon. & Wed. Tues. night we were in thick woods. One fellow sprained his ankle (the same as I made the tank movie with). Several others got their shins and faces scarred from logs and limbs. It was so dark that if I got five feet away from the others, they couldn't see me. I could see farther in the dark than most. So I didn't get my face scratched; although, I stepped in a couple of holes."

"Every morning from 7:15 to 7:45 four of us have to clean out 3 offices. I don't think that I told you this before."

"The fellows that didn't go out on the last 3 day war went out today. It is raining now. I'm certainly glad that I wasn't detailed to go out. Tonight I have to go to a meeting. It is usually about scouting and patrolling, map reading & military courtesy."

In response to questions from home, Bob wrote,[144] "They don't give us gruesome things to make maneuvers more realistic."

"The girl is very cute. I'm going to stay with her family the 9th and 10th. She is going to have a nice party at the house. Wolfkill, from Bremerton, is going up with me."

"I don't know of anything you can get unless it is a small sewing kit containing brown 4 holed buttons, and a small but good pair of scissors. I have needles."

"Tomorrow Dick Schultz and I are going to shoot a short (*movie*) on the M1 (Garand rifle). It rained today and last night. The fellows on the war (*maneuvers*) must have gotten wet. I'm glad that I didn't have to go."

"Last night we had a test on map reading. Every Thurs. night a Chief Marine Gunner gives lectures. I missed 2 of 15 questions and had only attended the 1st lecture on maps. I had help with one question. Navigation at Hi School and compass at movie (*school*) helped me."

Writing to Zelda about home and New Yorkers, Bob commented,[145] "The New Yorkers have a very definite accent. Each part of N.Y. has a different kind. Some have none and some have more than others. Monday another class starts in movies. We still have another month."

Bob wrote again about his food,[146] "We get milk almost every meal. From two to three quarts are allotted eight people. Our friends in the mess hall often sneak us extra quarts, so we get along OK. We've been having chicken lately and pies, too. The only thing that I get tired of is lamb."

"A new class in movie started today. We are the advanced class now. I'm going to start sending home a few odds and ends. My locker is getting too full. I'm sending back some pictures you sent."

Three days later,[147] "In case I didn't tell you before, we are now learning a type of fighting that is a combination of rough and tumble and Jujitsu."

"Wolfkill's and my color picture of a boat landing turned out swell. A (*film*) magazine jammed on me so I didn't get to shoot as much as I wanted. Wolf shot (*with*) a telephoto (*lens*) out of focus. Otherwise everything turned out damn good, especially for the first time."

In response to a question about a present for Christmas, Bob replied,[148] "I don't know what would be a good present for Christmas. If I don't think of anything, put $5 in the bank."

Reporting on his New York adventure, Bob wrote,[149] "I had a pretty good time in N.Y over the weekend. We went to a party across the street. We had quite a bit of fun and enough to drink. We got in bed around four. Sunday I took it easy."

"About eight fellows are going to New River, N. Carolina to make a movie of girl marines. They asked me to go but it was almost voluntary so I declined. Eleven fellows are shipping overseas pretty quick. I think that I shall be going to the W. Coast before the 1st of the year."

Bob gave Zelda some brotherly advice,[150] "Who won? You or Mom? I mean the letter to Dick. If he doesn't care to write, I don't see why you should go out of your way to write him. Tell Mom that it isn't up to her to see what you write. Although, you should tell her what you write. Don't ever hide anything from her."

"I tear up the letters after I get them. Most of the excess stuff that I have is pictures and a couple of books. Some night when I go to the PX, I will mail some of them home."

"Today our Captain (*Soule*) went to D.C. for the day. When he left he said that if he came back a private we would know that he stuck his neck out. He is a swell guy and will go to any end to do things for us that will help our class out."

"A fellow made a suggestion that we have a class picture made. It was done. Soon I hope to get a copy. I shall send it to you & the rest if things work OK."

Bob then told Jim more about school,[151] "School is working out OK. Friday Bob Bleier and I worked over at grips and props. That is the outfit that does special effects and makes scenery and such. We worked in the miniature dept. We were making a relief map of a coral reef in the South Seas. We worked one day and it takes 6 weeks altogether so you can see how little of the whole we did."

Continued on the 18th, "Today the uniform of the day was changed to greens. We look like Marines again."

While Bob and his classmates were learning the skills of combat cine-photography the three Marine divisions in the Pacific were training for planned landings on Japanese territory in order to advance to the final destination, Tokyo. The First Division was preparing to land on Cape Gloucester at the western end of New Britain; the Second Division was training for the capture of Tarawa in the Gilbert's; and the Third Division was practicing for the invasion of Bouganville, the largest of the Northern Solomon's.

26. Cinematography Class, L-R, F-B Robert S. Bleus, James Galloway, Bill Genaust, Alan R. Gray; Al L. Hota, Clay Mitchell, Wayne Nalvanko, Powe; Schultz, Sheppard, Walter A. Spangler, Robert Van Deveer; Albert Walavich, Robert Watson, Grant Wolfkill; Instructors: Rubalcava, Joe Davis, Capt. Karl T. Soule, Joe Franklin, Hewitt, Hoyt Rhodes

9

CINEMATOGRAPHY INSTRUCTOR

Robert and his class completed the course of instruction for Still Photography and Cine Photography. Some members began to receive orders for new assignments; a few to other stateside duties and others were sent to the Pacific War Theater. Bob did not know what his next assignment would be; then he happily learned that he was chosen to remain at the Photo School as an instructor.

Bob informed his family of his good fortune with a perfunctory statement,[152] "I graduate Saturday and that evening I'm going on a 72 hr. pass. It officially starts Sunday at 0600." "I think I'll go to N. Y. with Wolfkill. Our plans aren't definite yet."

"After my leave I shall be an instructor along with Wolfkill. We will be here from eight to ten weeks more."

"I've found something else that would be nice to have, a good shaving brush. I left mine in the head one morning and someone got it."

"Will you send me my camera and whatever film is left? Maybe I can find time to use it."

"The trip to N. Carolina had a return ticket but going to a new place for a couple of months with no towns around and very little to do isn't any vacation."

"If I go west again it will probably be a straight through trip, so don't count on me getting home again for sometime."

"The last few days we've been editing our film and then viewing them. They aren't too bad for a bunch of amateurs."

"A week later Bob reported on his 72 hour leave,[153] "I'm standing noon watch at the camera (*movie*) building. The movie section has the whole 3rd deck of this building. We have several departments: repair, editorial (cut & splice), animation, distribution, production, and school."

"I spent my 72 in Philadelphia and N.Y. Sat. night Wolfkill and I got into Phila. and left Mon. noon for N.Y. We picked up a couple of girls Sat. night, Sunday we ate dinner at one of their houses. That night we saw 'Salute to the Marines, Leathernecks on Parade' with Wallace Beery. I think that is the name of the show."

"A fellow here that taught photography at the Pratt Institute of

Technology in Brooklyn lined us up with two gals. The one I had wasn't the best looker in the school, but she's a swell kid. She has a personality similar to Carolyn Owens's. (*a high school friend*) She is studying to be an art teacher and is in her 4th year there."

"We met the girls at school, looked the place over and then went out. They have some very good artists there. The art building is very old but it is fairly well equipped."

"That night we went to a show called 'Thank Your Lucky Stars', I think."

"Tuesday afternoon Wolfkill and I left N.Y. We stopped off in Phila. for awhile. He went to see the girl that he had met and I came back here. It rained all Tues. all up and down the coast. I suppose you have seen in the paper that a 50 mph gale hit N.J."

"Zel, tell Mr. Kilby that military etiquette makes it almost prohibitive for a Private to visit a Colonel." (*Bob's high school coach wanted him to say hello to a Colonel friend.*)

While spending a Saturday night on station, Bob wrote,[154] "I had a swell time on my 72 hour pass, although I had to borrow $10 to do it"

"A fellow from here is going to make a portrait of me with pencil about 8"x10". He is pretty good. It will cost $3. If you want a photo I'll get it for you for a Xmas present, OK?"

"Wednesday I'm going to take the new students that start Monday, through Still School. From now on most of the students will not have gone through Still (*School*). We will have to start from scratch with them. Saturday I have to teach them how to pitch shelter halves and make up light marching and field transport packs."

A week passed before Bob wrote again,[155] "Last week Tuesday and Wednesday nights I had to work correcting papers and editing film."

"This weekend I went to N.Y to see the girl that I met at Pratt. I think I told you about her. She played a dirty trick on me. I had written to her asking if she would be so kind as to reserve me a room. She then answered in the affirmative, describing a swell room: blue wallpaper with airplane pictures for atmosphere, twin beds with Beauty-Rest mattresses (in case Grant came up). She then said that she had forgotten to ask the price. When I saw that I certainly got frightened. I had told her explicitly to get a moderately priced room."

"She met me at the station and she told me that the room was at her house. In fact it was her own. It is a two story house about 5 years old and nicely furnished. You see there are not any hotels out on that part of Long Island that she lives on."

"She mentioned several places that we could go to in Manhattan and then a barn dance out near her house. Then for the lark of it I said, 'We're going to the barn dance'. We then got on the L.I. train and went to her house. There I met her father and little brother. We got the car and went to the dance. We walked in and decided that it was too crummy. We left and drove to a nightclub. We got in about 2 A.M., drank some hot tea that she made and went to bed."

"I got up about 9:30 and even at that she had to wake me and everyone else was up before me. I met her mother and we ate breakfast. Then by 'hook & crook' I made Evelyn help me do the dishes. We read the papers and then went for a walk. We ate lunch and lazed around. During the course of the day we went for a couple of rides me driving. After eating the evening meal and loafing she took me to the L.I. R.R. station and I was on my way back to Quantico."

"Then after a weekend of little sleep I had to work until 10:00 last night. To top it off we had a thunder, lightning, and rainstorm. Last night we corrected papers and made out grades. We still have calisthenics and run the obstacle course every night. I hope this will make up for not writing sooner."

Back on his schedule of writing every other day, Bob told about a movie he watched,[156] "I saw 'Guadalcanal Diary' tonight. It was very good. The first show was so crowded that the enlisted men filled all empty seats in the balcony, which is officers' territory. The second show was filled to over-flowing far more than the 1st and a third one is to be shown at 10:00. This is the 1st time that has been done since I have been here."

A recent viewing of the film suggests that the movie "Guadalcanal Diary" would have made a significant impact on the young men, most of whom had not been overseas or experienced combat. Marine casualties, sudden death, and loss of close friends were depicted in the film, but unlike modern movies the killings depicted were generally bloodless and did not show the carnage of real war. The incessant shelling by Japanese ships and bombing by enemy airplanes that Captain Soule wrote about in his book "Shooting the Pacific War" was also depicted. There was enough realism even in the black and white format to give the young marines much to think about as they contemplated their expected participation in the bloody Pacific War. Continuing, Bob wrote, "It hasn't snowed here yet but the frost is on the ground almost every morning."

"Everything is working out fair. A bond drive or a purge is going on here. If you don't take out a bond every three months they make a fellow feel like hell. One thing though they just want it down on paper and it doesn't start until Feb. and we can stop anytime."

"I'm afraid Grant (*Wolfkill*) and I will have to move to another barracks, just because we are instructors. Our rates haven't come through and it looks as though they won't until after we ship out."

"Don't send me any money. I have a record that not many have. I've never taken money from my folks since I've been in. There isn't any use starting now. Of course little presents help, but don't send money."

"I haven't received the shaving brush yet. I should be getting it any day though."

Bob followed with more descriptions of his activities on the base,[157] "Yesterday afternoon we went for a little walk and run. We did 4 and some fraction miles in an hour. It was over hilly ground so it amounted to a little over 5 miles. This morning some of the fellows went up on a hill and did extended order drill. I stayed at the school and worked. Every Sat. afternoon, those that don't have liberty have a 'field day' (clean everything) and calisthenics. But today we just had a field day no obstacle course. We got through at 3:00"

"Thursday morning it snowed but melted the moment it hit the ground. It has been cold enough at nights to snow for the last week."

"I've been notified that I have '72' for Christmas. It will make up a little for not being home then. Maybe I can get a delayed transfer and go home on the way overseas. It is a very slim chance but I'll try. Don't count on it though. Many times things happen so fast when the orders come through that you don't get the chance."

Continuing the letter on the evening of the 16th, Bob wrote," I've moved into another barracks. It is made of wood, is small and is practically on the river's edge. It is less than 100 yds. from the water, in fact. We have single bunks instead of tiers of two. The springs are better. The fellows are neater and much more quiet. From what I understand stealing is practically unknown. It certainly sounds good."

"Yesterday while running I sprained my ankle. This morning I could hardly walk, so I went to sickbay. They made an X-ray and of course no bones were broken. The doctor then proceeded to fill my foot with Novocain, told me to put my shoe on and try walking naturally. I did so with but a very slight limp. It has hurt very little all day. Apparently it hasn't worn off yet. You notice that I didn't say anything about taping. Reason-he didn't tape it: With all of the exercise that it is getting I doubt that it will hurt me much. I also think that it will heal very fast."

In his next missive Bob discussed his recent date on Long Island and his plans for Christmas,[158] "The girl's name is Evelyn Zeph, brunette. Yes her folks are nice."

"The fellow who was going to make a sketch of me is shipping out as a combat artist, so he won't be able to make it. I'm going to have one of the fellows here make a picture of me. I'll send you the negative, you can have it retouched and have some prints made from it."

"I'm also going to try talking Evelyn into inviting me up for a Christmas '72', and have her make a sketch of me. I've already sent a letter to her. I hope that she will take the hint. It sounds a little on the sly side, but I want it done pretty badly."

"Last night the Captain (*Karl Thayer Soule Jr.*), Wolfkill, and myself took the new class, #3, out for a short compass course. It gets awfully cold here. But we have sheepskin coats and fur caps that we can get at school for fieldwork. They are nice to have, believe you me. Tomorrow night they are going to run a full fledged course through the woods. Last night they ran it on a parade ground so as not to get lost on the 1st time. Tomorrow night we will have parachute flares in case someone can't find the way to the finish."

"Dad- I don't think that I shall ever have cause to sell the camera (Follmer Graflex Speed Graphic) If I ever get a rate it will be Cpl. Our rates come under the E.P.R. (Engineering Personnel Reserve) classification and they don't have Pfc. warrant. The commandant gave an order that anyone that completed a school would go up one pay grade, so, we get nothing under that order. E.P.R. warrants are just as hard to get as line warrants. Most all of the rates here are school warrants."

Having just spent his first Thanksgiving away from home from the family celebration that usually involved the extended family, Bob started his next letter by commenting on the feast he had missed.[159] "I bet that the Thanksgiving festivities were something to remember."

"Spangler is still here, but the word came through today that he is to ship out next week. Six others are going too. They are from the class that Wolfkill and I were in. Some more fellows from all three classes are going to Chicago for a course in camera repair. I'm to stay though and so is Wolfkill."

During the war the services always attempted to make Thanksgiving Day special for the men and women in the military. Even in combat zones an effort was extended to provide special food including turkey whenever possible. Thoughts of family were always on the minds of the young people who could not be in their homes at that traditionally important time for most Americans. Bob's first Thanksgiving away from home was no exception as he reported.

"Our Thanksgiving banquet (for that is what it was) was the best meal that I've partaken of since I've been in the Corps. The mess hall was decorated with corn stalks, paper pumpkins, etc. They passed out cigarettes to everyone. Because all of the other tables were filled I sat at one of the tables for officers. I will send you the menu and napkin. That night I & another instructor took two classes out to start them on a compass course. The Captain and his guest ran the course. We met all of them at the end. Two fellows were slow getting in so I and the guest fired a rocket apiece, and the Captain fired two. It really wasn't necessary to fire them. We did it more for the fun we had doing it."

Three days later Bob described his activities as an instructor and told about other photographers' departure for new duties,[160] "I will have enough money for my '72'. I don't know for sure what I will do on my leave. My ankle is OK now."

"The only scarves that we wear are 'field scarves' or in civilian terminology neckties."

"Yesterday all day I did nothing but eat, read, and sleep. This week I'm on the 'head' detail from 0700 to about 0720 and thus I get out of instruction periods which we have at 0700 in the morning on military subjects. These instructions are separate from Cine School."

"By 0800 I was at school. The 1st two hours I helped class #3 get ready to shoot some pictures. About 1100 I projected some student film for the Captain and class #2. After chow I was placed in charge of all equipment, including cameras, film, and field equipment (tents, ponchos, etc.) We traded in some old cameras Sat. got some new today."

"About 1500 I projected the same film as in the morning only the students had done some editing and improved quite a bit. All day class #3 shot their stories. I took out 3 members of class #2 and we ran through the obstacle course. One of the fellows and I went back to the school and I got out some equipment for him. Tonight the instructors have to go back and make out grades and plans. I also have to get more equipment ready for tomorrow."

The next day, "We (meaning the instructors) just saw 6 of the fellows off for Linda Vista, Calif. It is a Marine camp about 19 mi. north east of Diego. From there they will go over, maybe stopping off at Frisco. The 7th fellow left this morning with his wife. He bought a car, and they are driving to Calif. You see, he was able to get a delayed transfer. They live in Fresno or Stockton, I don't remember which. His name is (*Hoyt*) Rhodes."

"The others' names are: Bleier, Galloway, Gray, Spangler, Van Derveer, & Walavich. In order they are from: N. Y. City; New Albany, Tenn.; Seattle; Vallejo; Ronal, N.J.; & Chicago."

27. Capt. Soule Sending his Boys to the Pacific: L-R Bleir, Soule, Van Deveer, Gray, Spangler Walavich and Galloway.

Years later Soule[161] described two of the photographers ordered to Linda Vista. "Bob Van Derveer was boyish, a little wild at times; but I could count on him when something had to be done right."

"Al Walavich was a blond kid from Chicago, big and hard, with a square-cut jaw and a strong grip. He knew his job, and knew he knew. Confident and aggressive, he got what he went after.
A fighter by instinct, slow to anger, quick to smile, he fit in well from the first."

Bob's first December letter described more activities,[162] "The other morning I had a watch from 0200 to 0600. I was a little tired during the day. Don't renew the newspaper subscription after the 24th, just send me clippings. I'm so busy I don't have much time to read them."

"Class #2 has 4 members. Class #3 has 8 members.

28. Cinematography Class 3, Instructors rear row: R L Watson, J P Franklin, Capt. Thayer Soule, Grant Wolfkill; Students L-R top to bottom: C. C. Winkler Jr., Charles D. Evans, Gus Paulette Jr., Robert W. Nye, Edward J. Sullivan, A. S. Tracy, Edward F. Carran Jr., F. McCockrell

"The fellows going to Chicago will have an easy time living in a hotel, every night off, an easy course. They needed two more instructors (here), and Wolfkill and I were chosen. I was told that we were chosen because they thought we would do better than the other students."

"The last few days have been fairly clear & warm. You might think that it was a nice fall day in the valley at home. I like it here just as much as going to Chicago. This afternoon the Capt. and I went out for two hours checking over trails to use on some conditioning walks. We covered about 7 miles in that time. The last mile and one half we went by compass using no trails. The last 1 ½ mi. we went lickety-split."

On the second anniversary of the Japanese attack on Pearl Harbor, Bob wrote,[163] "I got a letter from Father Houssell[164] inviting me up for Christmas. It was swell of them to send the invitation; but, if you hinted to them consider yourself bawled out." (*Houssell had been the Episcopal Church minister in Colusa where Bob served as an acolyte.*)

"Last night I ran the projector so that the Captain could view some films. We then made some changes in them (they were student stories).

After that the other instructor came over and we made the grades out for the classes. Tomorrow I'm taking Class #3 out on a field problem. Friday I may have to go out on another. This morning Sgt. Rubalcava and I made an inventory of part of our equipment. This afternoon I caught up on some of my bookwork, issued equipment for tomorrow, and then took the fellows out for a little game of touch tackle. It is the 1st time that I've played football since I've been in the Corps."

"Tomorrow, the O. C's. are acting as though they are advancing through territory that the enemy has retreated from. They have to search farmhouses, woods, etc. Just before the war or immediately after the beginning they bought a large amount of land adjacent to the Post. On this land are many farms that the people moved from after this transaction. This is where our mock wars & field problems take place." Bob saved 35mm film clips of the activity.

29. Officer Candidates Searching Farmhouse   **30. Officer Candidates Searching Woods**

Planning for Christmas Bob informed his parents,[165] "I think that I shall go see the Houssell's Christmas. Send me a good quart of Port, Sherry, or Muscatel wine and I'll give it to them when I go up. Make it a good brand and I'll pay for it when you tell me the price. It was very nice of them to send the invitation."

"Tomorrow morning I get up at 4 to go out in the field and I will get back about midnight. I'm in charge of Class #3 which is going out. This is the same as the 3 day war only modified because of weather."

In mid month Bob wrote about Christmas presents for the family,[166] "The weather last night was chilly, but bright. I got your letters of ninth and tenth, plus the package I'm supposed not to open until Christmas. It certainly is a temptation. I got some presents, one for Zelda and another for Mom. I will send them as soon as I get to the P.O. I will get one soon for Jim & Dad, can't find what I want for Jim."

"We had quite a wind here ourselves. It was from the north and freezing at that. Yesterday the puddles were still frozen at noon."

"Today, Class #4 started. Seven in it and one more due to come. Tonight we have to work (correct test, make out grades, make up liberty list, etc.)."

Two days later Bob complained about the cold,[167] "I would like to know how Houssell's knew about my pass and I apologize to you, Mom."

"No the girl in N.Y. didn't invite me up, although I got a note from her. I'm going to Houssell's."

"My work isn't bad but it's too damn cold here. The puddles stay frozen all day the wind is icy, and my cheeks and ears burn with cold if I stay out long."

"There is an aerating device here for the sewage just before it goes in the river. Icicles have formed the full length of pipes and are 2 to 6 inches long. (Rotating pipes eject) water from them out of holes the full length of the pipes. It was around 12 degrees above (freezing) here all day and it was colder than that this morning."

"2006 Saturday[168] I got your card with the money and note enclosed and your letter of the 13th. Thank you very much Mom. I haven't been able to find any good wine here in Quantico so far, but maybe I can find some in Washington."

"Thanks for the fin (Five dollar bill), Dad. Say, Jim, will you send me some football plays? There is an ex-coach here and I told him about our formation; he is very interested. He is also an instructor at our school. He is Cpl. J. P. Franklin. I have mentioned all of the other instructors before."

Thayer Soule wrote[169] his impressions, "Joe Franklin was older than I. A huge man of 230 pounds, he had played professional football. He had the sharpest mind that I had ever encountered, a thorough knowledge of photography, and a fine sense of humor."

Bob continued, "This afternoon after sweeping the hall and riding a bucking bronco waxing machine over floors of three rooms we went to the gym for calisthenics and wrestling. I wrestled Wallace of Class #4 and then the Captain. Wallace and I wrestled until we were pooped and so it was a draw. The Captain weighs at least 200 lbs. He won but it took him a couple of minutes to pin me. I have raspberries on my knee, and elbow and I have a few aches. Before we began wrestling all of us got in a circle on the mat, which is on the floor and had a free for all trying to throw each other off it. The one remaining person is the winner."

"I got two packages from you a few days ago, Mom. I certainly have itchy fingers to get at them."

"1900 Tuesday,[170] I leave for Millville, N.J. tomorrow evening. I'm going to pack tonight so that I can leave as soon as possible."

"My dress shoes that I got in boot camp finally have come apart. The top came loose from the sole. It happened just at the right time, after clothing inspection so that I can't survey them. All isn't lost though; I got the Captain to buy a pair for me. I finished fixing them tonight. You see we get Army Officer Shoes for dress. They are an orange-brown color and we have to dye and polish them to a dark cordovan color. I started last night and have them in pretty good shape now."

"The Captain is still trying to get our rates for us. We certainly are taking a screwing. The Photo Section is the bastard of the Marine Corps because we are new and no one recognizes us."

"I read the above to a few fellows here and they agree that it is a master piece of understatement. They also say that several volumes could be written on the dirt we are forced to eat. Several volumes can be written on this subject. It isn't as bad as that; although we aren't getting rates. If I were in the Army I'd be a Staff Sgt."

"Father Houssell is to meet me in Philadelphia. He then will take me to Millville."

On Sunday Bob described his visit,[171] "I got in from the Houssell's at 0445 this morning. I had a swell time there."

"Millville is a factory town of about 16,000. The people are very friendly and take an interest in the church. There are eight Methodist churches, one Presbyterian, two Catholic, and one Episcopal Church. Because of the Methodist power, shows can't open on Sundays."

"I got a taxi to D.C., a train to Phila. and a bus to Millville."

"The 23rd we decorated the church. The 24th finished up. Christmas eve the church was very beautiful. Candles on all of the walls and laurel ropes draped from arch to arch. Christmas eve about 5 we had a big goose dinner. We opened our presents after the service. I got Father Houssell a bottle of Portuguese Port wine, Ann two Irish linen handkerchiefs, and Mrs. Houssell (mother) a carton of cigarettes. I got a box of Fitch's hair tonic, shampoo, & oil, and a box of candy & a crucifix. Christmas I loafed around."

"The night of the 23rd I met a fairly nice looking girl. The hall at the church is used by the U.S.O. (*United Service Organization*) for dancing, and this girl was there with a soldier. She happened to be the nicest looking there so of course I wanted to meet her. I did. They were decorating for a dance on Christmas night and they started playing records as the night wore on. I asked her to dance. She accepted and as the crowd started to leave I took her home. I had to leave Sat. night so I couldn't go to their dance."

"The Houssell's took me to Phila. to catch the train."

"There is ice everywhere the sleet froze to everything. The sidewalks and streets are very slick."

"Thanks for the presents. The writing portfolio is swell, the gloves are just like the G. I. (*Government Issue*) only the G. I. don't have fur. I don't know how you did it. The nuts, apples and juice surely taste good. I had a lot of fun at the Houssell's. It took my mind off not being able to go home."

Out in the Pacific on the morning of December 26th the 7th Marines of the First Division led the attack on Cape Gloucester, New Britain, East of New Guinea, followed by elements of the 1st Marines thirty minutes later. The 5th Marines provided reinforcements on December 29. Bob's friend Ned Steele, who was wounded but survived the battle for Guadalcanal, was once again in combat. He called Cape Gloucester a "stink hole" a "swamp". Ned stated that the banyan trees, snakes and iguana were all three times bigger than normal. Capture of the airbase was an important objective to permit aerial attacks against the Japanese main air base at Rabaul a little over a hundred miles away on the east coast.[172] When a sufficient area was secured, marine patrols under the command of Colonel Chesty Puller, who had commanded the Seventh Marines on Guadalcanal, advanced into the mountains toward Rabaul in order to assess enemy activity. Ned, with eighteen men, was sent up the coast of New Britain to a small village called Iboki, the site of an old Copra plantation. With the help of natives from a village a half-mile away, Ned and his fellow marines repaired the decrepit headquarters building to provide a base for their operation. When organized, they patrolled up the river and reported their findings by TBX radio or by messages picked up by a Piper Cub aircraft.

One day Chesty Puller arrived and said, "If it's ok with you guys, I'd like to sack out with you for a few days while I check with my patrols up in the hills." Ned said that Chesty, who preferred the nickname to Colonel, never wore any indication of his rank and acted like an old private during the ten days there. He borrowed a pouch of tobacco from Ned when they shared a smoke together and taught Ned how to play two-handed Pinochle.

Col. Puller told Ned to get six guys and go to the beach to meet an LCPV (Landing Craft Personnel Vehicle) that was coming to meet him. They all boarded the boat and patrolled up river to check on Japanese bivouacs for activity. They found one with no activity and a second with two wounded Japanese soldiers "who were dispatched" on the belief that a good Jap is a dead Jap. After discovering a large encampment, Col. Puller decided to send a larger unit to deal with the Japanese unit and ordered the coxswain to head back down the river. The river was inhabited by large numbers of crocodiles and at Pullers suggestion Ned and the others spent an hour shooting them as the coxswain made S turns down river.[173]

Another time a motor torpedo boat tender and two squadrons of PT Boats (Patrol Torpedo) arrived and asked for Marine volunteers for night patrol to interdict Japanese barges. The boats were there for 30 days and Ned went out "eight to ten times" shooting at the barges. He was most appreciative of the good chow and remembered late dinner at three in the morning when they had ice cream.[174]

Several weeks after Bob visited Father Richard and Anne Houssell, Anne wrote to Bertha telling how pleased they were with his visit.[175] "Bet you think I'm the slowest mortal alive; owe you at least three letters by now. We were very happy to have Bob with us, at Xmas and he did have a good time. He said it almost made up for not being home. He made lots of friends here, who ask about him. He looked wonderful Bertha & handsome as anything in his uniform. For heaven sakes don't let him read this or he'll never come to see us again. He also said if he had anymore short leaves he'd come again. He not only helped decorate the church for service but he also helped the pretty U.S.O. girls and the soldiers from the airport decorate for the big dance. He also sandwiched in a couple of Xmas dinners and saw the town. We think it's grand that he is an instructor in photography or I should say cinematography. We were pleased to get Jim's announcement too, but gosh they are grown up. Zelda will be next.

"Please write again Bertha & I'll do better. And I'm praying Bob gets his leave to get home. My love to all of you. Anne."

Bob finally got the rating he was expecting,[176] "I left the evening of the 22nd on my '72' & got back the morning of the 26th, 0445."

"I still get the Colusa papers, but I don't have time to read them. I asked Grandma to stop them until I go overseas."

"This afternoon we swept, swabbed and waxed the rooms. (*Lt.*) Gen. (*Thomas*) Holcomb & (*Major General Archer A.*) Vandegrift are making an inspection (*General Vandegrift became the 18th commandant of the Corps*)." .It will be Holcomb's last as Commandant (*of the Marine Corps*).

"I got a letter from Aki Yoshimura today. He is in India. He doesn't like it there but says that it is a worthwhile experience."

Akiji Yoshimura, Bob's Assistant Scout Master had joined the Army before Pearl Harbor was attacked and was serving in the medical Corps. An FBI agent visited him after December 7 and asked if he was willing to fight against Japan and the Emperor. Akiji was saddened that the country he had been taught to respect had attacked the country he loved. He told the agent he was willing to fight against Japan and the Emperor. But because Akiji did not jump up and down and shout that he would fight, he was forcibly discharged from the Army sent to an internment camp along with all the other Japanese in Colusa. Later the Army decided he was needed and to prove his loyalty Akiji joined the Army again and was sent to Camp Savage in Minnesota at the Military Intelligence Service Language School. There he learned to use his Japanese language skills for military intelligence. At the time Yoshimura wrote to Bob he had been commissioned a 2nd Lt. and was serving along with six mainland Nisei and seven from Hawaii in Merrill's Marauders. Brigadier Frank Merrill was soon to take his rangers into Burma.

Slow U. S. Postal Service cheated Bob from visiting his N. Y. girl friend, "The girl in N.Y. sent an Xmas card and added this note, 'We're looking forward to seeing you at Christmas!' I got it Monday of this week."

"The day before yesterday Wolfkill & I got Pfc. rates. Yesterday we made Cpl. We got the warrants today. They are Engineering Personnel Reserve Rates and the only way that we can lose them is by a General Court Martial, transferring from photographic work, or by the ending of the war. If there isn't room for us to stay Cpl. at the end of the duration we would be broken, that is if we stayed in."

Then in a short note, Bob wrote,[177] "I got the wine ok and candy. You didn't make the candy did you? It certainly was good. The wine certainly is good too."

"It snowed early yesterday morning. It got to about two inches deep. It was so cold yesterday and today that the snow is still on the ground except where direct sunlight glared down on it for some time. It is a dry snow so it isn't sloppy like we have at home. We cross a gully on the way to work. On the side going down I slid all the way to the bottom. Several others had the same misfortune. Oh! What fun?"

And to Jim, "I got your letter of the 27th today. Sweater, gold football, the real pigskin, you're all set with a little collection. Thanks for the football plays. Now I have them for reference and to show to my buddy."

In his first correspondence of the New Year, Bob described his responsibilities and activities as an instructor,[178] "Monday morning I had the watch at the M.C.S. bldg. from 0200 to 0600. All last week the Captain was up in N.Y. at the M.C. film laboratory. Rubalcava now a S/Sgt. went to S.F. to see his father who was on the verge of dying. Wolfkill, Franklin, and I were left in charge of the school. Wolfkill left Wednesday for Wash. on a 72 so that the two of us were left. Sat. afternoon Franklin had liberty so I was left in charge. The only thing that I had to do was be with them while they saw a picture, conduct a discussion on it, and see that the fellows cleaned up the rooms properly."

"Saturday morning I gave a lecture on the compass. Today I had to meet the fellows at the end of a compass course after starting them. Yesterday I had to make up a film inventory report."

"I will ship out in March. The Captain is going to try to get me a 15 day delayed transfer. Don't count on it too much though."

"We wear wool sox and cotton underwear. I don't know of anything that you could get me. Grandma & Granddad (*Capito*) sent me a buck & Grandma W. sent me a fin. That is '30' for now."[179]

"Tuesday Class #4 ran a compass course.[180] Previous to that; Sat., I gave them a lecture on the compass. Tues., I started them out & met them at the end. That night they ran a short practice run after dark. Last night I gave them instructions for running the regular night course. I issued them equipment and got them all set before the Captain arrived. Taking rocket star flares the Captain & I rode to the start in a Jeep. Boy! Jeeps are OK for my dough. I thought that we were going to get stuck a couple of times and tip over, but we didn't. Two fellows were a little slow getting in so we sent a flare. We fired the rest (4 in all) because it requires too much red tape to turn them back in."

"Today Sgt. Franklin & Class #3 went out on a one day war. Tomorrow I am going to give a lecture on map symbols to Class #4. Today I made out next week's schedules for both classes."

Clarifying his status, Bob explained,[181] "I don't know how long my class will last because I'm not in a class. As I said in a letter before, I shall ship out around the fifteenth of March"

"The snow lasted about three days. It was a very dry and fluffy snow. Every few days it has gotten so cold that the river will freeze 1/5 of the way out from the shore. Looking out across the river many mornings I can see birds walking on the ice."

"Happy birthday Dad. It is a little late, but better than never. The last few days I've been looking for your brand of cigars. I tried to get them for Xmas, but no soap. Maybe they'll get to you by the end of the month. I haven't tried to slight you; I just haven't been able to get any."

"During the snow the cars packed the snow on the roads making ice of it. Some of the younger officers just loved to slide on it. We would wait until they got in the middle of a slide and then salute them hoping they would fall on their -------. None ever did, though, darn it."

"I got your letter today, Jim. You can't imagine how proud I am to know that you passed the test. It is an added pleasure to know that you chose to be a flying Gyrene. I hope that this is true. According to your letter they really put you through the paces. I knew that you could pass. Write and let me know more."

Jim had spent two days in San Francisco taking academic and aptitude tests and an extensive physical examination required for enlistment in the Navy V-5 program that involved two semesters of college, pre-flight school and then flight training.

Bob had fun playing in the snow and firing the 45 pistol for record,[182] "If you folks want the U. S. Camera Annual maybe you better buy it. I want to save all of the money I don't spend on essentials and liberty for my hoped for delayed transfer."

"It snowed last night. I had a fellow take two pictures of me in it. After the negatives are developed I shall send at least one to you for printing."

106

31. Bob Outdoors in Snow

"After noon chow one of my buddies and I were walking back to the barracks. Two fellows were waiting for us each with ready made snowballs. What a melee. Another fellow, and then another, came out from the barracks. We certainly enjoyed ourselves." "Sound effects: Wham! One just hit a tree behind me. Plop! One hit me. Swish! Another passed my ear. In the mean time I was by no means idle. I threw a few myself. Throwing and dodging kept me fairly busy."

"The other day, Fri., Class #3 and I took a course in handling the carbine & .45 pistol. We shot the carbine for familiarization and the pistol for record. I shot Expert, the highest grade. I don't get paid extra, but it goes in my record book and I feel a certain amount of pride in being able to wear the medal. Since the start of the war (Dec. 7), only a small amount of men get to fire the pistol and even fewer for record. You see, the pistol is being replaced by the carbine so it is a rare chance that I was lucky to get"

"Friday night I had the watch from 10 P.M. to 2 A.M. Sergeants have to stand watches too. So it isn't unusual for a corporal to stand guard."

Responding to questions,[183] "Yes I have gained quite a bit of valuable knowledge in the last year. No I don't drive government vehicles. No license. I don't know whether I would have been better off by going to college. Yes I got a package from the Turners for Xmas. I wrote to them sending thanks or at least I thought I did. Tell them for me that I'm sorry. Did they get an Xmas card from me?"

"I took 4 fellows out on a mortar problem today. Class #4, it was their 1st field shooting. Until today they had shot 2 pictures, for (*which*) they wrote scripts, had actors and props. On a field problem they can't do that of course. They have to make a story as they go along."

"I'm taking out a W.R. tonight (woman Marine)." (*The practice was to call women Marines, Women Reservists.*)

Five days later Bob happily reported,[184] "I finally got your cigars, Dad, El Roy Tan."

"I went to N.Y. over the weekend to see Pat Niedert. I met her at the station about 6 P.M. Sat. I checked my camera in a locker; we then went out for a bite to eat. I found a cigar store and got the last box of Roi Tans that they had. If I hadn't been a service man I wouldn't have been able to get them. Hailing a taxi we went to a show."

"After the show we went into a liquor store & bought her dad a quart of rum. It was very good stuff. After hunting for a nice place to dance and not being able to find one we went to Richmond Hills which is in Queens Borough which is on Long Island. We went into a little club, had a coupla' drinks and danced a coupla' dances. We then went to her home, had some milk and then hit the sack."

"I slept until 11 A.M. Sunday morning. Mrs. Niedert fixed me breakfast. About two we had dinner. I lazed around the house all day. We tried the rum that I bought; it was very good. About 6:30 P.M. we had a lunch. I left the house with Pat about 6:40 for the station. She went all of the way with me. She's a swell kid. I got the 9:15 train and got into Quantico and signed in at 3:50 A.M."

"Pat was to have mailed your cigars today, Dad; I almost forgot to tell you."

"Thanks for the clippings. I'm sending back the one about

32. Taking Train to New York, Bob in Center

Jimmy Midaugh. His death certainly is a helluva-note. He's a swell kid." (*Jimmy, from Colusa, was in the Army Air Corps training to become a navigator. He and several other students were plotting navigation courses on board an aircraft, which crashed, killing them all.*)

"I heard a lecture given by (*Norman T.*) Hatch and I've seen (*Obie*) Newcomb. They were on Tarawa." The four-day battle for Tarawa was one of the bloodiest in the Pacific Campaign with casualties nearly equal to those experienced in six months of fighting on Guadalcanal.

Norm Hatch had enlisted in the Marine Corps in 1939 and eventually became a photographer for Leatherneck magazine. The Corps sent him to the March of Time School of Pictorial Journalism in New York City and along with twenty-five others, most of whom had graduated from the March of Time School, became members of the newly formed Photo Section.[185] Hatch was assigned to the Second Division and staged from Wellington, New Zealand departing for Tarawa in November 1943. According to Hatch, the officer in charge of the 2nd Division Photo Section was "Cap (*tain*) Louis Hayward, the well known actor in the Man in the Iron Mask, The Son of Monte Cristo and Anthony Adverse. He was with us at Tarawa." Norm Hatch managed to get himself assigned to a unit destined for considerable action on Tarawa. He became famous for movie footage he shot that included enemy troops and Marines in the same frame. The only such film shot in all of World War II. His film was made into a short documentary that won an Academy Award. Newcomb was with Hatch on Tarawa.

Bob continued, "I had two pictures made of me outdoors. They are fairly good. I shall send them soon.

"Thanks for writing, Dad. I like to hear about your work. You often get jobs with quite a few men under you. You should be making snapper before long. I certainly hope so." (*Snapper was slang for someone in charge of a group of workers.*)

"Say Jim, what has the Marine Corps decided to do with you? Are you going to leave soon after the 1st of March or will you be around awhile?"

"I have to go to school now; it is almost 6:30. I have to help make out the grades for the past week."

"P.S. Please send me the suitcase unless Jim is going to use it. I'd like to have it by the 1st of March. I think that the metal one would be in the best shape by the time it got here. Send it R (*Rail*) W (*Way*) Express."

In his next report Bob commented on the weather and graduation diplomas,[186] "Everything goes good, the same with all of you I hope. Please send my jointed ramrod. I have been issued a rifle as I told you before I believe."

"Today and yesterday have been swell. They have all the symptoms of spring days. Dad, remember the weather that we had in April of the year that we went to the mountains to wire that lady's house? You know, the horsewoman. We have had that kind. It is too good to last."

33. Bob Wearing Marine Corps Issue Pith Hat

Sketch of Hand

"We got some diplomas yesterday for going through movie school. Starting with Class #3 all students that pass satisfactorily will get them. You see only those that have gone through the new 12 week course get them. I got one because I was an instructor. The other fellows in my class won't get them except Wolfkill."

"I'm enclosing a little sketch that I made using my hand as a model

Bob expresses his opinion of the Captain and discusses travel plans for a leave to visit home,[187]

"Saturday night I had the watch over at the MCS building from 10 to 2. About midnight the wind really blew."

"Yesterday everyone had the afternoon off except two students, the Captain and me. The Captain apparently never goes out. He is at the school every Sat. afternoon and his car is almost always in the parking lot.[188] Captain Karl T. Soule, Jr. is his name."

"Anyhow the students and I cleaned all 3 rooms, dusting sweeping, waxing, and doing a damn good job. I worked from 1 until 4."

"I'm afraid I won't save enough for the trip home. You see I want to go up to N.Y. every other weekend. (*Bob was obviously motivated to see Pat Niedert.*) If I do that I can only save from $50 to $60. It is a cinch that I don't want to go by coach, it is near to dying. I shall get a coach to Chicago and a Pullman to Vallejo. It will cost over$100. I shall go to Washington and get the exact price. They will give me 4 days travel time plus 15 days (I hope). Maybe it will only be 10. I hope not though."

"After March the M. C. should be sending you bonds that are coming out of my pay." "If you can send me some money I certainly shall pay it back. It shouldn't be at all hard to do that either my destination probably being a line-camp near San Diego."

"Two classes are always in session and I divide my time between them. Class #3 graduated, Class #4 is still in session, & Class #5 starts Tuesday."

"A kid just got in from Boot Camp. (*Glen*) Chittenden is his name. (*Glen graduated from Vallejo Senior High School in the class of 1943*.) I saw him at chow just after he got in. Jim & Zelda, what kind of guy is he? I think that he wants to go to movie school and we have to know all about him. Ask his teachers. What kind of grades did he make? Does he work hard? What kind of a person is he? I didn't know him very well."

Bob gained some new privileges and revealed for the first time the name of his secret love,[189] "The Captain has decided to give the instructors some privileges. One is to get our mail as soon as it comes in; another to have one afternoon or part of one off a week. That is why I am writing now. I just got back to the barracks and so decided to take advantage of this opportunity to write you. I am the first to get an afternoon off."

"My date with the woman marine was OK. She works in the Photo Section on the same deck as the school."

"I have been going to N.Y. quite often to see Pat Niedert. She is a swell kid. Someday I'll show you a picture of her."

"Class #5 started today. Evans of Class #3, formerly a Cpl., now a Sgt., started in as an instructor. Sgt. Rubalcava now a S/Sgt. left the school and is working on the production crew."

"Craig Wilson, Bill Pillsbury, and Lee Setterquist write to me once in awhile. Aki Yoshimura sends a V-mail from India occasionally."

"I'm going to N.Y. this weekend to see Pat, that is, if everything works out alright."

"In Class #5 there are 8 fellows."

No doubt in response to questions, Bob tells about his girl friends, especially Pat Niedert,[190] "I have been to the Niedert home several times. She is the first girl that I ever met in N.Y. I met her on my 1st visit. I'm going up to see her this weekend. She isn't the one I met at the art school. That was Evelyn Zeph. I met Pat in June while I was on mess duty. I had a weekend off and went to N.Y. with a fellow (*Martin McEvilly*) who used to go with her. No more does he. The W.R. marine was Mary Cook."

"I catch the 12 noon bus from Quantico, get the 1:55 train to N.Y. and get there about 5:45. I know when I've had enough to drink. Besides, I don't partake too frequently. It is about 300 miles from here to N.Y. City."

"Tonight I had charge of Physical Drill. We played basketball-15 min. I gave them the toughest set of exercises that they've ever had. I was fairly far on the road to being pooped."

"I pressed one set of greens & my field jacket tonight."

Martin McEvilly had introduced Bob to Pat who was attracted to him. As Pat later explained in a letter,[191]when Martin arranged a double date, Pat picked a friend "that I knew he wouldn't like so it was pretty easy for me. Mean trick but I just took a liking to Bob & nothing was going to stand in my way. Mart was angry as all get out because Bob started to write; to make it worse Bob asked Martin for the address when he got back to camp."

In his next letter, Bob discussed the invasion of the Marshall Islands and participation of photographers,[192] "Here I am on watch again (2000-0200). It is at the MCS building as usual. "

"Three of the fellows that were in Class #2, which I helped teach, are in the 4th Marine Division which is attacking the Marshalls. The Atoll that is under attack is Kwajalein. The two main islands invaded by the Marines are: Roi Is. & Namur Is."

The two islands were attacked on 31 January and secured by evening of 1 February when the Japanese that remained, following the pre-invasion bombing and shelling, were killed one by one. Garrison troops came to relieve the Marines a few days later, but the Seabee outfit failed to make the objective airfield suitable to receive aircraft and in the absence of Navy's carriers, that had left the area, there was no protection against Japanese aerial assault. On 14 February Japanese four engine bombers brought a Valentine's Day gift dropping bombs that set off an ammunition dump killing many marines and destroying supplies of vital food and equipment.[193] Meanwhile a well executed amphibious assault on Kwajalein by the Army's Seventh Division that had lost so many on Attu, near Alaska, secured the Atoll by 7 February.

Bob continued, "I took the new class, #5, for a tour through the Still Sec. this morning. This afternoon a still class paid a visit; so, I showed them around through the different departments. I had to cut this a little short in order to issue equipment to Class #4 that is going out on maneuvers. Class #5 consists of eight men: Brennan, Ewin, Hepfner, Hollander, Korach, Ridge, Schulz, & Vlahovich."

"A fellow made some portraits of me today. He will make some prints tomorrow for choice. I sent some pictures to you in an envelope, and some in a box. You should get them soon.

When Bob next wrote home he responded to a question about Captain Soule's age and told how he avoided being shipped out until later.[194] "Captain Soule is about 27 yrs. I got a letter from Raymond yesterday. I also received Jim's graduation announcement, thanks. It is very nice looking."

34. Formal Portrait CPL Watson

"After spending the weekend in N.Y., working Monday, I took the fellows for a conditioning run through the hills, and helped make out the grades for last week, in the evening. I got to sleep about 10:45 P.M."

"On the spur of the moment Capt. Decided I was shipping out this week. I had one 'helluva' time talking him out of it so that I could stay until March. Even now I don't know that it is settled for certain."

"It is time to be on my way back to work. Love, Bob.

P.S I'm sending a picture of Pat.

Signs of early spring got Bob's attention and he had more information about his leave en route to the Pacific theater,[195] "I am sitting on my foot locker using my bed and writing folio you sent me, Mom, for a desk. It was very satisfactory.

"Yesterday was clear, but the wind blew making it cold. Today is nippy, but the sun is beaming down and a very slight breeze is causing the treetops to sway slightly. Just before chow we saw the first robin of the year. It was the first time for one of the fellows. He is an artist formerly of L.A. Some people certainly have missed a lot."

"Friday I took three students out on a boat landing. It was so cold that the spray froze on our coats and the decks of the boats. It's been much colder here. I think that I told you about our coldest day- about 12 degrees."

35. Pat Niedert

"Upon returning to school after the landing I found a cake awaiting me. Pat Niedert sent it to me. It was very nice of her."

"Saturday afternoon we had our usual field day. They stained woodwork, dusted, swept, swabbed, waxed, straightened up equipment, shelves, and did numerous other things. We secured at 4:45."

"By rushing I took a shower, changed clothes, ate chow at the Hostess House-for a change, and saw the show 'Madame Curie'. It was very good."

"I just got back from taking time out to press two pairs of trousers and three field scarves. On the weekends that I stay in I catch up on my housework as it were."

"Concerning my delay en route, my best bet will be to catch an Army plane west or go out to San Diego with the rest of the fellows and go home from there. Either way I won't need any money from you. We can't make any reservations for trains because we aren't notified soon enough. I certainly don't want to ride coach all of the way. "I'm enclosing a picture of three fellows and myself while we were in just before leaving for our first three day war.

Upon receipt of a telegram from Jim informing Bob that he would be on active duty in the Navy V-5 program by March 1st, Bob responded with a telegram,[196] "GOOD LUCK ON VENTURE JIM. LEAVE HERE ABOUT MARCH 15= BOB."

He then wrote to his parents,[197] "Mom, get Jim some Seaforth's talc & after shave lotion. I shall repay you."

"I don't think that I shall need any money from you, Dad. If I do I shall send a telegram. I shall leave here on or about the 15th of March. I think the government will pay my way to S.D. From there I can get a train home. If that takes place I won't need any money."

"I'm enclosing a picture that I took of Pat Niedert in her front room using just the light from the windows. Thanks for the candy, cookies ramrod & suitcase. All safe."

36. Going on Maneuvers: CPL Albert Walavich, PFC Wayne Nalvanko, CPL Watson, and CPL Wolfkill

37. Pat Niedert at Home

Bob sent a longer response to Jim,[198] "I got your letter and telegram, OK. I'm sorry as hell that I won't get home in time to see you. I sent a telegram to you the evening that I received yours. As I said in my telegram I will leave here on or about 15 March.

I'm proud to know that you're a life member of the C.S.F. (*California Scholarship Federation*)."

. "Col. Pierce, Officer in Charge of the M.C. Photo Sec., was here from Hdqtrs. Today. He likes the school very much and says that we are doing a swell job. We are teaching better and more practical stuff than the Navy or Army. The Col. didn't say that, I do. I have seen some of their text books and heard reports on them. According to all information we are doing much better with less. At the beginning of the war Army and Navy went 'hog-wild' and bought up everything. We have to get equipment wherever we can find it, second hand or otherwise. Here is an example: The Army bought tons of Kodachrome. It has become out of date so they gave it to us. Knuckle heads, I say. Good Luck, Bob"

Bob described a sudden move,[199] "Thursday evening at 5 the fellows in my barracks were told to pack and to be out of there at 6:00. After a little mad scramble we made it. We are now all in H barracks where I started. Before the Photo Section personnel were quartered in #919 where I was, the MCS Detachment bldg., where I ate chow, (not MCS where I stood watch), and H barracks. Now the whole photo sec. personnel are in 'H'. I am in almost the same bunk that I had before."

"As far as I know I shall be home about the 20th of March. I shall send a telegram the day that my orders come through, which should be anytime from the 12th to the 16th."

"Earl Wells is here at Quantico. He is the only one left of the 5 of us that came out together. I saw Pat again this last weekend."

"Our new Class #5 is just about the dumbest that we've had. I'm speaking of the class as a whole."

Bob tells about his role as an actor,[200] "We just got through with a footlocker, wall-locker, and personnel inspection."

Class #4 is making a picture on the movie school. I acted in three scenes of it. I was supposed to be teaching the students compass use. If the story is good and filmed correctly sound will be added after it is edited. It will then probably be distributed to marine posts."

"I hope that Jim leaves his camera home. I would like to take it overseas. I believe that I could take some very interesting pictures."

March weather, a possible promotion and travel are the subjects on the docket,[201] "March came in like a lion, here. We had freezing weather and the wind blew quite a little. Yesterday it snowed quite a bit although it melted as it touched the ground. First the snow came down almost a sleet; then it came down in big flakes an inch in diameter. Later they became small wet flakes, all melting immediately."

'Yesterday I got the film inventory straightened out, for the month. Today I sent in some extra equipment to the quartermaster.

Tomorrow & Friday I have to get all inventories straight so that the new instructor will have something to go by. Every time I take over books or equipment they are always in a mess. I then have to straighten them out. Oh, well."

"Saturday afternoon I shall leave for N.Y.; I have a '72'. After spending 3 days there I may need some money from you to ensure my getting home; $20 will certainly be enough."

"I'm glad that Jim took my shirts.[202] At (least) they go with him, even if I don't get to see him."

"My 15 day delay enroute is almost a cinch. I believe that the only thing to keep me from getting it is a sudden call for photogs in the field, which is very unlikely."

"Yesterday the Captain sent in a request for my promotion to sergeant. Things are really happening: a '72', a 15 day delay enroute, and maybe a sergeant's rate, Woo! Woo! It is almost too good to be true."

Bob shares a secret with Jim who is now in the Navy,[203] "I see that you are getting underway there at Flagstaff. (*Navy V-12 program at Arizona State Teachers* College) I'm very glad to see that you like it. That makes it much easier."

"I got a 72 hour pass beginning 5 Mar. 0530 and ending this morning. I was lucky and got away Sat. afternoon early. I got to Pat's house about 9 P.M. I ate; some of Mr. Niedert's friends came over so we drank beer and talked. We got to bed at 5 A.M. Sunday. I got up at 9. Sunday night Pat, Phil, her brother, another girl, and I went to the Rockefeller Center to the theater there. We saw the movie 'Up in Arms' with Danny Kaye. I think that's his name. It was a swell musical and damn funny. The stage show consisted of a symphony orch., singing, dancing, and a comedian. The comedian supposedly drunk climbed upon a lamp post, took off his coat and shirt, pulled his undershirt out of his trousers, and pulled out a newspaper. Squatting on his haunches with his undershirt pulled down to his ankles, he looked as though he were taking a crap. It was very realistic."

"Pat and I are engaged. I didn't buy her a diamond though. Her folks will let us get married now, but we both think that we are a little too young. (*Bob was still nineteen years old and Pat was only sixteen.*) If everything goes right we'll get hitched after I come back from overseas. Don't tell Mom. Mrs. Niedert cried when I left, so you can see that they approve of me."

"The date of my leaving isn't definite as yet, but I shall probably leave the latter part of next week (that is from Wed. on). I am going to the 1st Marine Division. It is now under MacArthur, part of the 6th Army at Cape Gloucester. According to some scuttlebutt that the Captain got (I think at HQ.), the 1st Division will be in Burma oattack some more islands pretty damn quick. He thinks that I shall get out there just in time. <u>Keep this under your hat.</u>"

In another letter, Bob told his parents about his last trip to N.Y with less detail about the Radio City visit.[204] "My '72' started 0530 Sunday. The rule is that a man may pick up his papers at 1700 the night before. I was very lucky and got mine at 1220 Saturday. I wasn't able to catch a train out of D.C. until1455 though. Even at that I arrived at Pat's house about 2100."

"Her Dad had some friends over and Pat & I weren't expected to go out so I drank beer with them until 0500 Sunday. We didn't drink too much. I didn't get drunk and I had a fairly good time. That morning I got up at nine. During the day we fiddled around the house. That night, Pat, her brother, another girl, and myself went to Radio City. We got to bed about 0300 Monday."

"I got up about 1130. Monday being Pat's birthday, we went to a store got a cake and ice cream. I found some Christian Bros wine, Tawny Port, and so we had a little party. That night everyone was out so Pat & I took care of the kids."

"I got up late Tuesday morning. That afternoon we saw some friends of Pat's. I got the 10 O'clock back to D.C. that night. I got back to the barracks about 0430 Wed. All in all I had a <u>damn good time.</u> She bought me a silver I.D. bracelet without me knowing it, the little so-and-so."

Bob mentioned waiting for his orders and expectation of joining the First Division. He promised to tell more when he arrived home.[205]

"I won't be going through Flagstaff[206], I go south of there."

(*Jim had tried and failed to get liberty to see Bob for a few minutes and did not know until years later that Bob did not go through Flagstaff.*)

"I have all my G.I. clothes clean now. I washed them all yesterday afternoon. At 10 min. to one I called the Captain and asked to have it off. He surprised me and said yes. The only thing that I have to wash now is some shorts & handkerchiefs from home."

"I made up two packages to send you. One contains my iron and the other has my correspondence lessons in it plus some letters. The latter is marked personal property; <u>so do not open it.</u> The 1st is heavier than the last."

"I took two fellows of Class #5 out on a mines & booby trap problem Friday P.M. Sat. A. M. I issued equipment to some fellows in Class #5 so that they could leave on a problem early Monday A.M., 0645 to be exact. It is probably my last time to do that. I certainly am glad, too. That job gets quite monotonous."

Bob learns that Captain Soule had written home about him,[207] "I am glad that Ray (*Uncle Raymond*) got to see Theron (*Cousin Major McDaniel*). Maybe I shall see Ray overseas someday."

"I had to go to the instructors' round-table last night. While there, I asked the Captain if he had written to you. Of course he said yes. He didn't tell me what he had written though. Your letter was the first I'd heard about it, Mom."

"I went to school for about 1¼ hrs. this morning and then came back to the barracks. I have some shirts to press, but the barracks iron is in use and I sent the other to you. Instead of doing that I sewed a belt loop onto my blouse that had come loose."

"MT/Sgt. Tate, formerly an assistant director in Hollywood, and now a 1st Lt. will be the photo officer of the 1st Div. He is leaving for S.F. Monday. He is a swell egg & not in the least changed by the bars on his shoulders."

"Up to now our orders haven't come in. (By our, I mean Cpl. Howard Foss, Cpl. John Ostermeyer, Cpl. J. E. Wallace, and myself.) Foss was given the nickname Wilbur by Ostermeyer. All three fellows are of Class #4. Oh, yes, Pfc. Frank Adler is going too. We are all going to the 1st Div. I think that Gray & Spangler are in the 1st Div. now. Both of them were in my class."

10

DEPARTURE FOR SOUTH PACIFIC

Transfer orders finally arrived. After ten months at Quantico as photographic student and then instructor, Corporal Robert LeRoy Watson now knew that he was headed to the Pacific Theater and the duty for which he had been trained and that he had wanted. When his orders arrived, Bob wrote,[208] "My orders came in this morning without providing for a 15 day delay. The Captain went to the Colonel though so we get them. Wallace and I leave Friday sometime so I should be home the 22nd or 23rd. I'll send another telegram from Southern Calif. letting you know."

"All of my clothes, except those I have on, are clean and I'm getting some more tomorrow. I shall get paid Friday morning most likely."

"I'm not going to the 1st Div. as I was told unless I get assigned to it after I get out a ways. I am slated for the 1st Marine Amphibious Corps. It supplies men to the 1st Div. so I may still get in it. I don't know."

The orders read in part: "Corporal Robert L. Watson, #490975, will proceed via rail to Headquarters, Fleet Marine Force, San Diego area, Camp Elliott, Linda Vista, California, leaving this post on 17 March 1944, whereupon arrival he will report to the Commanding General, thereat, for further transfer to the First Marine Amphibious Corps, for duty with the Photo Section of that Corps."

"Corporal WATSON is authorized fifteen (15) days delay in reporting to Camp Elliott, Linda Vista, California and has given his address while on delay as: 642 Louisiana St. Vallejo, California."

Captain Karl Soule wrote[209] to Bob's parents and gave a good report of his performance as an instructor and his development as a leader of men. It made them very proud of their first born.

"Dear Mr. and Mrs. Watson: I can't let this week go by without dropping you a few lines to tell you how much I have enjoyed working with Robert."

"It has been quite sometime since he first came into the school, and he has really grown up with it. During the past few months that he has been an instructor, he has made considerable progress in developing qualities of leadership. It was a pleasure for me to recommend him for sergeant."

"During my work in the Marine Corps, and especially since I have worked with the school-men like Robert, I have become increasingly aware of what marvelous material we have in the Corps. It is a pleasure to work with men like Robert. He is a man, you know, though it may sound a little odd to you who have seen him grow up, and remember him as he was when he left you."

"I seem to have wandered off into a rambling lot of talk, which was not my intention. However, I do want you to know that it has been a great pleasure to have Robert here for the past several months. He has worked hard and well-never losing patience, nor forgetting courtesy. You can be proud of him in every way, and I know that I am glad he is going out into the field as a representative of the school."

"You will be glad to know that his tentative assignment is to the most seasoned unit in the Corps, one that is well led, and has experience in the ways of war. He will be with good men, and I know he will do a grand job."

"Sincerely yours, <u>Karl Soule</u>"

As promised Bob sent a telegram to his parents informing them of his departure and expected arrival home for leave on his way overseas.

"MAR 16 PM 8:40 LEAVE HERE TONIGHT BE HOME ABOUT 21ST WILL SEND ANOTHER TELEGRAM WHEN I GET IN CALIFORNIA=BOB."

Upon arrival he sent another telegram.

"LOS ANGELES CALIF MAR 20 PM 6:50
WILL ARRIVE TOMORROW MORNING ABOUT 11:00 =BOB."

Bertha documented Bob's arrival in her diary with the following entry, "The Big Moment arrived about 11 a.m. when a taxi stopped in front and Bob steps out. Gee we were happy to see him."

Bertha, Earle and Zelda lavished attention on Bob. Very conscious that he was soon to leave for the South Pacific and where he might well be in harms way, they relished every minute with him..

The young mother was most concerned and feared for Bob's safety but did her best to remain calm and maintain a good attitude.

Bob spent much of his time "loafing", but managed a trip to San Francisco and took Nadine McKinney, Bill Pillsbury's girl friend, to the high school Inaugural Ball. He also played some tennis. According to Bertha's diary Bob had a good time at the dance but none of his old buddies were there. Many were in some branch of military service by that time or out of town.

Bob also revealed to his parents the deep feelings he had for Pat Niedert to whom he wrote a loving letter every day. Bob kept himself looking every bit the Marine he was proud to be and took time to show Zelda how the Marines had taught him to shine his shoes using spit and cordovan polish demonstrating as he went along."[210].

38. Last Family Portrait, Earle, Bertha, Zelda, and Robert, Photo by   Jimmy Turner

On Saturday April 1st, Bob and Bertha went to the Southern Pacific Railroad Office and obtained a coach seat assignment for his trip to San Diego. The next day, Earle, Bertha, Zelda and Bob attended Sunday services at the Episcopal Church in Vallejo. Bob's Uncle Osmond and Aunt Maxine came from Yountville for a visit that same afternoon.

On April 4th the family said tearful goodbyes at the Greyhound bus station when Bob caught the 6 A.M bus to San Francisco to board the train to Los Angeles. Jimmie Turner, landlord in Vallejo, drove the family to the station and joined in wishing Bob good luck and God speed in his new adventure. When Bob was telling Zelda goodbye he told her she could "wear his football sweater until he came home." Zelda had been wishing she could do that "because so many other girls at Vallejo High were wearing the sports sweaters and it was comfortable and warm."[211]

After checking into Camp Elliott, Bob reported his arrival,[212] "Well I'm here. I got in L. A. about 6:05 last night (April 4). I got a hotel room, took a shower, ate, went to a show, came back, wrote a letter, and went to bed. I got up at 0600, shaved, got a street car to the station, ate, and caught the 0720 train."

"I arrived at Linda Vista at 1005. It is just a telegraph and freight office, and a siding. I called transportation. Arriving at Camp Elliot and being sent all over the place, I finally reached my correct outfit. There certainly is a lot of red tape here."

"I'm staying in wooden barracks, comparatively new, stucco inside, and fairly nice though a little crowded. The chow is good. We eat cafeteria style."

"The fellows drill in the morning and go on marches from eight to ten miles in the afternoon. All here are waiting to go overseas and they do that to keep in condition. As yet I haven't been issued any arms or other field equipment. Until I get that I won't go on any of these things, I hope."

"Things aren't too strict for the fellows. On the whole, they have it fairly good, except for liberty. We get liberty over night only and L. A. is the only decent place to go."

Bob also wrote to Jim repeating information about conditions and activities at Elliott, then added[213] "I had a good time on my furlough. I went to Frisco with 'Goober' Anderson, took out Nadine McKinney (*Bill Pillsbury's girl*) several times, played tennis with Teeny, and went on one of his trips with him. I saw Lee Monroe. Much of my time was spent loafing."

"Write soon. I don't know when I shall leave."

Four days later on Easter Sunday,[214] "Thursday afternoon a fellow by the name of King and I went swimming in the camp pool."

"That night we went to a stage show at the main camp theatre. We saw Helen Parrish, (she is very pretty); and Danny Kaye."

"Friday morning we had 'Rocks and Shoals' read to us. It is the Navy regulations." (*The Articles for the Government of the Navy were called Rocks and Shoals suggestive of ships running aground, and by implication the trouble military personnel can experience if failing to comply with the regulations. The Articles were usually required reading when personnel reported to a new base.*)

"Friday afternoon we had field day." (*General housekeeping or policing the quarters in military parlance*) Saturday morning we had quarters' inspection. That afternoon late, King and I went to S.D. We ate, saw a show and came back."

"Today I sharpened Wallace's and King's knives. Tonight I saw the show 'Tornado.' Saturday bout 4 P.M. Adler, Carothers, Foss, and Ostermeyer left for overseas. I have to shave now."

On Monday Bob continued,[215] "I got your letter of the 7th this morning, Mom."

"I'm glad that Os got the deferment. (*Uncle Osmond was deferred from the draft because he was married with two young children.*)

"Thanks for the pictures. I'm sending one back. This afternoon I went swimming. Tomorrow I get paid."

"Tonight I went to the show and saw 'Son of Dracula'. I have to shave and shower now."

Two days later Bob informed his parents that he had his orders to ship out,[216] "Yesterday they read off a list of names, the fellows that are to leave. I'm on the list. M. T. /Sgt. Abrams that I taught in Quantico is in charge. I hope that because I know him I may have a good deal."

"We will probably get our equipment today and leave before the week is out. All of us will probably be issued knives. We get rifles, helmets, cartridge belts, gas masks, shelter halves, and mattresses. We already have packs, leggings, and dungarees."

"Abrams just told me that I was to be his right hand. I'll probably be a flunky. I've always gotten along with him though; it shouldn't be so bad."

"I just finished signing for the equipment. I'll probably get my issue today."

"You had better stop writing until I send you a P.O. number. That may not be until I get over there somewhere. As yet I don't know. We have to be ready to leave at anytime."

"I'll probably get a rifle but I hope to get a carbine. If I do get a rifle I'll pick up a carbine over there. It is now 0850. I shall write Jim now."

124

Continuing to report,[217] "Yesterday I got a letter dated the 9th and 3 dated the 7th, 10th, & 12th."

"I'm glad that you are going to school, Zel."

"They say that we are leaving tomorrow or Sunday for certain. I wonder though."

"I got some of the letters from Pat that you sent, Mom. Maybe I got them all. Thank you very much."

"I don't know what I want for my birthday."

"I think I'll get my teeth cleaned now."

"I went down and they found seven holes; I got them cleaned. I didn't eat chow. After chow I went back to get them filled. While filling them he found two more. He filled all nine in 1 ¼ hrs. counting time out for a smoke. My jaw aches from all of the gadgets he had in my mouth."

"We have barracks inspection tomorrow morning. The uniform of the day is khakis here and greens for liberty. I don't think we'll leave until Monday or Tuesday, maybe Sunday."

"We were supposed to have sea-bag inspection tomorrow, but they called it off."

A note added the next day, "Yesterday morn we had inspection, barracks and some training films. At noon a S/Sgt. and I went to L.A. and fiddled around. We came back; there wasn't anything to do. I slept all morning. After noon chow I put some clothes to soak. I don't know when we'll leave."

Bob's next message was on Monday,[218] "Dear Mom; They took our sea-bags out to be hauled away. We will leave in a day or two."

"I'm enclosing some money to get Jim and Zel presents for their birthdays. I got Dad a pipe and am mailing it to you. Give it to him on Father's Day."

In one of his rare mentions of possible danger Bob admonished his mother, "Be sure to send Pat the colored pictures. In case I should by some slight chance get wounded and can't write and you find out, let her know."

"I'm going down to get the money order now."

Then to Zelda,[219] "This will probably be my last letter to you for a little while. We don't get liberty tonight; we just took out our sea-bags to be hauled away, leave soon day or 2."

"I'm enclosing some money for you to get Mom something for Mother's Day. Get her a flower plant or perfume, or something else appropriate."

"Thanks for the card. It is very nice. Your loving brother, Bob"

The next day to Jim,[220] "I got your letter yesterday. That's a helluva note getting Scarlett Fever again[221]. I hope that you are feeling better now."

"We drew all of our equipment that we get here except knives and our sea-bags are at the docks. Now I think that the orders have been changed. I have a few clothes in my pack, thank gosh. I don't know when the devil we will leave."

"I called Pat last night. I put the call in a little after 1730 and I didn't get her until 2200. I went to the show and fiddled around for awhile; at least I wasn't next to the phone all of that time."[222]

"It was about 0100 back there and of course she had been asleep when the call went through. She sounded very nice. It was swell to talk to her again. I said hello to her mother too. She got Pat up I guess."

"We haven't been doing anything except police up our areas. Pvt's. & Pfcs. get all of the shit details such as swabbing, cleaning the heads, etc. Once in awhile they call on Cpls. but I've been lucky most of the time."

"I've been swimming twice since I've been here and I went to L.A. Sat. and came back Sun. morning. I didn't get any sleep so I slept most of Sun. taking time out to write a couple of letters and wash clothes."

"Pat sent me some cup cakes for Easter. They were very good. Brother, Bob"

A day or two later a cadre of troops including Corporal Robert Watson arrived at a dock in San Diego Harbor in order to board a troop transport for the long voyage to the Pacific War Zone. After boarding, Bob searched for the deck where he would be quartered on the crowded ship and located his duffle bag that had been previously loaded.

When the transport steamed out of the harbor Bob no doubt scanned the harbor area searching the surrounding landmasses attempting to identify familiar sights. If it were a clear day he would have seen the famous Point Loma lighthouse originally put in service in 1865, but taken over by the Navy at the start of the war to use as a signal station. It is easy to speculate that Bob reflected on the training he received at the Marine Recruit Center in the first three months of the previous year and more recently his time spent in Quantico, Virginia learning to be an expert cinematographer and also teaching the skills to other marines. He probably dwelled for a moment on the combat training and exercises he had experienced under the tutelage of Captain Thayer Soule; and may have wondered if he had learned well enough to survive the rigors of island warfare. Now headed for an uncertain future and the greatest adventure of his young life, Bob would have quickly settled into the routine of daily ship life along with other young men with similar fears and thoughts.

After being at sea for several days Bob's thoughts turned to the day the ship would cross the equator and he along with all the other Pollywogs would be subjected to harassment from the Shellbacks. At least since the days of the Portuguese explorers there have been ceremonies associated with crossing the equator. Before a sailor or marine has crossed the equator he is known as a Pollywog. After enduring the ritual conducted by the ad hoc King Neptune and his assistants, supported by the crew that have previously crossed, he joins their ranks as a Shellback. It is possible that the custom originated as a religious ceremony in which the participants thanked God for seeing them safely across the equator. Later it may have been a rite designed to assure the old timers that the new crewmembers could survive the rigors of a long voyage.

After making the transition from Pollywog to Shellback and crossing the International Date Line Corporal Robert Watson found time to describe his first ocean crossing plus a perfunctory report of his transition from Pollywog to Shellback.[223] "I'm writing this on board a transport. I've been on it for some time and am at sea quite a distance out."

"The inconveniences are many but not as many as I had supposed there'd be. Being an NCO helps out more here than where I was before except while I was actually at work. NCO's aren't in such a large proportion here."

"We crossed the equator a few days ago and underwent the initiation. Here is what happened to me: short belt-line, a hunk cut out of hair (I had it cut short a coupla days before so it didn't hurt it much), some bitter liquid to swallow, ran through a stream of water from a fire hose, a longer belt-line. Oh! Yes. They put oil and graphite on our hair after cutting it. Some of the things that fellows got in whole or part for resisting or ditching: more hair chopped off, oil and graphite rubbed on neck, shoulders & torso, fish fat rubbed on face, and harder swats in belt lines."

"We crossed the international date line so that it is Wednesday the

3rd at home now as I'm writing this."

"The first two days at sea I had a headache and felt a little woozy, but I didn't lose any food. I'll have to stop now; we are going to have roll call."

"It was for the fellows to wash clothes and all of mine are clean so I don't have to wash any."

"We are able to buy things from the sea-stores and the Red Cross gave us soap, cigarettes, books and writing paper plus playing cards. We are doing alright. I'm in good health. Love, Bob"

In a side note he added, "I took Holy Communion here. (*He either meant on board ship or at Noumea, the first port.*) 2 Army Chaplains are priests. One knows Father Houssell."

Bob added a page before mailing the letter from Guadalcanal. The military censor cut out the top right hand corner of the letter, which presumably had the date and location. "When I wrote this I was at Noumea. (New Caledonia) "Dear Folks, Well here I am in camp now."

"I've seen two movies since I've been here. The first was 'Appointment in Berlin' and the second 'Youth on Parade'."

"Has anything new happened around home?"

"I'm now at Guadalcanal."

"There isn't anything new to tell. There are so many restrictions about what we can tell."

"The scenery is nice here; that is about all that I've seen so far."

The same day Bob wrote a V-Mail letter,[224] "I have arrived safe and sound. We had no raids or scares while on board ship."

"We left San Diego and went straight across to New Caledonia. We left there and arrived here a couple of days ago. I know about everyone here. I met most of them at San Diego, Quantico, or New Cale."

"From what little I've seen the Photo Section is fairly well set up, much better than I expected."

"I'm going to check up and see if any of the old timers knew Ned Steele."

"I've been swimming twice since I've been here. Walavich and I washed a truck called a carry-all. It isn't a dirt mover. It has seats for nine besides drivers and can carry supplies. I will write you more as I learn about things and the restrictions are removed."

Corporal Robert Watson arrived on Guadalcanal May 14, 1944 from New Caledonia where he had arrived two days before. He was assigned to the Photo Section of the powerful Third Amphibious Corp formerly known as the First Amphibious Corps. Major Halpern and twenty-eight year old Lt. Harold Palmer led the Section. Bob settled in quickly as he indicated in his next letter.[225] "Things are going good here. For the last two days I've been making inventories and checking equipment with Walavich."

"Of course I've washed clothes and straightened out some of my gear. I'm fairly well straightened away by now."

"The night before last we made some pineapple ice cream and last night we made chocolate."

"Every night or so we get coke or beer rationed to us. Being in a rear area we have to pay for it."

"I just finished washing some more clothes."

"I've had more clothes and gear issued so I have just about everything required."

"I'm thinking of going for a swim today."

The censor tore the next sentence out, but the tops of the letters were partially visible. It seemed to say something like, "I'm going or flying on a mission." According to Hal Palmer, Bob went on an aerial reconnaissance mission in a PB-J (Billy Mitchell B-25 twin engine bomber, the same type used by Lt. Col. Jimmy Doolittle in his raid on Japan) to take pictures near the straights of Kavieng,[226] the capital of the province of New Ireland. Bob made no mention of the reconnaissance flight in any of his letters other than the possible reference mentioned above that the military censor removed. He did confirm in a later letter[227] that he had been up in an airplane for trips to Tulagi and Bouganville.

39. PB-J on Bouganville

Always attentive to his family, Bob wrote[228], "I got your letter today of the 13th, Mom. Boy! Was I glad to get it. I'm a little concerned, Zelda. I sent you a $5 money order to get Mom a present for Mother's Day. She didn't mention it in her letter. However she said, 'Your address made a lovely Mother's Day present tho.'

Now I'm wondering if she got the money order. If she didn't, I'm sending my receipt."

"Today I rode around the island a little and visited a few places that I hadn't before."

"The 2nd morning that I was here I met a kid that I went through Boot camp with, Fields" (was his name.) The other day I met another by the name of Menke. I also met a kid from Quantico that was on mess duty at the same time I was. He wasn't in the Photo Section. He is red-headed and named Montgomery. He is now a meat cutter."

"We have a black and white female cat here that gave birth to six kittens yesterday. It was a little excitement for us. They took down the time for each birth."

"I believe that Theron McDaniel[229] was here a week ago Friday. I didn't get to the Section until Saturday so I missed him. I think he has gone back to the States; I'm not sure though."

"P.S. I'm glad to see you are in P&E, Dad." (*Earle Watson, an electrician, had been promoted to the electrical Planning and Estimating Department. at Mare Island Navy Yard.*)

Major James Theron McDaniel, Bob's first cousin once removed, was mentioned in an article written by Raymond Clapper[230] posthumously published on February 5, 1944: "Major James T. McDaniel, Eureka, Cal., had recently led a full scale raid into Rabaul. He said the Japs were fighting better and harder than ever in the air".

Theron had returned to the States to attend a command and staff school at Quantico, VA. As leader of a dive-bombing squadron, he had been on numerous bombing and strafing missions over Japanese held territory, and was credited with two direct hits on Japanese ships. McDaniel was awarded the Distinguished Flying Cross during a ceremony at the Quantico air station.

Bob described[231] efforts to have some normal fun in a war zone staging area, "Last night some of us had a party on the beach. We had a lot of fun singing and drinking six cases of beer and eating crackers and sandwiches. The sandwiches were tuna, turkey, cheese, and pineapple. The fellows did quite a bit of bumming to get everything. That is one good thing about this outfit. They made lots of contacts and came out OK."

"Today we had an inspection of us with field equipment. Some still pictures were made of us."

40. Third Amphibious Corps Photo Section in Field Gear First Row L-R: Gallagher, Kempe, Carroll, Rohde, Brunk, Abrams, Gas, Plaine; 2nd: Johns, Hager, Whittingham, Lt. Palmer, Cusack, Major Halpern, Rogers, Cannistraci, Clement, McEvilly; 3rd: Rhodes, Sarno, Foss, Calnen, Watson, Wilson, Hudson; 4th: Adler, Carothers, Ostermeyer, Davis

41. Photo Section, sans Officers. R. L. Watson sixth from left second row

42. Carryall Truck with Members of the Photo Section, Bob is standing on the left side.

In reply to a letter from Zelda, Bob wrote[232], "So Pat had been telling on me? My! My! Oh well, I don't mind. I got the blues (*dress uniform*) from a buddy of mine. They fit me almost perfectly." Pat apparently wrote about how handsome she thought Bob was in his dress blues.

"Lately I've been testing cameras and doing both painting and carpentering work. I've also been driving quite a bit lately. From that you can see that I haven't been completely idle. The other day we fixed up our tent. It was beginning to sag badly.

Then later to Zelda[233], "I was glad to hear from you mentioning what you did with the $5 eased my mind a great deal. I'm glad that you got Mom the prayer book."

"I just got through digging a drainage ditch. I didn't do it all by myself, about six of us worked on it." Ever resourceful, Marines find ways to improve their circumstance as Bob narrates, "One of the fellows picked up a radio for the Major (*Halpern*) and when he isn't busy we listen to it. It's a good one.

Bob and several of his fellow photographers were about to have a dramatic change in their circumstance. They were soon to be ordered to participate in a major campaign to retake Guam and capture Saipan in the Marianas Islands.

11

FIRST TASTE OF BATTLE-GUAM

In January 1943 President Roosevelt and Prime Minister Winston Churchill met in Casablanca, Morocco where they agreed that unconditional surrender would be required of the axis powers. The Combined Joint Chiefs of Staff also agreed to a Central Pacific offensive aimed toward the Philippines by attacking through the Marshall, Carolina and Marianas islands. As a consequence of planning and approval by the American Joint Chiefs of Staff (JCS) it was decided to attack three islands within the Marianas group: Saipan, Tinian and Guam. Known as project Forager, the goal was to establish air bases on the islands so that the new Boeing B-29 Super Fortress could bomb the Japanese mainland. Guam was also intended to become a major naval base so as to shorten the long logistics path currently dependent on shipping from Hawaii. Admiral Spruance, Commander, Central Pacific Task Forces, was responsible for all the military forces involved. In addition to the naval task groups, Project Forager planned employment of the Second, Third and Fourth Marine Divisions, the First Provisional Marine Brigade and the Army's Twenty-Seventh and Seventy-Seventh Infantry Divisions.

The Third Marine Division and the newly formed First Provisional Brigade were designated to conduct the invasion and recapture of Guam as part of the III Amphibious Corps Southern Troops and Landing Force, under the command of Major General Roy S. Geiger. The Third Marine Division commanded by Major General Allen H. Turnage and the First Provisional Brigade under Brigadier General Lemuel C. Shepherd with the Army's 77th Infantry Division, under command of Major General Andrew G. Bruce, were to provide the bulk of the forces scheduled for the recapture of Guam, code named STEVEDORE.

The 1st Provisional Brigade had been activated on 22 March 1944 at Pearl Harbor with only a minimal headquarters staff. Now on Guadalcanal, command of the Brigade was taken over by General Shepherd on 16 April. At the end of the month the Fourth Marine Regiment Reinforced (Fourth Marines) arrived on Guadalcanal after successfully occupying Emirau. The 22nd Marine Regiment

Reinforced (22nd Marines) also arrived after capturing Kwajalein to provide the bulk of the strength of the Brigade.

The Fifth Amphibious Corps-Northern Troops and Landing Force that included the Second and Fourth Marine Divisions and the Army's Twenty-Seventh division were assigned to capture Saipan and Tinian under the command of Major General Holland M. Smith. The landing on Saipan was scheduled for the morning of 15 June. The invasion of Guam was scheduled to commence three days after the Saipan D–Day on 18 June.

While Bob was testing cameras and improving the facilities used by the Photo Section, the Third Amphibious Corps' Northern Attack Group, not to be confused with the V Amphibious Corps, Northern Attack Force, practiced amphibious landings at Cape Esperance. The III Corps' Southern Attack Group rehearsed in the same area on 25-27th. After training, the Third Division, assigned to the Northern Attack Group, embarked on transports and LSTs from docks at Tetere,[234] located 24 miles east of Honiara the current main port of Guadalcanal.

The newly formed First Provisional Brigade assigned to the Southern Attack Group that included the Twenty Second and Fourth Marine Regiments participated in training exercises at Tulagi from 10 to 28 May. Bob joined the Second battalion, Twenty-Second Marines on board the U.S.S. Leedstown (APA-56) on 3 June 1944.at Kukumbona Anchorage, just ten miles east of Honiara. On 4 June the Leedstown sailed as part of Task Group 53.2, enroute to Kwajalein Atoll, Marshall Islands. Leedstown and eleven ships in Transport Division Six were protected by a ten Destroyer Screen.

Leedstown went to General Quarters each day of the sail and on several occasions conducted anti-aircraft firing exercises against targets towed by aircraft. On 8 June Leedstown anchored at Anchorage "A", Kwajalein Atoll and loaded provisions. The next day troops were disembarked to various LSTs at anchor. Bob, along with his friend Martin McEvilly and Master Tech Sergeant Brunk, boarded LST-270 with the assignment to film Company G, commanded by Lt. Col. Don C. Hart, in combat during the attempt to recapture Guam.[235]

Bob and most of the Photo Section under Master Tech Sergeant Brunk,[236] were photographed before leaving Guadalcanal. Claude Winkler, Howard Foss and Cannistraci were not present when the photo was snapped.

43. 1st Provisional Brigade Photo Section L-R Bottom up; Rhodes, Watson, Catnen, Johns, Gallagher, Sarno, Brunk and McEvilly

The Southern Troops and Landing Force (TG 53.2) under command of Rear Admiral L.R. Reifsnider, that carried the First Provisional Brigade and the Third Marine Division, included Leedstown and eleven more attack transports (APA) and three cargo transports (AP). Destroyer Divisions 90 and 94 protected the transports. The Southern Attack Force included the Northern Tractor Group, TG 53.16, and the Southern Tractor Group, TG 53.17, whose LSTs carried troops and Landing Vehicle Tracked (LVT), transported elements of the Third Marine Division and the First Provisional Brigade respectively.

At 1450 hours on Friday 9 June, LST 270 was underway from anchorage as ordered by the Commander Task Group 53.17 proceeding enroute as part of Tractor Group Four for Forager Operation, Task Unit 53.4.4 steaming on base course 294 degrees true at nine knots.[237] During the next four days the LST convoy continued toward the Marianas with only routine activity that included gun firing and abandon ship drills, receipt of guard mail from another LST and supplying a minesweeper with fuel, water, bread and potatoes.

To the extent permitted Bob would have explored the ship and been entranced by the maneuvering of the convoy's several columns. Transfer of supplies to the minesweeper surely caught his attention and mail from the LST would have raised his hopes for letters from home. Typically guard mail included orders and information for the skipper of the ship, but did not include mail for the troops. Without these diversions the long days at sea would have been boring; and Bob no doubt spent time talking and laughing with McEvilly and Brunk. Surely some time was spent discussing their upcoming photographic assignment and concerns about their first time in combat.

By 12 June the faster ships including the Leedstown had sailed, and the "entire task force had left in convoy formation,[238] bound for the" Marianas Islands where it was to be held in reserve for the Saipan operation before being committed to landing on Guam. The Fifth Amphibious Corps, Northern Attack Force, had already sailed from Eniwetok to the Marianas with the last ships leaving on 11 June. Aerial bombing of Saipan, Tinian, Guam, Rota and Pagan, by carrier planes of Task Force 58 began on June 11 for a three and a half day bombing campaign. Fast battleships of the Task Force blasted Saipan and Tinian with their big naval rifles. The Second and Fourth Marine Divisions landed on the beaches of Saipan on D-Day, June 15, as scheduled.

American submarines alerted Admiral Spruance that Japanese naval units were sailing toward the Marianas when the Marines landed on Saipan. Japanese ships were observed emerging from San Bernardino Strait between Samar and Luzon headed east. Land based Japanese airplanes also made an unsuccessful attack on American escort carriers on the same night.

At 1600 hours on 15 June, Task Group 53.17 was in reserve steaming on course 265 degrees true, when lookouts on LST 270 sighted four enemy aircraft off the port bow at an approximate altitude of 1000 feet. The call to general quarters was sounded. The aircraft identified as Bettys (Nakajima B5N2 torpedo planes that had attacked Pearl Harbor and sunk aircraft carriers Lexington, Hornet and Yorktown in an earlier battle) attacked two of the columns of LSTs. No doubt those on board LST 270 who were not at combat stations found cover where ever available as they watched a Betty attack their ship off the port quarter at 1729 hours. The commanding officer ordered all engines to flank speed as the gun crews opened fire. The "attacking aircraft was hit by anti-aircraft fire from" the "stern batteries and crashed into the sea 1000 yards off starboard beam."[239]

As Bob watched the Japanese torpedo plane press the attack his adrenaline gland pumped epinephrine into his system and his blood pressure rose. He along with his fellow Marines were relieved to see that their ship received no damage and were elated when they saw the torpedo plane crash into the ocean. No doubt there was yelling, cheering and laughter accompanied by slaps on the back. Yet Bob's report was matter of fact when he wrote[240]home about the attack, "Four Jap torpedo planes attacked our convoy one day. Two planes were shot down that I saw. Our ship was given credit for one."

The only casualty onboard was a Baker 3/c who fractured his ninth rib when he bumped his head as he rose from his bunk when general quarters was sounded.

The next morning Admiral Spruance indefinitely postponed the attack on Guam scheduled for 18 June "until the enemy carrier force had either retreated or been destroyed."[241] Because of the impending naval battle Spruance ordered unloading on the Saipan beaches to cease at dusk on 17 June and also ordered all transports and LSTs not vital to the operation to sail eastward from the island. Also the transports and LSTs scheduled for the Guam invasion were ordered to a position 150 to 300 miles east of Saipan. Admiral Spruance delayed the landing on Guam, scheduled for 18 June, indefinitely as his task force engaged the Japanese navy in what became known as the Battle of the Philippine Sea. As part of that battle, U.S. Naval air forces destroyed 330 of 430 Japanese airplanes[242] that attempted to obliterate the American fleet. Fifty more enemy planes were destroyed in American attacks against Japanese airfields on Guam. Only thirty American planes were lost, thirteen of them in attacks on Guam. In American Naval Lore this became known as the "Great Marianas Turkey Shoot."

The Northern Attack Group 53.16 was not as fortunate. On 17 June, LST 274 reported, "Convoy repelled an enemy air attack by 3 torpedo bombers of Kate type. Manned GQ (*General Quarters*). One plane destroyed, another plane probable. LCI 468 blown apart by the explosion." Torpedo planes "damaged one LST so badly it had to be scuttled", and Yap[243] based "fighters, torpedo planes and dive bombers damaged an LST that was retiring with the transports."[244]

Although the Battle of the Philippine Sea resulted in a major victory for the U. S. forces by 20 June, the battle on Saipan had forced the commitment of the Army's 27th Infantry Division, which was intended to be the reserve for the battle of Guam. As a consequence

Admiral Nimitz released the Army's 77th Division, currently in Hawaii, as the reserve for the Third Amphibious Corps. One regimental combat team was then scheduled to leave Hawaii on 21 June with the rest of the division to follow.

After the attacks on the Southern Attack Force, until the end of June, there was little activity with the exception of reports of enemy planes in the area that did not result in attacks. A destroyer did fire on and sink a surface target 12 miles distant. Otherwise the convoy ships of the Southern Attack Force cruised on station east of Saipan. There were a few exchanges of supplies from 270 to smaller ships and from a destroyer to 270. At one point a sub-chaser delivered 1000 Atabrine tablets to prevent the Marines from contracting malaria.

During this time Bob and his photographer friends along with the Marines of the 22nd Regiment coped with boredom as they waited to learn when they would be ordered to land on Guam. They whiled away the hours cleaning weapons, playing cards, and basking in the sun acquiring tans. Marines on some ships set up virtual tent cities for protection from the hot sun. Some engaged in exercises in an attempt to stay in good physical condition. Others told stories, reminisced about good times and sang familiar songs, especially if someone had a harmonica. Some of the troop transports had facilities to conduct boxing matches. When a chaplain was on board, religious services were conducted. Surely on June 24, 1944 Bob and his friends took time to celebrate his birthday and was congratulated on reaching the ripe old age of twenty.

Many of the members of G Company had been together as part of a cohesive unit since its formation as part of the 22nd Marines in 1942 at Linda Vista, California near San Diego. The Regiment was used in the capture of Eniwetok in February 1944 and also for mop up of the many atolls in the Marshall Islands. Replacements for the casualties from those operations had ample time to become integrated into the regiment when it returned to its new base on Guadalcanal. As a newcomer and outsider assigned to photograph the men in combat, Bob no doubt used the time at sea to become acquainted with them and to gain their confidence. This would have been essential so that he would be accepted in combat, not firing a rifle, but filming their action. Bob's friend and fellow photographer, Grant Wolfkill described the importance of being accepted by the unit to which a photographer is assigned.[245] "When you gained their confidence and if they knew you were serious they were very helpful and would look after you and help you if they thought you needed it. They would warn you if you needed to be warned. I know they would carry you out if you were wounded."

While the Southern Attack Group continued to cruise the waters east of Saipan, the Northern Attack Group containing the Third Division was ordered on 25 June to Eniwetok, located on the western fringe of the Marshall Islands, for restaging in anticipation of landing on Guam. On 30 June, Bob learned that the First Provisional Brigade was no longer to be held in reserve and was to proceed for restaging at Eniwetok. Taking advantage of the pending stop over, Bob wrote a V-Mail letter and submitted it to the censor for review and dispatch. He informed his parents,[246] "I'm with the *twenty-second regiment* and have been for a little while. I certainly am seeing a lot of water". (*Italics indicate censored words.*)[247]

"The last mail I received was just before I left Guadalcanal. I kept hoping that I'd get a letter from Pat, but I wasn't that fortunate. Someday they'll all catch up with me though. I got two letters: one from Zel and one from Mom back at the last place that I was." How did my pictures turn out? How is Jim doing? Send me a fountain pen if you can. Someone swiped mine."

"I'm in good health and am acquiring a little tan." I've taken very few pictures and those that I did take were not very good."

LST 270 sailed in convoy on base course near 100 degrees true until lookouts sighted land off the port bow 20 miles distant at 0640 July 5, 1944. At 1020 Bob saw Japtan Island off the starboard beam as LST 270 entered Eniwetok Atoll and proceeded independently to anchorage.

From July 6 to 15 LST 270 was at various anchorages taking on ammunition, water and other supplies. The Marines were allowed to go ashore in groups for a brief respite after 28 days at sea. Bob was included in one of the R and R groups and in anticipation of immediate departure for Guam wrote[248] to his brother followed by another to his parents.

"Dear Jim, Yesterday I got four letters from you. Excuse the V-mail please. Unavoidable, must hurry. Glad to hear that you are getting along OK and that your grades are good. Your course sounds fairly tough. I got some letters and pictures from Pat, also a bunch from home. It certainly was good to hear from all of you. It was quite sometime since I last got some. I'll write more as soon as I can. I have to get this censored and mailed immediately. Brother, Bob."

"Dear Folks, Excuse the use of this paper, please. I don't have any other available at this time[249]. Yesterday I got about 36 letters from you including 3 from Dad, 3 from Zel, and 30 from Mom. These are the first for quite sometime. I also received 3 or four from Jim, one from the Turners and one from Grandma. Please acknowledge the receipt of these. I doubt if I shall have time. I got a whole slew from Pat, 2 or 3 from her mother, one from the Captain (*Thayer Soule*) and one from Nadine McKinney. I'm glad to see that she and Bill got engaged. (*Bill Pillsbury*)."

"Each day out here is very similar to the one before. When I have time I shall write you all about this. I got the money order that you sent to (*Camp*) Elliott, Mom. I hope you all like your presents, although of course I don't know what Zel got you. Excuse this poor letter; I'll try to make up for it later. Thanx for the stamps; they are very handy right now. I shall close now so that this will get out in time."

Although the Southern Attack Force had been held in abeyance until the Saipan situation was clarified, the Navy proceeded with the planned bombardment of Guam to support the original schedule. Carrier airplanes from Task Force 58 began bombing Guam on 11 June. The Orote Peninsula received its first shelling from a two-hour naval bombardment 16 June. The task force then attacked Japanese ships in Apra Harbor on 27 June. Destroyers from Admiral Mitscher's TF 58 celebrated Independence Day by lobbing five-inch shells near Agana Bay, Asan Point, and Agat Bay.[250] Then on 8 July the task force commenced a daily bombardment of Guam at a level unprecedented in World War II.[251] The attacks continued from destroyers and airplanes followed by battleships and cruisers. Unfortunately, 16 U.S. navy planes were shot down before the invasion day known as "W day".

On 10 July DD 400, U.S. McCall, spotted a signal coming from one of the hills on Guam that said, "I have information." The McCall responded by telling the sender to come to the shore. The captain sent a small boat with volunteers to pick up the messenger who swam out to meet them. It turned out to be Radioman First Class George R. Tweed who was the only survivor of the 555 navy and marine personnel present when the Japanese invaded Guam in 1941. Tweed had survived by constantly moving and hiding in caves. Native Chamorros also helped him with food and shelter; and for their trouble the Japanese executed some.

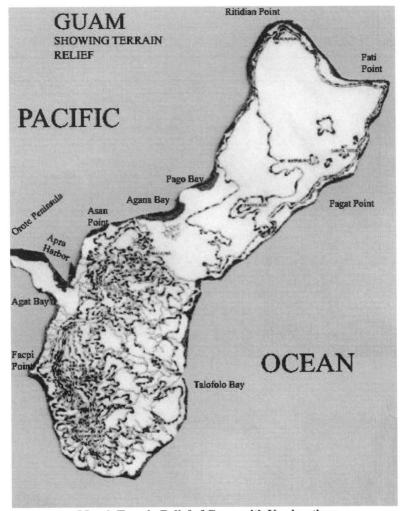

Map 1, Terrain Relief of Guam with Key locations

Back on at Eniwetok the Guam invasion force made preparations to sail, the Northern Attack Group carrying the Third Marine Division and the Southern Attack Group bringing the First Provisional Brigade. LST 270, part of the latter group, took on board its final load of 40 mm ammunition and got underway at 1124 July 15. Sailing in LST convoy and eventually joined by the faster ships, 270 reached the approach to Guam. By 20 July all the ships in the invasion force were either on station or almost in position off Guam. "H-Hour" had been confirmed for 0830 on W-Day 21 July.

142

After the long delay leading up to the invasion, almost 55 days at sea, the men would now make sure all of their gear was in order. While the riflemen were cleaning and oiling their rifles several times, checking bayonets and hand grenades, Bob checked his Eyemo 35 mm movie camera and made certain he had an adequate supply of film cartridges. He also inspected and cleaned his 45-caliber pistol one more time and checked again his supply of back up loaded ammunition clips. Master Tech Sgt. Brunk gathered his team of photographers for one last meeting to discuss their mission and to wish them all well during the landing and subsequent combat. He had one of his cinematographers record the event.

44. Sgt. Brunk wishing his Men well. L-R: Unknown, Brunk, CPL Watson, and Pvt. McEvilly. National Archives Photo

On the 21st, Bob responded to early reveille and early chow, then prepared himself mentally for the ordeal ahead as he anticipated landing on Yellow Beach 2 with G Company Second Battalion. He wondered how he would perform during his first time in combat, but after reflecting on the intense training he had endured at Quantico, some under live fire, he knew he was prepared and would acquit himself well. He was determined to do his best and resolved to accept whatever may come.

The transports maneuvered to positions off shore that would permit landing the Third Division's three regiments on the 2,500-yard beach between Adelup Point and Asan Point. The 3rd Marines were scheduled to land on a beach area designated Red 1 and 2; the 21st Marines centered on Green Beach; and the 9th Marines to the right on Blue Beach. The First Provisional Brigade ships were positioned for landings between Agat village and Bangi Point, a mile apart. The 22nd Marines were to land on Yellow Beaches 1 and 2; and the 4th Marines to the south on White Beaches 1and 2. LST 270 arrived to within four miles of Guam bearing 090 degrees True at 0245 hours on Friday 21 July.

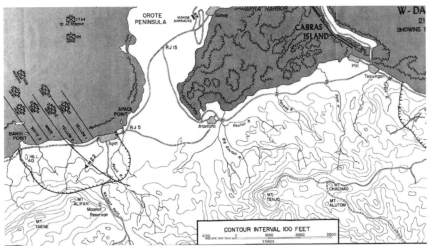

Map 2, Landing area between Bangi Point and Apaca Point from L-R White Beaches 2&1 and Yellow Beaches 2 & 1, where First Provisional Brigade was scheduled to land.

The sky above Guam glistened with stars until first dawn at 0445. Forty-five minutes later the destroyers, cruisers and battle ships were all at their assigned stations ready to fire shells onto the landing beaches. At 0535 four battleships started firing their twelve 14-inch guns. The rest of the support ships laid rounds on the designated landing beaches, and adjacent areas to the sides and inland. Fifteen minutes after sunrise, at 0615, a combat air patrol (CAP) of 26 carrier planes was over the island. Nine bombers of the CAP dropped missives on buildings, machine gun nests and antiaircraft installations.[252]

At this time marines began boarding LVTAs and LVTs (Landing Vehicles Tracked Armored and Landing Vehicles Tracked) in preparation for the landing and assault on their assigned beaches. On board LST 270 a marine from Company G, Bob's assigned unit, slipped when he jumped into an LVT an caught his arm on an unknown metal surface and fractured his wrist. Depending on his mental state he may or may not have been happy to go to sick bay and miss the chaos and danger of the impending landing. No doubt some of his buddies envied his circumstance. Bob lowered himself into his assigned LVT and checked his camera equipment one more time as he realized his introduction to combat was only minutes away.

Marines and sailors above deck on the transports were treated to another aerial display between 0715 and 0815 as 85 fighters, 62 bombers and 53 torpedo planes strafed the 14 miles western beaches while ships provided gun fire. The trajectory of the projectiles was no higher than 1200 feet and the aircraft stayed above 1500 feet.[253]

The sixteen LSTs carrying the assault troops of the First Provisional Brigade moved into the launching area about 1200 yards off Yellow and White Beaches by 0700. Five minutes later LST 270 opened its bow doors and lowered the ramp gate at 0722. It took only four minutes to launch the LTVAs, five minutes later the last LVT was launched carrying the last of the assault troops. Nine gunboats LCI (G) s armed with 42 rocket launchers plus 40 mm and 20 mm guns led the assault, shelling the beaches after they crossed the line of departure. LVT (A)s followed within seconds as six waves of LVTs formed up ready for the attack. Bob was in the second wave sharing the ride with about 29 marine riflemen headed for Yellow Beach 2. At the same time the Third Division was headed for Asan Beach to the north.

45. Part of First Wave, Photo from 16 mm film shot by Hoyt Rhodes

About 0810 the gunboats were firing salvos of rockets at the beaches and the armored LVTs in the lead assault wave moved forward from the launch area. At this time air observers dropped white parachute flares as a signal for the ships to cease firing their 14-inch guns. Then 32 carrier planes dropped depth bombs and strafed the beaches until the marines were almost ashore. Twelve more planes immediately strafed inland from the beaches. As the armored amphibians crossed the reef they fired their 20 and 40 mm weapons at any Japanese troops within eyesight. There was little or no enemy opposition except for sporadic firing from a few locations, including a Japanese field piece sighted firing from Gaan Point, located half way between Agat and Bangi Point. Naval guns silenced the weapon that was later determined to be a 75 mm field piece.[254]

As the amphtracs crossed the reefs, mines and enemy fire suddenly created havoc. Twenty-four of the Brigades tractors were put out of action by enemy fire, damage to the treads from the coral, or mechanical problems. The first wave of the 22nd Marines was hit by intense enemy fire when 100 yards from the beach. The fire came from a 75mm gun stashed in a concrete blockhouse on Gaan Point where a 37mm gun was also protected by concrete. Several of the LVTs headed for the Yellow Beaches were damaged and some of the marines on board were hit. The leading waves suffered ten LVTs and LVT (A) s destroyed. Crossfire raked White Beach 2 where the 1st Battalion of the Fourth Marines landed. Pillboxes between Agat and Bangi Point, and other well concealed guns on the south side of Orote Peninsula fired on the landing troops. "Casualties were numerous at Yellow Beach 2, where marines received savage fire from the concrete blockhouse on Gaan Point; and small arms, mortar, and machine gun fire from well concealed positions overlooking the beach."[255]

As Bob's LVT approached the beach he could see boats near him being hit and fellow marines being killed as the enemy projectiles exploded on the boats and in the water. He began to feel nauseous as adrenaline kicked in preparing him for the ordeal ahead. It reminded him of running the hurdles in high school track meets when he would feel nauseous waiting for the starting gun. The nausea would always go away as soon as he started running and concentrated on clearing the hurdles as smoothly and as fast as he could. This time was different, a matter of life and death, his. But he was determined to carry out his mission of filming the combat in spite of the death and destruction around him.

Bob rushed out of the LVT after landing at 0832 and scrambled up the beach seeking cover. While the riflemen aimed their weapons in search of enemy soldiers, Bob readied his Eyemo camera and proceeded to film the action.

"The 22nd Marines suffered a considerable loss of men and equipment while landing, but once the troops were some 200 yards inland, out of range of the Japanese guns aimed at the beaches, progress was easier. The 2nd Battalion had advanced to high ground about 1000 yards inland before noon, when it began to receive artillery fire, a foretaste of resistance beyond the beaches. The fire increased as Lieutenant Colonel Hart reorganized his troops on the high ground and prepared to move out at 1250. His objective was a line that included the crest of Mt. Alifan and the village of Agat."[256]

While the battalion was advancing and taking casualties, Bob was engaged in filming the fighting. He concentrated on getting good scenes of the action while forcing himself to ignore the cacophony of sound, the confusion and danger. Grant Wolfkill described combat photography,[257] "When you are filming, you forget a little about the enemy. You line up a shot and concentrate on getting it in the key moment. Remember, we used cameras that wound down in no time at all, and if I remember correctly a whole roll of film only lasted 2 ½ minutes, a 100 foot roll."

Bob took advantage of the training he had received at the photo school under the tutelage of Captain Thayer Soule who had insisted that the photographers learn to judge the amount of light available so they could set the F-stop[258] accordingly. He argued that there would be no time to use a light meter in combat; also, light meters were fragile. If a photographer intended to film a particular action, he could miss the opportunity if he had to take time to read a light meter.

The limitations of the Bell and Howell Eyemo 35 mm movie camera added to the difficulty of capturing an intended action. There were three lenses mounted on a turret, which had to be rotated to select the appropriate lens for wide-angle, normal, and telephoto viewing. An optical viewfinder was used to compose the shot. The version used in World War II had a clockwork (spring) motor wound by a ratchet key. This permitted filming for about 20 seconds at 24 frames per second. Bob had to rewind the spring after each shot and remove the cartridge after seven or eight sequences, stow the cartridge in his pack, retrieve a fresh cartridge and reload the camera. Under those circumstances, filming satisfactory footage was challenge enough. Add to that the tremendous noise of battle; confusion and terror it demanded intense concentration by Bob to accomplish his task.

"Progress (for the 2nd Bn.) that afternoon was measured by inches."[259] An air strike was called in to knock out a Japanese gun that stopped the progress of Company E in the 1st Bn. Unfortunately the strafing hit marines in the front line and bombs fell on members of

Company F. The accident delayed the advance so the units had to dig in for the night. "Before dark the marines of 2/22 could see the 4th Marines to their right across a deep gulley."[260] By the evening of W day, 1/22 was on the outskirts of Agat. Japanese counter attacks during night kept Company G on the right flank of the lines of 2/22 busy "fighting and killing 30 enemy troops between 0100 and 0500."[261] Some of the enemy managed to infiltrate the rear areas where they harassed the 22nd Marines command post until daylight, when they were dispatched by headquarters troops. After the first day and night of fighting the Japanese regiment defending against the 22nd Marines ceased to exist except for one battalion that pulled back and retreated to the Orote Peninsula.

On 22 July the 22nd Bn was tasked with opening the road to the Orote Peninsula that the Japanese had managed to block. The rest of the brigade proceeded to secure the "Final Beachhead Line that ran from the Alifan-Taene massif, crossed the Maanot Pass, and reached the high ground leading to Mt. Tenjo."[262] The Army 305th Regiment that had been held in reserve landed to join in the fighting and to provide some relief to elements of the brigade. The 22nd Marines, reinforced by the Army 305th Regiment began an attack at 0900. The few Japanese met by 2/22 were eliminated with little difficulty aided by naval gunfire that knocked out several pillboxes. The logistics of getting ammunition and weapons to the troops delayed the advance because LVTs were in short supply as they were required for off loading supplies on the beaches.

During a relatively quiet second night there were a few infiltration attempts, but no serious threats to the front line. Bob along with the men of the rifle squad nearby had dug foxholes in order to hunker down during the night and to provide some protection against incoming rounds. The regiment was now supported by the III Amphibious Corps Artillery, 1st and 2nd Battalions, equipped with 155 mm howitzers. At 0800 on 23 July, the 22nd Marines supported by the 305th Infantry moved out to "seize a line that ran across the neck of the Orote Peninsula to Apra Harbor and then southeast to the ridge leading to Mt. Tenjo and south along commanding ground to Maanot Pass."[263] The 22nd Marines faced light resistance during the morning attack and were strengthened by noon with the arrival of tanks.

Before attempting to close off the neck of the Orote Peninsula the regiment received support from air attacks, artillery and naval gunfire. The Japanese fired on the marines with artillery that caused them to believe their own artillery rounds were falling short into their lines. This tactic, often used by the enemy had the effect of confusing the marines and delaying their attacks. Consequently the 22nd Marines failed to meet their objective after repeated attempts during the afternoon. The fighting resulted in over a hundred casualties and as darkness approached the pinned down marines were able to withdraw about 400 yards to more defensible terrain. Around 0200 the Japanese hit the leathernecks with mortar and artillery fire as well as counter attacks by small enemy units.

On 24 July the 22nd Marines were ordered to attack in a flanking movement to overcome the opposition of the preceding day. The attack scheduled for 0900 was preceded by aerial bombardment, artillery and naval gunfire, and then delayed until cruiser and destroyer bombardment could take out Japanese gun emplacements along the southern coast of Orote Peninsula. Battalions 1 and 3 moved out at 1000 to drive to the shore of Apra Harbor. Lt. Col. Hart's 2nd Bn, with Bob attached to Co. G[264], moved out at 1000 from Old Agat Road and experienced enemy fire. Naval gunfire supporting the attack landed along the front line delaying the attack until the firing was moved forward. Finally at 1300 after a counter attack by about 100 Japanese was aborted by mortar and artillery fire, patrols from 2/22 overran several abandoned caves that they closed off with flame throwers. The Bn reached its objective and then advanced east along the coast until it was able to occupy the village of Atantano. In late afternoon as 2/22 moved into position through heavy brush it was subjected to harassing enemy fire. Because of its exposure, the Bn was reinforced by F Company of the Fourth Marines as it set up night defenses. By evening 1/22 was dug in at its objective, but 3/22 was 400 yards short. Fortunately this gap was covered by the Second Battalion's success in reaching its position.

The failure of the Brigade to reach all objectives on the 24th caused General Sheperd to delay the attempt to overrun the Orote Peninsula until 26 July. The 1st and 3rd Battalions of the Brigade attacked on the 25th to shore up the lines in preparation for the attack on the 26th. The 2nd Battalion sent patrols from Atantano and mopped up enemy holdouts between the Old Agat Road and the front lines. These actions closed off the neck of the peninsula. However the Japanese had built a series of fortifications across the peninsula just beyond a mangrove swamp along the 0-3 line, the initial brigade objective for the 26th. On the night of the 25th, Company L received the brunt of a counter attack from 500 enemy troops that had been fortified with sake. Company L supported by 26,000 rounds of artillery shells held off the attack that resulted in 400 enemy dead sprawled in front of marine lines. The Brigade attack commenced at 0700 on the 26th, but 3/22 and 2/22 were forced to delay their attack until 0815 because of heavy enemy shelling. The 22nd Marines received little resistance and patrols from 2/22 received only sniper fire as they penetrated deep into the mangrove swamp. Elements of the brigade were subjected to intense enemy fire from well-placed gunners. The brigade 4th Marines dug in at 1730 along the 0-3 line, but the 22nd Marines had to set up in the swamp.

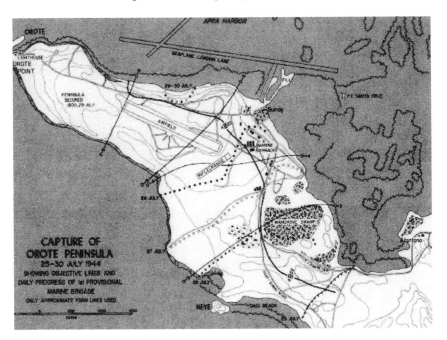

Map 3 Orote Peninsula: See Airfield, Sumay and Marine Barracks

Bob was with G Company all this time until the afternoon of July 25th or morning of July 26th when he returned to the Photo Section headquarters in order to replenish his supply of film and catch a short rest. He was able to write his first letter since he left Eniwetok,[265] "Dear Folks, This is my first chance to write to you in a long time. I'm safe and sound. I participated in the initial assault on Guam. I've been right in the thick of it. I shall write more of the action later after I find

150

out what will go through and what won't. Tell everyone hello for me, especially Jim. I won't have time to write anymore. Drop Pat a line for me giving her my love. It is late and I am very tired. Be sure to write me Zelda, Your loving son, Bob"

On the morning of 27 July the brigade attacked enemy forces following heavy bombardment by air, Navy ships and marine artillery. The 22nd Marines supported by tanks as Company G led the assault in a narrow zone between the swamp and the road being careful of the minefield that had held up the attack on the 26th. The Sherman tanks fired smoke shells to obscure the regimental bomb squad as it disarmed mines so that the tanks could move up with the riflemen. Fire from Japanese positions across the Orote peninsula caused heavy marine casualties. Three of the four company commanders and Major John Schoettel who had relieved Lt. Col. Hart at 1430 were wounded. The 22nd Marines dug in at 1700 on high ground. Carrier aircraft, that were called in to strafe and bomb the enemy positions, were effective in suppressing enemy defenses and some strafing was "too close" for safety. Apparently the unrelenting attack was too much for the enemy troops who fled the area at 1835. The marines pressed after the fleeing enemy stopping on the high ground overlooking the old marine barracks as darkness approached.

Bob returned to the 22nd Marines on the 28th when the brigade resumed the attack at 0830 following preparation by air strikes, naval gunfire and artillery shelling. The 22nd Marines, Second Battalion (Bn) concentrated on capturing the old marine barracks area. Tanks supported the assault but were forced to halt in the face of the rubble and litter from Sumay. One Sherman tank and its crew were completely destroyed when it hit a 1,000-pound bomb mine. On 29 July 1944, the "22nd Marines was able to seize the barracks ruins, the whole of Sumay, and the cliffs along the harbor shore before dusk."[266] At 1500 hours, a ceremony took place at the ruins of the Marine Barracks. The American flag was officially raised on Guam for the first time since 10 December 1941. Witnesses included Admiral Spruance, General Holland Smith, Generals Geiger, Larsen, and Shepherd and the brigade regimental commanders. General Sheperd spoke to the assembled troops, "On this hallowed ground, you officers and men of the First Provisional Brigade have avenged the loss of our comrades who were overcome by a numerically superior enemy three days after Pearl Harbor. Under our flag this island again stands ready to fulfill its destiny as an American fortress in the Pacific."

46. Old Marine Headquarters with American Flag,

Bob returned again to the Photo Section headquarters to reload and was able to write home again. "Evening of July 29th. I'm very sorry that my letters have been so far apart. I'm sure that you'll understand, though. I'm on Guam and the other day was the first time that I was able to write. I landed with the 2nd wave. I just got back from the front again this evening. This is the second time." (*This was followed by a list of letters received.*) "I'm writing this with a Japanese pen. It writes fairly well and the point is in good condition. Tell Jim that I'll write to him as soon as possible and that I haven't forgotten him. The good Lord had been watching over me very carefully and I'm very thankful. 'Hello' Zelda, be sure to write. I'm closing now and I'll write again soon."

True to his word, Bob wrote, "Dear Jim, I got your letter of July 7th the other day[267]. This is my 1st chance to reply for some time. I'm at Guam; I landed in the second wave. I was with the assault troops for five days after they landed and then came back for a rest. I then went up again for two days. I went from Guadalcanal to here stopping off at Kwajalein Atoll and Eniwetok Atoll in the Marshalls. Three of our photographers were killed and one wounded[268]. The Lord must have given me a guardian angel. I'm whole & healthy although tired and dirty. Enough for now."

Bob's two letters provided no details of his nerve wracking experience photographing the riflemen in action. Men were being wounded and killed all around him, but he remained unscathed. He was kept busy operating his camera filming the infantry shooting at the enemy and destroying positions with hand grenades, satchel charges and flame throwers. He, like the riflemen, dug foxholes in an attempt to protect himself whenever defensive positions were established. He also endured the counter attacks as he tried to get some rest hunkered down in his foxhole at night.

The next letter written in the evening[269] said in part, "In case I didn't tell you before, I received the money-order while Enroute to Guam where I now am. My body is clean although my clothes aren't. I'm just now beginning to get somewhat rested. And it looks as though I'll be going out again. We've been fairly busy." (*The last sentence was an understatement typical of Bob.*)

"A picture was made of me at the front; it is a group shot. I shall try to send a print as soon as possible[270]. It will probably be some time though because official film has all priorities of course."

47. Photographers in front of Old Marine Barracks ruins: L-R 1st; Cannistraci, Sarno 2nd; Watson, Brunk, Johns

"Our section seems to be doing a pretty-good job. I'd better not count the chicks before they are hatched though."

Bob shared his experience[271] with Jimmie and Rita Turner, landlords and friends, "I was very glad to get your letter written May 30th. I received it while enroute to Guam where I am now. We had three or four air attacks while enroute and our ship shot one down. We were very elated that day as you can imagine. Quite a few of us photographers landed with the assault troops. I've been very lucky; I have no battle scars except for a few blisters made from digging foxholes and scratches from the bush."

"Mom used to holler about keeping dry and clean, but since I've been in the Marines I've found that men can go through hell and still come out alright. I've come to realize that more and more after making this beachhead. We have a pretty good set up here now. We have a headquarters from which to work and keep our gear. Things are much better than they were before and I'm very thankful."

Then in a letter home, "Today[272] four of us photogs and 3 other fellows went quite a ways beyond our defense lines to take some pictures of Jap caves. We were in no danger; there weren't any live Japs present."

Contrary to Bob's statement, Hal Palmer remembered the event differently[273]. "There were several of us, about a squad, and we were armed and went well into the Jap territory. We stumbled upon a Jap battalion. I have never seen a group of Marines stand so still and be so quiet in my life."

In response to a question, from home, about going into Japanese held territory on Guam, Bob wrote,[274] "The reason that we knew there were not anymore Japs beyond the lines at that place was because we went to take pictures and none bothered us. There may have been some hidden in the vicinity but we didn't see any."

August 6th Bob acknowledged receiving a "pile of mail". "In case you don't know it Mom, Pat copied my name onto the Mother's Day card and sent it to you. She wrote and told me about it later. I haven't received any packages. They probably were sent to Guadalcanal. Thanks for paying my camera insurance."

Recognizing there would be a need to take care of the native population when the recapture of Guam made satisfactory progress; civil affairs officers had set up a camp at Agat to accommodate the Guamanians. Since 31 July there were about 5,000 natives in the camp and more were coming in each day. By 2 August it became apparent there was no organized enemy activity in southern Guam. According to a Marine Corps report an order was issued "stating that all Guamanians living south of a line from Agat to Pago Bay would be encouraged to remain at their homes, resume their normal pursuits with emphasis on agriculture, and obtain food and medical attention as necessary from the Agat Camp."

Bob began to encounter natives himself which he mentioned in a letter dated August 8th. "Nothing new today except that the natives are coming down from the hills fast. The little kids certainly like to ride in our vehicles. They stand along the roads hitch hiking. After picking them up, we ask them where they're going and they don't know. They just go for a ride. They will get a ride in one direction, get off and catch another going back."

On 10 August at 1131, General Geiger announced that all organized resistance on Guam had ended. On the morning of the 11th, after the last battle was fought, General Obata, the Japanese commanding officer, took his own life. General Geiger and his staff flew to Guadalcanal on 12 August leaving command of the Southern Troops and Landing Force to General Turnage. Admiral Spruance ordered Geiger to take charge of the planning for the pending operations against the Palau Islands.

Four days after his last letter, Bob described an impromptu barbeque,[275] "One day up at the front things had quieted down and we shot a chicken. After barbecuing it we ate it. It tasted fairly good even though we didn't have salt or trimmings. During the last week and a half I've been taking it easy just going out on a few jobs to take pictures. I've shot both black and white and color on this island. You should be seeing some of our pictures in the newsreels by the time you get this letter. You've probably seen some still pictures in the papers."

The "few jobs" included taking pictures of Chamorros, Guamanian natives, as they attempted to return to their normal lives. Bob was also assigned to photograph atrocities committed against the native by the Japanese soldiers. He sent home some 16mm film in a box that was not to be opened until the war was over according to his admonishment to his parents.

The recapture of Guam cost the First Provisional Brigade 368 killed in action, 96 died of wounds and 1,600 wounded in action. Total U. S. losses were 1,407 KIA, 376 DOW and 6,010 WIA. The dead included three photographers assigned to the First Provisional Brigade: Claude Winkler, Howard Foss and Bob's friend Martin McEvilly.

48. Ceremony at First Brigade Cemetery

After the major combat ceased, Bob and his friends were able to take pictures of each other at interesting sites much as a tourist would. He posed for one picture by a Japanese bayonet target that he later described,[276] "It was taken after the island was secured, in the city square of Agana. I'm wearing a Nip army cap and they had workouts with bayonets on those dummies (the straw ones only) to impress the natives."

49. Japanese Bayonet Target

50. Japanese Signpost, Town of Agana in Background

Bob also posed in front of a newly created cross-roads with direction signs typical of those created by American troops in the aftermath of battles in many locations during the war in Europe and the Pacific.

51. Bob at Recently Established Cross Roads

Referring to the destruction of two ammunition ships near Vallejo, Bob's letter continued, "I'm glad you told me about the explosion. I was wondering about its effect upon Vallejo and you folks."

On July 17th a catastrophic explosion destroyed the SS E. A. Bryan and SS Quinault Victory docked in Port Chicago. The Bryan was loaded with 4,600 tons of high explosive and incendiary bombs, depth charges, and ammunition. The Quinault was being loaded with ammunition and explosives for its maiden voyage.

There were 98 black enlisted men loading the Bryan and a 13 naval- merchant crew of 31armed guard on board; the Quinault had a crew of 36 and 17 armed guards on board. There were 460 tons of ammunition on the pier, a locomotive with 16 boxcars, and a three-man civilian crew and a sentry. The explosion caused the Bryan to completely disappear along with the 1,200-foot long pier, the locomotive and 320 people. The stern of the Quinault was upside down 500 feet away and the rest of the ship that had been blown out of the water was in scattered pieces. Vallejo did suffer some broken windows

And, "Today I received a very pleasant surprise in the form of a promotion order from III Amphib. Corps notifying me that I've been promoted to Sergeant. It became effective on my birthday. A very nice present, Eh Wot? I believe that I got it through the recommendation of Capt. Soule.

Bob received orders to return to Guadalcanal aboard the Weltevreden[277], a Dutch transport, and embarked on 16 August. He arrived ten days later on 26 August reassigned to the Third Amphibious Corps photo section where he waited for new orders. Two days later Bob was transferred to the First Marine Division that was preparing for the attack on Peleliu in the Palau Island Group.

12

"NO REST FOR THE WICKED"- PELELIU

While the Third and Fifth Amphibious Corps were securing Saipan, Tinian and Guam, General Douglas MacArthur's forces had reached the western extremities of New Guinea. Neutralization of the Japanese base on New Guinea paved the way for McArthur's forces to attack Mindanao in the Philippines. High-level planners concluded that the Palau Islands in the Western Carolinas, Japan's main threat to MacArthur's invasion route north from New Guinea, had to be eliminated. As a result, they decided to invade the islands of Peleliu and Anguar in the southern Palaus and the Ulithi Atoll in an amphibious campaign code named Operation Stalemate. See Map 4 on page 160.

The Palau Islands cover about 175 square miles and extend 100 miles northeast to southwest. Situated just north of the equator approximately 500 miles east of the southern Philippines, the Palau Group's main islands are Babelthuap, Koror, Arakabesen, Urukthapel, Eil Malk, Peleliu and Angaur. Although Babelthuap, in the north, was the largest island of the group, the planners decided to capture Peleliu and Anguar in the south. "The main military value of Peleliu and the Palaus was the southern lowlands where the Japanese had built two unusually good runways in an X pattern"[278]. The airfield was suitable for bombers and fighters with ample areas for maneuvering and taxiing.

Peleliu is located inside the southwest tip of the Palau reef. The island has an odd shape with two elongated arms of land resembling the claw of a lobster. The coral limestone island is approximately six miles long and slightly more than two miles at its widest point. The southern section is relatively flat while the northern section is dominated by "an irregular series of broken coral ridges, narrow valleys, and rugged peaks." The ridge system named after the 550-foot Umurbrogol Mountain was honeycombed with natural caves, crags, pinnacles, and coral rubble. The Japanese military took full advantage of this terrain, supplemented by added man-made caverns with

159

connecting tunnels and reinforced gun emplacements, to create their main defensive fortress.

The southern part of the island terminates with two promontory points separated by a cove. The southwestern promontory called Ngarmoked Island is larger than the southeastern promontory that is connected to the main island by a small spit of land. There is also a small island off shore from the southwest promontory, identified as "Unnamed". There was no natural water supply on Peleliu and its inhabitants depended on collected rainwater stored in cisterns. See Maps 5 and 6 on pages 162 and 163 respectively.

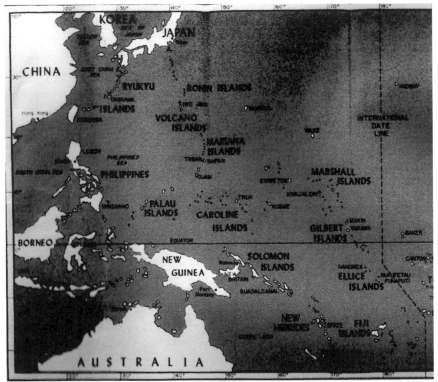

Map 4 Location of Palau Islands Relative to other strategic Land Masses

The First Marine Division was given the task of invading across the 600-700 yard reef that extended all along the prospective beachhead. The Division, after its New Britain campaign, was reorganizing on Pavuvu in the Russell Islands located about 65 miles northwest of Guadalcanal. Plans called for the three regimental combat teams of the division to land abreast on the 2,200-yard beachhead on the western side of the island. The First Marines were to land two of its battalions abreast on the "White" beaches on the left (north); the 2nd Bn was to be held in reserve. The Fifth Marines were to land in the center over Beaches Orange 1 and 2; also with two in assault and one in reserve. The Seventh Marines were to land in column of battalions on Orange 3 with the Third Battalion in the lead with Sgt. Robert Watson assigned to I Co. The First Battalion would come in second with Battalion Two held in reserve. The Eleventh Marines with artillery were to land on Orange Beaches when ordered an hour after H hour. (See Map 6 page 163.)

There was some controversy over the necessity of attacking Peleliu because of the progress MacArthur's forces had made in the invasion of the Philippines. MacArthur still argued in favor of the attack, but Admiral Halsey voiced strong opposition, arguing that it was unnecessary and would be too costly in lives lost. Although Admiral Nimitz had some doubts about the necessity of the invasion, in the end ordered it to proceed. General Rupertus, Commander of the First Division, had been in the states during the initial planning and was apparently unaware of the debate.

The Marines had boarded ships by 26 August and final rehearsals were held off Cape Esperance on 27 and 29 August. When General Rupertus observed the Division's preparatory exercises, he declared, "We're going to have some casualties, but let me assure you this is going to be a short one, a quickie. Rough, but fast. We'll be through in three days. It might take only two." He also thought it would be a good exercise for the Marines that had no combat experience.

The Japanese defenders had a different idea and had prepared extensive defensive positions. There would be no troops defending the beaches or futile banzai attacks as there were on Guadalcanal and Tarawa. Instead, reliance would be placed on large and extensive caves connected to each other. Some cave entrances had steel doors and were large enough to house infirmaries, mess halls and dormitories. Artillery pieces were mounted on railroad tracks for ease in moving out to fire and then roll back into caves for protection. Many of the gun emplacements would be invisible to the attacking naval forces and would not be destroyed by the planned pre-attack bombardment.

Some of the LSTs scheduled for the attack did not arrive at Pavuvu until 25 August, but by 31 August all of the 30 LSTs, 17 transports and two LSDs (Landing Ship Dock) assigned to carry the division were fully loaded for combat.

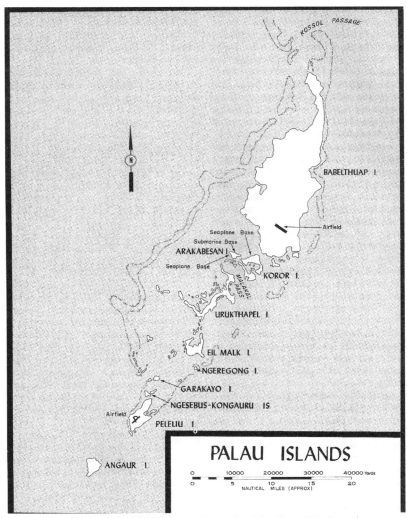

Map 5 Airfield on Peleliu was the main objective of the invasion.

After the landing exercises at Guadalcanal, the marines went ashore for conditioning hikes, small unit maneuvers and recreation. Sgt. Watson joined the First Marine Division on 28 August and then boarded attack transport APA-41, DuPage, at Guadalcanal on 30

August. At this time Bob was able to write a letter that started with the usual report of the number of letters he had received and from whom. Then he expressed minor irritation.[279]

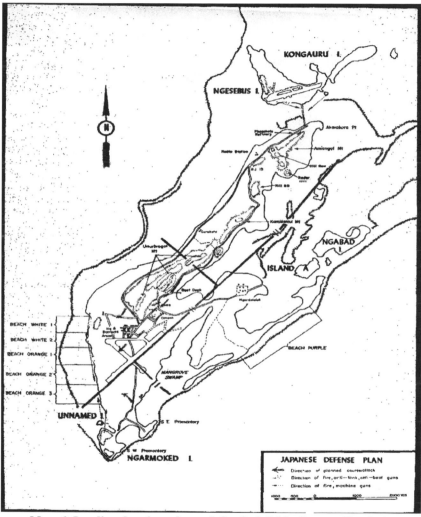

Map 6 Landing beaches shown left of airfield; Orange Beach 3, most southerly, scheduled landing area for I Company 3rd Battalion Seventh Marines.

"All of these addresses are very nice that you've been sending me, but I have hardly enough time to write you, let alone everyone else."

"I got a letter from Jim telling about the closing down of V-5 and his chance to stay in school. I told him that it would be foolish not to stay in and become a Naval Officer. He has good sense; he will."

"No I haven't run across Ned Steele, but I may have a good chance in the near future. You see I'm in the 1st Division now." Bob was now assigned to Hq. Co. Photo Section 1st Marine Division.

"Since I left San Diego, I've spent more time on board ships then I have on land."

"I met Wolfkill out here. He is in sickbay with the mumps, otherwise he's OK."

Back in Quantico, VA Captain Karl Soule wrote[280] to Bob's parents with a nice report about him and other news of interest. "I am so glad Bob's sergeant warrant finally caught up with him. It was a long time coming, as I wrote the original recommendation back in March."

"Major Halpern[281], who was Bob's officer, has just returned here after two years overseas. He tells me Bob did a fine job for him, and that he was very glad to see his warrant come through."

"We hear that Bob has been moved to the First Division. It was due to a mix up in orders, but I hope it sticks, as all his old friends are there."

"The First Div. was supposed to get Bob and 4 others some time ago, but they were delayed for Guam. Thinking they weren't coming, the Division asked for five men from here, whom we sent. Now Bob has gone after all, so they have 10 instead of 5! They are all grand boys, and are all old friends, so I hope they stay- But how I wish I was there!"

"Incidentally, I expect now to go out again in October, and hope to see all my boys again. By the way, if Bob stays where he is, he will soon have excitement again."

Because of the mix up in orders, Capt. Soule was asked to send five photographers from the school at Quantico. In his book, "Shooting the Pacific War", Soule stated, "The First Division, about to attack Peleliu, urgently needed photographers, the best we had. I could pick the men, but there was no question: Evans, Franklin, Herring, Lundigan, and Wolfkill would go." [282] Wolfkill traveled to the Pacific via military air transport rather than by sea because of the urgency.[283]

On Saturday 2 September Sgt. Watson, Sgt. Hoyt Rhodes, PFC Franklin Adler and Galloway were transported to Togoma Point, on Guadalcanal. Small boats lowered from LST-734 picked them up along with riflemen from I Company, 3rd Bn Seventh Marines. The contingent embarked early on the 4th for the landing on Peleliu, a distance of 2,100 miles.

All of the LSTs carrying the first assault troops departed with their naval escort ships for the Palaus by 4 September. Between 0800 and 1200 LST-734 formed into column with a Flotilla of six LSTs; and conducted a General Quarters drill followed by an "abandon ship drill for ship's crew and passengers." The crew and Marine passengers experienced several calls to General Quarters but with no enemy action. On 7 September the ship "slewed out of column to starboard" to repair the starboard engine that had a breakdown; repair of a fuel pump allowed the ship to return to its convoy position.

Bob began to write a letter the next day and on Saturday was able to observe the ship's fifteen-minute gunnery drill. Different LST's came along side on three different days to deliver mail and Bob's letter that he finished writing on the 12th was picked up on the 13th but was not post marked until 1 October.

"8 September 1944. At Sea. I'm in the 1st Division now and am going into action again. No rest for the wicked. The war certainly is moving along, both here and on the other side."

"Rhodes, Galloway, and Adler were transferred with me. You've heard me speak of them before."

"Wolfkill (I've seen him), Franklin and Evans are overseas now. Wolfkill has the mumps." (*Wolfkill actually had some unknown tropical fever from which he recovered.*)

Then on September 12th in the same letter, he added, "I'm still on board ship, playing cards, reading, shooting the breeze and sleeping. I've nothing to tell so this shall be very brief."

"We had one alert, but nothing came of it. I've made some good friends and am enjoying myself."

"We have good quarters considering, fresh water showers, and excellent food. Most of the meals consist of food as good and as well prepared as stateside Marine meals. Some of them are better meals than some meals that I've eaten at posts back there, of course not counting maneuvers"

"I'm in good health and am getting along swell. We also hear records broadcast over a speaker system, nice? "Tell them all hello for me."

Bob probably spent some time reviewing his assignment along with Sergeant Hoyt Rhodes to make a "Motion Picture Record of Communications[284] Operations." The instructions stated in part:

"This picture record in all echelons and branches should include the functioning of communications in: Companies, Battalions, Regiments, Divisions......."

"There are three major divisions of shooting. These are: 1. Preparatory which includes planning, embarkation and rehearsal phases. 2. Enroute to the target area, including activities aboard ships, briefing and bombardment. 3. D-Day to securing of campaign, which includes debarkation movement ashore, and communications in actual combat."

"This intelligence report and pictorial record is being made primarily for instructional purposes. It should demonstrate all phases of communications; technical activity and operation." Instructions for the cameramen followed:

"Photographers assigned will confer at all times with Signal Officers and NCO's (Non Commissioned Officers) when taking pictures of signal equipment. The cameramen should include on their dope sheets the standard designation for all equipment and the organizations using such equipment. Always include on your dope sheets, locations according to the grid map."

"From D-Day on, the shooting will be more intensive and the scenes to be looked for and photographed are: (*There were 37 scene descriptions*)."

Number 34 was most applicable to Bob. "Communications in Divisions-Rifle Company, 60 mm mortars, 81 mm mortars, etc." The order concludes with, "The Corps Photographic Section in cooperation with the Corps Signal Officer and the Corps Signal Battalion is making this Communications film in order that students, officers and enlisted men will see demonstrated the phases of communications in a combat operation."

The assembled attack force was made up of 886 ships with 129 assault vessels. Submarine chasers guided the fleet, which was guarded by destroyers, while mine sweepers cleared the path of mines. Command, survey, repair and hospital ships followed the attack forces. Anti-submarine net layers, oilers, salvage vessels, tugs, PT boats and a floating derrick were included. Assault ships included LSTs, DUKWs, LSDs, cargo ships and 770 landing craft. (LST's averaged 7.7 knots while the transports cruised at 12.1) There was a similar number for the Army's 81st Division that had sailed from Pearl Harbor[285]. Altogether the attacking force presented a vast array of ships that had to be impressive to any observer on the sea or from the air.

In preparation for the assault, carrier airplanes had bombed the islands in March. Additional carrier plane attacks followed in July and August with subsequent Fifth Air Force B-24 Liberator bombers in August. The Fire Support Unit and the Escort Carrier Group of the attacking forces arrived at the islands on 12 September and began bombing and shelling selected targets. The bombarding ships included five battleships, four heavy cruisers, four light cruisers and fourteen destroyers. During a lull in shelling carrier planes attacked targets within the interior of Peleliu. The heavy naval guns resumed firing after the aerial bombardment. The ships and aircraft continued to alternate their attacks for three days. Although the intensive attacks appeared to turn the island into "a barren wasteland", it would soon be revealed that the Japanese had greatly increased the number and extent of underground defenses, including artillery behind steel doors, such that the enormous tons of naval shells and aerial bombs had little or no affect. By 14 September the faster moving troop transports joined the slower LSTs and each ship took up its assigned station 18,000 yards off shore from Peleliu in preparation for disembarking the assault troops.

In the early morning darkness on D-day, 15 September, Bob prepared himself for the ordeal that lay ahead. Even though General Rupertus had postulated a short but tough fight, Bob's experience in the hell of Guam had forewarned him of the extreme danger that lay before him. Clear skies and calm surf provided ideal conditions for the trip to the beach but Bob knew the enemy welcome would not be friendly. He loaded his pack with a supply of film cartridges each containing 100 feet of film, extra sox, loaded clips for his .45 caliber pistol that he had cleaned one more time, added at least one canteen and his pre-loaded 35mm Eyemo movie camera. When the support ships started shelling the island LST 734 moved into its assigned position 4000 yards from Orange Beach 3; and at 0610 the ship's crew lowered the small boats to the main deck level so that the Marines of I Company could board them in preparation for the assault.

Bob and the riflemen he was scheduled to photograph boarded their assigned LVT's and at 0700 734's bow doors were opened, the ramp dropped and its entire complement of LVT's launched within ten minutes.[286] At the same time the other ships in the LST Flotilla discharged their complement of LVTs, troop-carrying amtracs that proceeded toward their designated beaches in waves as the support ships increased the intensity of shelling.

While the naval bombardment continued, 50 carrier planes

bombed enemy positions on the beaches at 0750. The trajectory of the naval shells was limited to an altitude below the pull up altitude of the diving bombers. Destroyers covered the Japanese artillery positions with phosphorous shells to obstruct the enemy's view of the approaching landing craft. At 0800 the first wave of armored LVTs crossed the line of departure followed by 18 LCIs equipped with 4.5 inch rocket launchers that fired salvos of 22 rockets each when they came within 1,000 feet of the shoreline. Immediately following the rocket salvos, 48 navy fighter-bombers attacked the beaches with bombs, rockets and machine gun fire. When the first wave approached the shore, the aircraft moved their attack inland staying at least 200 yards[287] from the LVT (A) s. The Third Battalion, 7th Marines, leading the assault on Orange Beach 3, received intensive fire from enemy machine guns, antiboat guns and mortars enfilading[288]the beach from Unnamed and Ngarmoked islands on Peleliu's south tip.

Bob, with I Company riflemen, 3rd Battalion, landed in the second wave at 0833 followed by succeeding waves in one-minute intervals. The reef off the beach was cluttered with natural and man-made obstacles that caused the amtracs to land in columns. Some veered to the left depositing some elements of the 7th Marines on Orange Beach 2. As Bob and the riflemen hurried from their LVT and ran up the beach they could see burning amphibious tractors as well as dead and wounded. (Official reports listed 26 LVTs destroyed with dozens damaged.) They joined the first wave in holes scattered along the beach that had been made by naval gunfire. Moving inland they were greeted by increasing volume of artillery, machine gun and rifle fire. According to Ned Steele[289], "the Japs had a 150 mm stove pipe mortars located on hill sides that dropped shells on the beach. Each shot would kill 18 to 20 marines crowded on the beach."

PFC Warner Pine, a member of the 11th Artillery Regiment, landed after the rifle companies and recalled, "Oh my God, what a sight! You could see marines lying all over the place, some dead and other(s) wounded, wrecked landing craft of all types, abandoned equipment everywhere-just a gruesome mess."[290]

Bob's assignment to take movie film of communications as employed by Rifle Company I, 3rd Battalion 7th Marines, meant that he had to go ashore with men while under fire from the defenders, move up the beach and photograph the action with emphasis on communications. To comply with the order, he had to choose which action to shoot, compose the picture in the viewfinder, focus the lens, and estimate the required exposure, make the f stop setting, wind the spring motor; and then shoot film for 15 to 20 seconds. Then rewind the spring and repeat the whole operation. This all had to be done in the highly confusing intense combat situation accompanied by an incredible cacophony of high decibel explosive sounds with fellow marines falling around him from debilitating and mortal wounds. Without regard to his own danger Bob had to concentrate on getting a good shot with his camera; wait for the right moment, trigger the shutter, shoot ten to 15 seconds of film, rewind the spring motor, shoot again until he had about two and a half minutes of exposed film, remove the cartridge, grab another from his pack, insert and shoot again; all the while jumping in and out of foxholes and advancing with the troops while exposed to enemy fire, because as Norm Hatch[291] said, "You can't take pictures lying down."

ASSAULT FORCE *under enemy fire at Orange Beach 3. Note burning amtracs in background. (USMC 94937)*

52. Assault Force on Orange Beach 3

As the 7th Marines advanced it was hit by Japanese antiboat, mortar and machine gun fire from a promontory and a small island that had not been shelled by American naval gunfire. Third Battalion moved inland with I company on the left and K Company on the right after disposing of about thirty enemy troops that had survived the shelling of the beach.[292] (See Map 7 on page 171.) Mines, barbed wire, and enemy fire from pillboxes and trenches hindered the battalion.

Fortunately a spotter plane sighted an antitank trench inland on Orange Beach 3, which the marines were able to use as temporary shelter as they advanced. Sometime later, Bob sent home a newspaper clipping, with a photograph of the trench, stating, "I spent a very short time here in the ditch pictured. It was made to stop tanks, but they bypassed it." At one time the trench became the Command Post for Major E. Hunter Hurst's Third Battalion (3/7).

53. Battalion CP in a Ditch just in from Orange Beach 3

According to Garand and Strobridge, "3/7 had seized the beachhead by 0925 at a cost of 40 Marine casualties", and had advanced 500 yards in little over an hour. Early in the afternoon I Co. was stymied by a well organized defense built around a large blockhouse, the concrete ruins of a barracks area, several pillboxes, concrete gun emplacements and mutually supporting gun positions."[293]

The battalion delayed further attack while it waited for tank support that it expected to receive in short order. Unfortunately the tank commander mistakenly operated with I Company Fifth Marines until he discovered his error. The delay in tank support for I Company 3/7 kept the battalion from reaching the east beach on the first day.

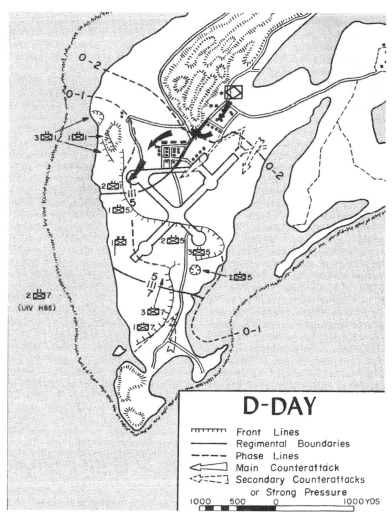

Map 7 Location of Bn on D-Day Map from Vol. IV History of Marine Corps Operations WW II

In an attempt to make up lost time, 7th Marines continued the attack until dusk, and dug in at 1715. Bob along with members of I Co. 3rd Bn. dug foxholes and hunkered down behind Orange Beach 3. They got little rest as enemy light machine gun teams acting in coordination pressed against their hastily drawn defenses. Marine artillery responses to localized counter attacks and occasional star shells and flares, fired from support ships, shattered the darkness in attempts to expose attacking enemy troops. The strongest attack was against C Company that was repulsed at a cost of 50 Japanese casualties. The shore party and support troops replenished ammunition and water at the front during the night; and evacuated wounded.

On D-Day General Rupertus had expected the Division to seize territory inland 300 yards behind the northern beaches and all of Peleliu south of the airfield. By the end of the day, the marines achieved the 300-yard objective behind the northern beaches, but "held only a narrow wedge of terrain across the island behind Orange Beach 3."[294] The first day effort caused heavy losses including 210 dead and 901 wounded to which must be added those suffering from battle fatigue and heat prostration. By nightfall, 12,000 marines were crowded on the beachhead with each man limited to his personal few square feet of coral and sand inundated with insects.

The Division resumed the attack at 0800 following a half hour of aerial and naval bombardment. The temperature rose to 105 degrees in the shade making it difficult for the attack to progress as the men emptied their canteens and struggling men collapsed to the ground, some with "tongues so swollen as to make it impossible for them to talk or to swallow."[295] Never the less, the attack continued against enemy artillery, mortar and machine gun fire emanating from blockhouses, pillboxes and other fortifications. The marines, supported by Sherman tanks, countered with supporting arms fire, flamethrowers, and demolition charges.

Photographers Rhodes, Adler, Clements and Watson had organized their camera equipment at First Division Headquarters in a makeshift cache, covered by a tarp among battered palm fronds, in preparation for photographing the day's action. Bob moved with the 3rd Battalion as it pushed rapidly across the island gaining the eastern shore by 0925. Company I set up defensive positions on the beach in anticipation of possible enemy counter attacks. Company K led the assault south toward promontories defended by pillboxes and concrete gun emplacements. Flamethrowers and bazookas were freely used to eliminate the defenses thereby allowing the battalion to reach the southeast promontory. The troops were forced to delay the advance because lack of water severely reduced their ability to press on. By the time the water arrived at 1500 there was insufficient daylight left to continue the attack. Much of the water had been stored in fuel drums that had been improperly cleaned. The contaminated water temporarily incapacitated many of the infantrymen. The battalion dug in for the night while a detail of combat engineers removed and disarmed enemy mines placed along the sandspit.

54. 2nd Day on Peleliu First Division Headquarters Orange Beach; Rhodes, Adler, Clements, Watson

The 3rd Battalion was prepared to move out on the morning of 17 September after an air strike on the southeast promontory at 0730. However the attack was delayed for an hour and a half while combat engineers, protected by rifle fire and Sherman tanks, disabled a minefield in the path of the advance. Supported by napalm dispensing flamethrowers, the Battalion captured the entire southeastern promontory by 1215. Seizure of the promontory made it possible to site weapons to provide supporting fire for the First Battalion's assault on Ngarmoked Island. In the two days of fighting the battalion lost seven dead and 20 wounded. Whereas the Japanese suffered 441 killed.

The early morning attack by the First Battalion against Japanese forces on Ngarmoked met heavy opposition from fortified positions that prevented expansion of the bridgehead that had been achieved. The troops were withdrawn to allow naval gunfire, artillery and mortars to pound the defensive positions. The success of the attack by the Third Battalion permitted release of tanks and weapons support to aid the First Battalion's attack on the island. Company A, which broke through the weakened Japanese positions and continued southward supported by tanks, replaced the badly mauled Company B. After an hour, Company I was established as reserve for the First Battalion so that Company C could join the attack on the right of Company A. By nightfall the two rifle companies had control of the eastern and western shores and had been able to destroy the Japanese artillery units that had been shelling Orange Beach for such a long time.

The following day, 18 September, the riflemen and supporting weapons moved into advantageous positions and resumed the attack after intensive artillery fire. Company A attacked on the left of a large swamp located in the center of the promontory, while Company C attacked on the right. The two companies joined forces once they had reached the other side of the swamp. The units were ordered to ignore bypassed enemy troops that were to be annihilated by demolition teams. The Japanese tactics allowed their positions to be overrun so they could then attack the Marines from the rear. During the attack around the swamp, Company C left fifteen riflemen behind to guard cave openings and pill boxes in case they still harbored enemy troops. As soon as the main body of marines advanced around the swamp, a large number of Japanese soldiers emerged and began firing at the Marine detachment. The attack was so strong that the Division Reconnaissance Company and most of Company I were needed to control the bypassed areas.

Companies A and C of the First Battalion seized the southern shore of Ngarmoked Island by 1344. Company B moving toward the Eastern shore ran into extensive Japanese fortifications. The attack proceeding yard by yard against heavy opposition stalled at 1354 when the Sherman tanks withdrew to rearm and the half-tracks became mired in the boggy ground. The effort cost the Japanese 350 dead; and reduced their defensive area to 50 yards. While the marines waited for bulldozers to come and dislodge the mired halftracks, they could hear enemy troops committing suicide by shooting themselves. Others attempted to escape by leaping into the sea in order to reach the southeastern promontory. The Third Battalion promptly killed 60 of them. Company B resumed the attack after the bulldozers were extricated and overran the remaining enemy troops. The estimated enemy killed that day was 425.

The 7th Marines completed its initial mission on Peleliu and so informed division headquarters at 1525 on 18 September. The regiment completely destroyed an excellently trained and well-equipped Japanese infantry battalion when it seized the southern part of the island. The First and Third Battalions accounted for an estimated 2,609 enemy dead; none surrendered. The regiment lost 47 killed, 414 wounded, and 36 were missing in action. The seasoned marine troops using proven small-unit assault tactics succeeded in destroying the enemy units entrenched in strongly fortified positions. The four-day battle resulted in a surprisingly disproportionate ratio of enemy killed to the small number of marine losses, considering that the Japanese were entrenched in fortifications while the Marines were forced to fight unprotected.

The First Marines, on D-Day at 0832, had landed its Third Battalion on White Beach 1, and Second Battalion on White Beach 2. The First Battalion landed at 0945 on White Beach 1 as the regimental reserve. The objective of the First Marines was to drive inland, help seize the airfield, and then attack the high ground north of the airfield. Upon landing the First Marines were immediately confronted by heavy fire coming from a long coral ridge that jutted up 30-40 feet. The ridge, not shown on any of the maps or photographs provided the marines before the landing, was honeycombed with caves and dug in positions manned by multitudes of Japanese soldiers. The heavy fighting reduced the strengths of the attacking marine platoons to that approximating a squad. Failing in a frontal attack, the infantrymen attacked the bastion from the rear destroying each pillbox and emplacement using grenades thrown into openings. Company K subdued the enemy positions by 1015 killing 110 of the enemy at a cost that left the two attacking marine platoons with only 32 survivors to set up a perimeter defense for the night. The First Marines resumed the attack on the morning of 16 September and gained the high ground on the coral ridge with the help of the last company of the regimental reserve supported by two Sherman tanks.

By nightfall, the tactical situation had been improved, but the marines were confronted by a counter attack at 2200 hours, preceded by mortar fire and grenades, when about 500 enemy troops attempted to retake the Point. The marines responded with supporting artillery, grenades and automatic weapons. In spite of the concentrated fire, 30 Japanese managed to infiltrate and had to be taken out in close fighting. The attack was stopped by 0200.

On 17 September, all three battalions of the First Marines had to be put on line to continue the attack, because the regiment had over 1000 casualties in the two days of fighting. The Second Battalion, 7th Marines that had landed the previous day to support the drive south, was diverted to provide a reserve for the 1st Marines. The attack proceeded until it encountered a heavily fortified group of reinforced concrete blockhouses with four-foot thick-walls and 12 pillboxes.[296] The battle ship Pennsylvania was called upon to destroy the defenses with 14-inch armor piercing shells. As the attack resumed the 2nd Battalion encountered the Umurbrogol ridges, "a misshapen conglomeration of soaring spires, sheer cliffs, and impassable precipices that would become infamous in the weeks ahead."[297]

The intense fighting caused so many casualties that a company from 2/7 had to be rushed in from reserve to support the depleted strength of the 1st Marines. After three days of continuous assault the 1st Marines had suffered 1,236 casualties. Replacements were derived from supporting units including 200 from regimental headquarters. Prior to the morning attack on 18 September, the 2nd Battalion 7th Marines relieved the 1st Battalion of the First Regiment. In spite of valiant attempts to take the commanding heights, the marines were thwarted by severe artillery and mortar fire and the precipitous coral ramparts that defined the Umurbrogol Pocket which became the final defensive position of the Japanese forces. By day's end the 1st Marines total casualties were over 1,500.

In other fighting, the Fifth Marines had succeeded in capturing the primary objective, the Peleliu airfield, driving the defenders out of the area. By the fifth day of fighting most of the remaining Japanese, who were able to, withdrew from the fight and joined the main forces in the Umurbrogol pocket. Here the Japanese commander intended to make his last stand in a prolonged bloody battle. At 0700 hours the First Marines resumed the attack all along the front. The 3rd Battalion "moved up the western coastal flats for some 400 yards". Still under operational control of the First Marines, 2/7 seized control of the forward slopes of Hills 200 and 260 for an advance of 300 yards. Company A, First Bn. First Marines passed through 2/7 to continue the attack, but a 150-foot cliff and intense enemy fire stopped them. Only six men of the rifle company regained the lines established by 2/7 without being killed or wounded. The Second Battalion, 1st Marines, advanced 500 yards into the dominating terrain that became known as the Five Sisters, five peaks that averaged 250 feet in height, separated from each other by steep cliffs. The Marines called this "Bloody Nose Ridge".

55. Looking toward Bloody Nose Ridge, Photo courtesy of Grant Wolfkill

56. Bloody Nose Ridge, photo courtesy Grant Wolfkill

Sergeants Watson, Rhodes, Wolfkill, Pvt. Spangler and other Photo Section photographers recorded the combat activities of the three regiments. Embedded with the troops, they stayed in the combat situation until all their film was exposed. It was then necessary to return to the Photo Section headquarters, near the Division Command Post, deliver the film and obtained a new supply. The film along with other regimental or division documents was transferred to ships off shore for further transport to another location, probably Hawaii.

A photographer could also receive a new assignment based on intelligence and/or command decisions regarding attack plans. While some photographers were sent out to cover specific actions, others were attached to a regiment to film the combat action of their designated unit. In that case they exercised considerable discretion in choosing the particular activity to film. But photographers, such as Rhodes and Watson, who were assigned to film communications in combat, would emphasize that activity. But no doubt they would shoot film of any action they deemed worth recording.

Grant Wolfkill stated that when on assignment with a combat unit, there could be days of boredom with considerable discomfort hunkered down in a foxhole. Conversely, there could be an intense firefight that demanded the photographer's skills to record the action while under duress. A photographer had to be a marine first and a cameraman second.[298] If a firefight got out of hand the photographer would put down his camera and use his firearm, either a rifle or a .45 caliber pistol. If wounded needed to be returned to the beach and no one else was available, the photographer had to grab a handle on the stretcher and help.

According to Wolfkill, returning with the film could be more dangerous than being at the front with the riflemen.[299] Whether it was 50 yards or 500, the return trek covered ground already taken, but often harbored hiding enemy troops that had been bypassed. Wolfkill told of two experiences when he encountered Japanese during his return to headquarters with film. "I saw two legs sticking out under a piece of corrugated metal. And that was right at the foot of Bloody Nose (*Ridge*), and it was the furthest shot I ever took with a 45, it was probably 50-60 yds. But I could tell where I was hitting because of the sheet metal and I braced my hand against a stump there. And at the first shot he pulled his feet up and I knew he was alive. I emptied into the thing. And we heard later that where we were the Japs would come out of the caves at night to get water. And apparently he got caught in the daylight out there. I never went down to him, but I know I got him."

"Another time I came around the corner and this was in brush and all. There had been a sort of a camp there with streamers of bandages and blood and stuff. There was a canvas cover or something with two feet sticking out. I looked at them and there were no flies on them. The first thing that struck me was that there were no flies."

The fact that there were no flies was a sure indication that the Japanese soldier was alive. Peleliu was inundated with flies because of the suffocating heat, unsanitary conditions and rotting corpses. When the marines opened their rations to eat, they had to immediately cover the container to prevent the ubiquitous flies from landing on their food.

"I had somebody with me, I don't remember who. Just on a chance I fired in, and the damndest thing. The guy hollered out 'Banzai', I fired again, 'Banzai', I fired again, and (heard a) weaker, 'Banzai'. It was really, really strange. It turned out he was a medic. And I got his medical kit. Just because-- it was terrible—"

Although the Command Post was removed from the front line action there was still danger from Japanese mortar and artillery fire so returning photographers often took shelter in a foxhole. On one occasion when Bob was present, Walt Spangler had come "back from the front and was sitting in a foxhole. He had just started to eat when he fell asleep, utterly exhausted. In one hand he had a sandwich, one bite gone, flies crawling all over it and on the deck lay an apple untouched, which had fallen from the other hand. His mouth was wide open. After he had been asleep a few minutes some mortar shells began dropping in about 75 yds. away during which he slept. It was very funny at the time. Too many began dropping in, although we were fairly safe, so we woke him."[300]

Sgt. Watson was with the 7th Marines 2nd Bn when it relieved the 1st Marines 1st Bn prior to the attack on 18 September. As the attack was pressed the next day to Bloody Nose Ridge and the final defensive area in the Umurbrogols of the Japanese, shrapnel hit Bob as he filmed the action.[301] Although the wound was small, he was temporarily blinded in one eye and the medics were concerned about infection. He was evacuated on 20 September[302], by small boat, either to the USS Fayette (APA-43) or the USS Tyron (APA-1), two of the troop transports in the attack group now employed as hospital ships. By this time the Fayette was filled to capacity with wounded and sailed on 20 September, as did the Tyron, to Manus Island in the Admiralties group.

Bob spent two days in the ship's hospital and then was ashore at Manus where he received orders to proceed to Pavuvu. No doubt, had he been in a rifle company and not a cine-photographer Bob would have been sent back into action. Presumably the mix up in orders that resulted in ten photographers being assigned to the battle instead of the originally planned five, kept him out of further action. While waiting for transportation to Pavuvu, Bob happened to see George Tyrrell, (a classmate of Jim's) standing in a navy chow line. They only had time for a brief greeting and exchange of a few words[303]. George, a Torpedoman, was waiting for the USS Oberrender DE-344 to which he had been assigned.

George was going over a sea of mud to the chow hall on a long wooden stairway from the top to the bottom of the hill when he came face to face with Bob.[304] "I made the exit from the chow hall with a satisfied smile on my face, and full of good will toward men. My good humor was soon dampened for descending down the one-way ladder was a single line of MARINES as far as I could see. I uttered, (as usual) an oath, and asked my buddy who those Gyrenes (marines) thought they were, holding up us Navy men, and consequently delaying the entire war."

"Well, we waited about 15 minutes before we sighted the last Marine stumbling over the crest of the hill, and someone exclaimed, 'Well, I'll be danged! George Tyrrell!!' I looked up, and coming down the trail stumbled Bob Watson. I have only been on this isle a month, but anyone from home looks good, and Bob looked like an angel. He looked good, he was in fact, the best looking Marine in the bunch, and I have a feeling in his case, looks aren't skin deep."

Meanwhile the fighting on Peleliu continued with the marines stymied at the Five Sisters. By the evening of 20 September the First Regiment had sustained nearly 1,700 casualties, more than half its original strength. The 5th and 7th Marines had fewer casualties, but the total division suffered nearly 4000 casualties by this time. On 21 September, General Geiger visited the command post of the First Marines and concluded that the regiment was finished as a fighting force. Over General Rupertus' objection, Geiger ordered the First Regiment relieved by the 81st Infantry Division's Regimental Combat Team 321, commanded by Colonel Robert F. Dark.

Back in the States, Captain Karl Soule wrote to Bob's parents indicating that he might be able to stop in Vallejo for a visit on his way to the Pacific.[305]   He had "at long last received my orders to return overseas, so I am packing and about to shove off."   Referring to the current campaign he wrote, "We have heard nothing from Palau, but we hope the boys are OK.   Headquarters says the casualties are not excessive, so that sounds good-but that the living conditions are terrible.   Bob certainly has seen his share of action since he went out-But that is what he wanted, and he is with friends.   I wonder if Wolfkill recovered from the mumps in time to go."

After recovering from his wound Bob took the time to inform his parents that he had survived the still continuing battle for Peleliu, "Just a note to let you know that I'm OK.[306]   I got hit by a little piece of shrapnel in the left cheek.   I was in a hospital for just two days.   It's completely healed now and I'm at a receiving station (*probably Manus Island*) standing by to leave for my outfit.   I certainly had a swell vacation, they treated us royally.   The chow was wonderful."

"I was finally able to cash the money order, Mom.   It certainly came in handy."

"Say a little prayer thanking Him."

"Dad, I had a Jap dynamotor and a book on simple electricity but I had to leave them behind."

Bob sailed to Pavuvu where he was assigned to Headquarters Battalion, Headquarters Company First Marine Division.   In correspondence home he wrote,[307] "I'm on land again, taking it easy and enjoying myself as much as possible.   Things aren't too bad here.   Of course many improvements can be made."

"My physical condition is good.   The weather is fairly good and the island is kind of pretty.   Our camp is situated in a coconut grove and the area is covered by grass short and green similar to a lawn."

"Mom, I'd like to have you send me a box of Dixon's 'Best' colored pencils, Assortment 110.   Also send two sketch blocks size 8" x 10".   I'll send you the money immediately after I get paid."

"Tell Nadine McKinney 'Hello' for me and get her address; I lost it and I owe her a letter.   Give the Grandparents and Jim my love.   I'll write them as soon as I get squared away."

"Send me a couple of bottles of Soretone" (*An analgesic solution*).

Acting as a travel journalist for his family, that had no travel experience except a radius of 200 miles from their home, Bob reported about his exotic surroundings.   "I'm enclosing a couple of sketches that I made.   The parrot isn't like the ones out here, but houses can be found out here very similar to the one in the other sketch."

"The huts are supported by poles and cross pieces, which were originally saplings, tied together by the shredded stems of palm fronds. The siding and roof is made of whole fronds woven together. They are cool, and a well built one will keep out the rain but they deteriorate very rapidly. They are very picturesque in their proper setting but of course they don't compare with houses for stability, durability, and conveniences.

Sketch of Parrot

Hut on Pavuvu

57. Bob with Parrot at 1st Division Headquarters on Pavuvu

Seven days later Bob wrote again[308]. "In the last three or four days I've received 17 letters from you plus some packages. The letters range in dates from July 31st to Sept. 20th. The packages contained stationery and the tooth paste, shaving cream, etc. Thank you very much. I also got a package of candy and stationery. The box was mashed and only one bar remained."

"You needn't send me candy unless it's fudge or similar. I don't eat candy often and what little I do eat I can usually get here." After enumerating additional letters he had received, including several from Pat, he continued, "So you can see my spare time is nearly accounted for."

"Thanks for renewing the insurance on my camera." "How do you like working in the farming out section, Dad?" (*Earle was in a group that assigned him to whichever section or ship needed his talents.*

In response to a letter discussing the possibility of purchasing a Speed Graphic camera, Bob wrote, "If you can get a graphic, hop to it, but don't pay an outlandish price. The war will be over soon and they'll be on the market again. Keep on using mine. I won't want it at least not until I can get squared away and have a place to keep it."

"If any of you see Lee Setterquist, tell him hello for me and congratulate him on his second term as Master Councilor (*Head of the DeMolay Chapter*). That is <u>very unusual</u> and a <u>great honor.</u> Congratulate Teeny (*Albert Watson, Bob's uncle*) for me on the First Degree, (*first level in Free Masonry*) or what ever the correct expression is."

"About my food Mom: lately it has been swell, but often times it is lousy as hell."

"I'm glad to hear what the Capt. and Maj. had to say about me."

Like so many young men in the service, Bob purchased war bonds to help the war effort and to save money for use after the war. "$6.25 comes out of my pay each month for a bond, so one every 3 Mon. Gotta close now. Love, Bob"

On Sunday 15 October, the date of Bob's last letter quoted above, Captain Karl Soule visited the Watson's in Vallejo and had dinner in their home. And on the same day Bob wrote to Jim, "I suppose that Mom has told you that I was transferred to the 1st Mar. Div. and that I was on Peleliu in the Palau Group. I landed with the second wave and was evacuated on the 6th day because of a slight cheek wound."

"I'm awfully sorry that I've neglected to write you. Since I've been overseas I've spent 3/5 of my time on board ship and that means no post office."

"I received two letters from you today dated April 20th, just after I left Camp Elliott and one 13 Sept. I haven't read them, will do so now." During World War II letters were the only means of communication between servicemen stationed overseas and their families. Sometimes these precious letters from home were delivered to the men months after they were mailed, as in the case of the letter written by Jim on 20 April.

"I'm glad that you didn't like smoking that time you tried it in sick-bay. It is filthy and I sometimes wish that I had the 'guts' to quit."

"The courses that you have lined up don't look like 'breezers' but they are damn good and you have a swell opportunity."

"'Good ole' football, I'm glad that you are playing. Tell me how your first game turned out."

"Did I tell you about seeing Kenji Uesugi (*A Nisei from Colusa, one of many who served his country during the war*) on Guam? He is in intelligence (army of course). He is Masai's brother. (I've forgotten how to spell it)."

"Pat seems to like writing to you and says that you are 'great'"

Incredibly, after surviving intense combat in two invasions Bob tells his brother who is in a safe stateside assignment that he needs to take it easy.

"Have you taken out many girls down there or are you tied up with work? Don't forget that you need relaxation once in a while."

"I've received about 2 letters from 'Doc' Pierce (*former Sea Scout master*) since I've been out here. He is stationed at a hospital in New Guinea. I have also gotten some from Raymond" (*Uncle Raymond Capito who had enlisted in the army*).

"I must close now. Bob."

"P.S. I saw Geo. Tyrrell just after I got out of the hospital. He's waiting for a ship and in fine shape."

Captain Karl Soule now with the Third Marine Division Headquarters Company informed Bob's parents,[309] "Bob's officer has just written me from Palau that all the boys are doing a grand job. I knew you would like to know. Quantico is very happy with what has come in already (*film from the battle*), and is eagerly awaiting the rest of it."

Shortly after Bob wrote the last two letters he received orders to rejoin the Third Amphibious Corps Photo Section. According to Sgt. Hoyt Rhodes,[310] Bob rejoined the Third Amphibious Corps on Guadalcanal on October 18, 1944. "There he worked with (Sgt. Mitch) Plaine and myself cutting the Guam picture." Officially Bob was still in the First Marine Division on temporary duty with the III Amphibious Corps.

Bob wrote[311] to the Turners from Guadalcanal, "I wish to thank you for writing to me. I haven't been very faithful with my answers."

"I got a letter from you written in July and the other day I received one that you wrote in September. Thanks for the congratulations. I am very lucky and pleased at making sergeant."

"Talking about the 'Ice Follies', which you mentioned seeing, a way of expressing our desire to be home is, 'I'll be glad when I can wear an overcoat in comfort again; or I'll be glad when I get to a place where I have to wear an overcoat.'"

"Tell Ira[312] that I hope he had a good time on his vacation in the Sierras. I don't see how he couldn't have enjoyed himself. Thanks for the snap of him."

"Tell Jim (*Turner*) that he can surprise me by adding a footnote to the next letter"

"I saw quite a few fellows in the 1st Div. that I knew back in Quantico. (*Walt*) Spangler from Vallejo is one." Bob related the story about mortar shells landing near the exhausted photographer sleeping in a foxhole when incoming mortar rounds prompted Bob to wake him. Then he added, "Many times we'll be almost scared to death, and afterwards we'll get to talking or thinking about it, and burst out laughing about some ridiculous incident or an expression on someone's face. What Lew Lehr[313] says is true, 'Peoples are the cwaziest things.'"

Bob never wrote about how bad the situation was on Peleliu. His comments were always matter of fact or made light of the situation. But as Ned Steele commented, "There was no escaping harm. Anywhere on the island you were in the fighting.[314]

While Bob settled in with the Headquarters Photo Section of the III Amphibious Corps on Guadalcanal, bitter fighting on Peleliu continued until General Murai and Colonel Nakagawa committed suicide on the night of 24-25 November. "At 1100 (hours) on 27 November 1944, Colonel Watson, commander of RCT 323, reported to General Mueller that organized resistance on Peleliu had come to an end. General Rupertus' two-three day exercise for the marines that had no combat experience, had turned into more than a two month protracted battle that resulted in the Marines losing 1,050 killed in action, 250 died of wounds, 5,450 wounded and 36 missing. The Army's 81st Infantry Division casualties were 208 killed in action and 1,185 wounded. Japanese dead were estimated at 10,900 including those lost at sea in reinforcement attempts.[315]

13

CALM BEFORE THE STORM

After seizing Peleliu, the official plan for further conquest in the Pacific involved an amphibious invasion of Formosa (now known as Taiwan) in an operation dubbed Operation Causeway. However, Admiral Chester Nimitz became concerned that American casualties might be as high as 150,000 killed or wounded.[316] Nimitz had previously supported the invasion of Formosa, but now in addition to his concern about casualties he believed that Okinawa, closer to the Japanese mainland than Formosa, would provide a better launching pad for the invasion of Japan. Plans had already been made for MacArthur's invasion of Leyte in the Philippines, set for October 20th, followed by taking Luzon, the main island. Admiral Ernest J. King, Chief of Naval Operations, met in San Francisco with Admiral Nimitz who argued for bypassing Formosa. Persuaded by Nimitz' arguments and knowing that logistic support for such an invasion could not be made available until the end of the European war, King returned to Washington D.C. and argued that offensive operations should be undertaken against Luzon, Iwo Jima and Okinawa in that order.

Invasion of Luzon, as MacArthur had argued, would show that America had not abandoned the Philippine people and would make good his promise to return. Iwo Jima, with two airfields and a third under construction, provided a base for Japanese fighter airplanes to threaten American B-29 bombers operating from the Marianas. Capture of the island would eliminate the threat and provide a base for support of naval operations in Japanese waters. The airfields would permit fighters to escort bombers attacking the mainland, provide for emergency landings of crippled B-29's returning from bombing raids. Capture of Okinawa in the Ryukyus would permit the interdiction of Japanese sea lanes to the homeland, and provide a land mass, 350 miles from Kyushu on the southern tip of the mainland, on which to build an invasion force for the ultimate battle of the war.

As a consequence of America's tremendous war production capability and the Navy's ability to rapidly train men and officers in necessary skills, the forces under MacArthur's and Nimitz' command "outnumbered the Japanese four to one in ships, and overwhelmingly more in combat power."[317]   Fortunately, the Two Ocean Navy Act passed by Congress in 1940 had allowed Admiral King to expand the Navy aggressively. According to Max Hastings,[318] the navy's tonnage swelled from three million in 1941to almost thirty in 1945."   To achieve this ten-fold increase, navy yards, on both coasts, made enormous expansions of their production capability. As an example, Mare Island Navy Yard in Vallejo, CA increased its 1939 work force of 6000 to 40,000 in 1944.[319]

By the end of 1943 the Navy had 713 ships in service with another 1,229 under construction. As of late 1944 the Navy had 3000 carrier-based airplanes, and during the year 8000 men aspiring to be naval aviators entered training. Also at this time the Marine Corps had six full divisions and according to Richard Wheeler, "was now the largest, best trained, farthest ranging, and most consistently victorious body of amphibious troops in history."[320] The First Division was recovering on Pavuvu after the battle for Peleliu; the 2nd remained on Saipan following defeat of the Japanese forces there; the 3rd was encamped on Guam still cleaning out remnants of Japanese defenders; the 4th was at camp on Maui in the Hawaiian Islands after fighting on Saipan and Tinian; the 5th, on the Big Island of Hawaii on the Parker Ranch, had been formed recently around disbanded Marine Raider and paratrooper units; the recently formed 6th Division, built around the First Provisional Brigade that served so admirably on Guam, was in training on Guadalcanal. Lt. General Roy Geiger also made his III Amphibious Corps headquarters on Guadalcanal.

The ensuing Leyte Gulf landings on October 20, 1944 were relatively easy compared with earlier landings on other islands. The American flag was raised "less than an hour and three quarters after the first troops landed."[321] The forces arrayed against Leyte included MacArthur's Sixth Army supported by Admiral Kinkaid's Seventh Fleet with 738 ships (157 combatant ships, 420 amphibious types and 157 minesweepers and service craft) supplemented by Halsey's Third Fleet with Mitscher's Fast Carrier Group made up of three escort carrier divisions 22, 24 and 25, code named Taffy 1, 2, and 3. Escort carriers were created by converting cruiser hulls to small aircraft carriers, also known as escort carriers or "Jeep" carriers or baby flattops. Each ship carried a complement of about 28 planes. Halsey and Mitscher's Third Fleet contained four task groups: TG 38.1, 38.2, 38.3 and 38.4. The Japanese determined to fight a decisive battle sallied forth with a plan based on deception, division of forces and surprise assaults. The result was a four part battle for Leyte Gulf. The first action was in the Sibuyan Sea on October 24; followed by the Battle in Surigao Strait during October 24-25; then the Battle off Samar on October 25; and finally the Battle off Cape Engano from October 25 to 26. Counting all four engagements as one, Morison dubbed it the "greatest naval battle of all time."[322] The largest battle to date had been the Battle of Jutland on June 1, 1916 during World War I involving 151 British ships and 99 German. The Battle of Leyte Gulf had 216 U.S. Navy and 2 Royal Navy ships arrayed against 64 Japanese. Morison estimated there were 143,668 officers and men in the Allied forces and 42,800 Japanese and that "there were more American sailors in the battle than had been in the entire Navy and Marine Corps in 1938." The Battle of Leyte Gulf was a significant victory for U.S. Naval forces that dealt a severe blow to the enemies fighting capability, with substantial loss of skilled aviators. U.S. forces were not without losses, particularly during the battle off Samar, but the Japanese Navy was prevented from stopping the invasion of Leyte.

While the Battle for Leyte Gulf raged far from Guadalcanal, Bob was adjusting again to life in a slightly more civilized environment. Establishment of the Third Amphibious Corps headquarters on the island brought better mess facilities, tent accommodations and administrative buildings, not to mention the Post Exchange that now made it possible for the Marines to buy many of the personal supplies they needed. Furthermore, the American population on the island was substantially increased when the Sixth Division was activated in September 7, 1944 at Tassafaronga and began training for the future invasion of Okinawa. The 22nd Marines that Bob had landed with on Guam were part of this most recently activated Division, the only one organized overseas.

Back in the Photo Section of the IIIAC, Bob and Sgt. Hoyt Rhodes were organizing, cutting and editing film to make a movie of the Battle of Guam to be shown to troops overseas. Bob took time from his demanding task to write to his parents[323], "Rhodes and I are still working on the Guam film. I didn't know so much had been exposed until we started cutting it."

"My scouts tell me that you had a visitor[324] Sunday the 17'th? Tell me about it. There must have been a bit of excitement at he 'ole homestead."

"I'm enclosing a money order for a $25 war bond for you (both)

58. Robert Watson viewing film for Guam Movie

as a Christmas present. .Mom take the rest[325] to pay for the stuff I asked you to send me, to help pay for my portrait, and if there is any left, put it on my account. From time to time I shall send you more money-orders. These you can deposit in the bank. Please let me know each time you receive one of these money-orders."

"Things are going well here. A crazy program is on the radio named 'Suspense'. It is an awful thing to be listening to but we don't have much choice due to the fact that we can get only one station. Programs are re-broadcast from the states; we get good news coverage; and they have a large selection of records, all varieties. I enjoy listening to the programs very much except for a few of them."

Then three days later[326], "I got several letters from Mom yesterday. They were dated 24, 26, 27, 30 Sept. and 3 and 4 Oct. plus a card. I also got some letters from Pat, also got from Ray, Os and Max, and a card and note from Jim Turner. Receiving mail from Jim was almost unbelievable, but it made me feel very good.

"Thanks for sending the clippings of Doc Pierce[327] and everyone else."

"I met a Miss Johnston, Ensign, U.S.N. that knew Mable Claire (*A navy nurse and first cousin twice removed*) at Mare Island. You see I went to the hospital to have a small piece of shrapnel taken from my cheek. The surgeon that took it out is very good and only a very minute scar will be left, after it heals, if any."

"If you send me any more stamps please put wax-paper between the mucilage and any paper."

189

"The wound scar is 1/4" long and 1/32" wide. It is barely noticeable. It's damn silly to send measurements of such a slight cut, but you asked for it. The only reason that I was evacuated was because I couldn't see for a while with my left eye and because of so many germs being present on the island."

"I'm enclosing another money-order this time for $100. You can put it in the bank."

Two days later,[328] "I forgot to enclose the money-order last time. I hope that you weren't worried."

"We are coming right along with our Guam story. It is going to be very good."

"I now have a locker box to keep my gear in. It is very helpful."

"I'm catching up with my correspondence now. About the time that I'm caught up though a stack of mail will come and I'll have to start all over again. I don't have anymore news."

Although Bob made light of his small wound it could have been very serious.

Captain Tom Barry recalled that a marine was killed on Guadalcanal during the fighting around the Matanikau River after being "hit with a shrapnel splinter no bigger than a toothpick. It went straight through him. Blood poisoning set in and before they could stop it, he was dead." Barry went on to say, "Never belittle a man's Purple Heart, no matter where he was hit. Any wound can kill, particularly in the tropics where infections can run rampant."[329]

Continuing to communicate with the Turners, Bob wrote,[330] "I certainly was 'snowed' the other day. You see I received your card, Jim. I had almost given up hope. Yes I was in on a few things as the papers indicated. I was also very lucky."

"I've been enjoying myself very much lately. Last night being Halloween we had a little party. Four of us had saved our beer ration for 1/2 month and we decided to get rid of it then."

"We talked about many things but of course we ended with stateside duty and girls as most conversations do out here. We had a good time having beer and girls even though the girls weren't real. Sincerely, Bob"

A week later, Bob wrote[331] to his parents with some urgency. "I have some favors to ask of you. Send me my birth certificate and be sure that it has the official seal on it or what ever it's supposed to have. Send my diploma of high school graduation. Get a copy of my scholastic record at high school and have it signed by the hired clerk if it will be official and if not by the principal; send it to me along with the other stuff."

"Please do these things for me immediately. In other words don't waste anytime. Don't ask me what they're for because I won't tell you yet."

"I'm getting along OK. I'm enclosing a money-order for $100. Put it in the bank. Love, Bob"

Naturally Bob's parents and sister were curious about his request for school records and wondered if Bob was being presented some opportunity that required the information. They were hopeful that it might result in a transfer back to the States.

Then in response to news that Bertha was developing and printing photographs at Corbin's photo store and Earle was taking portraits for paying customers, Bob wrote,[332] I got your 10 October today, Mom. It is the first in a long time."

"I have a couple of professionals in the family now. You'll have to give me some pointers when I get back. You really went into photography in a big way. I didn't realize that you'd go this far, but good luck and I hope that you have lots of customers."

"Don't let the 'ole-crabs' get you down Mom." (*This was probably a reference to customers or employees at Corbin's Photo Store*).

"Rhodes and I have almost finished cutting the Guam picture. All we have to do now is iron out the rough spots. Next week we start on the sound. We hope to include sound effects, narration, and music. It is going to be very hard, but here is hoping."

"I received three letters from Pat today, and one from the Turners. It is getting late now so I shall close. Yours with love, Bob

Bob's next communication was written on Japanese stationery so he emulated the Japanese method of writing from top to bottom and right to left, but after the first sentence he reverted to the American method: left to right, one sentence after another.[333] "I received several letters from you yesterday plus newspapers and my Xmas package."

"I got the paper on Peleliu and I started writing from top to bottom and right to left as the Japs do."

"It is a little something for a souvenir that you can keep if you wish."

"I have a special souvenir for you, Dad. It is a Jap book of elementary electricity. I'll send it someday when I get around to it. Don't be too anxious."

"We are still working on the picture (*Battle for Guam.*)."

"Every day the fellows play volleyball for exercise and recreation. Rhodes and I have been so busy with the picture that we've played not more than 1/2 dozen times since we've been here."

"I got the box as I mentioned above, and I'm going to open it tonight because it looks like food and the ants may get in it. They are thick out here."

"Last night we made ice-cream. It was very good. Love, Bob"

Bob wrote along the left side of the page, "We are not allowed to name the islands that we are on. The enemy will then know our base of operations."

I'm glad to hear that Jim has a chance to come home. I got two letters from him yesterday. He didn't tell me anymore than you know already."

"I also received a letter from K. T. S. (*Karl Thayer Soule*) telling about seeing you."

"I saw George Tyrrell on one of the islands in the Admiralty Group[334]. He was in good spirits. I just had time to say 'hello' and 'goodbye'"

"I think that K. T. S. is OK, too. I'm glad that you liked him."

"I don't know what the H--- you want me to write. How about asking a few questions and I'll try to answer them."

"I was wounded next to 'Bloody Nose Ridge'. I saw an enemy mortar that fired a shell almost 6" in diameter and I understand that they used bigger types along with that size and smaller ones on Peleliu. I know that they had a damn big wallop. (*This was one of Bob's rare mentions of his experience in combat. He was referring to the 150 mm stove pipe mortars that Ned Steel said could kill 18 to 20 Marines in one blast*). Your loving son & brother."

"P.S. I opened the box but it doesn't look like food, so I put the small packages in my locker-box to save."

Responding again to Jim and Rita Turner,[335] "I received your letter of 11 October just the other day; thank you very much."

Tell Ira that I send him congratulations for getting his first deer. I'll bet that he was very thrilled."

"We were vaccinated, given a tetanus booster shot, and another shot of some kind. Apparently they don't want us to get sick.'

"This is just a note to let you know that everything is OK and to let you know that I got your letter."

No longer on temporary duty, but now officially assigned to the

Corps Photo Section, 3rd Phib Corps, with access to a typewriter, Bob composed his next letter,[336]   "I got your letter of 1 November yesterday, Mom. That is fast work compared with the time it has taken some letters to reach here lately."

"I certainly am glad to hear that Jim got to go home before going to the eastern part of the States. I certainly would have liked being there."

"We have started writing the dialogue for our picture on Guam. We have another man working on it with us. He is T/Sgt. Mitch Plaine and he is in charge now."

"I doubt that fudge would be any good by the time it got here. It would probably be dried out by that time."

"Dad, don't be foolish and buy a camera for some outlandish price. It isn't worth it. You can use mine. When the war is over, get a good one for a fair price."

"I'm very glad to hear that you sent Pat some film. I'll be looking forward to getting some pictures from her. They mean an awful lot."

"I got an Xmas package from you, the one in the wooden box, but I haven't gotten the pencils, etc. yet. It should be along soon though."

"I have the watch today. I stay in the clerk's office during lunch hour, and all night to answer the phone, take any messages, call roll, and sound reveille and see that the lights are turned out on time at taps."

"Our Guam picture is on the documentary side. We are trying to show the 1st Brigade's part in it from the beginning to the end. The story follows this outline: Loading (troops and equipment), Enroute, Landing, Battles, Securing."

'I'm sure that it will be a very good picture and outshine The Tarawa story. I believe that our cameramen did a much better job than they did. Our version will be shown in the field only.

Another will be shown back home."

Full of bravado and confidence of the work he and his associates were doing, Bob must not have been aware that the film Norm Hatch shot on Tarawa had been included in a short documentary that won an Academy award. He probably had not seen the film, but never the less proud of his work, concluded that Plaine, Rhodes and he surely had put together a superior product.

Bob wrote to his parents after a special noon chow celebrating Thanksgiving on Guadalcanal. Before describing the menu he referred again to the cats that had given birth to six kittens on May 19 1944.

"When the fellows moved camp (*while Bob was on Guam and Peleliu*) the mother cat and a kitten ran off, so that we have only four kittens with us. They named 'Midnight', all black (male), 'Little John' alley-cat color (female), 'Helen', black and white (male), and 'Big John' alley-cat (male). The fellow got his sexes mixed when he named them."

"Little John' is going to have kittens. She is less than a year old. I guess one of the males couldn't wait."

"The sound for the Guam picture was completed this morning about 0400. I didn't work on the sound. Those that did went to the radio station to get the sound effects and make the records. We don't have any sound film systems. From what the fellows tell me, it is a good job."

"Early this morning the maintenance man and I patched a tube and he surveyed a tire." (*Surveyed in Marine parlance meant to return for a replacement.*)

"We have holiday routine today so no more work."

"Adler, one of my former students, and I are going to cut a black and white artillery film."

"This last week I received a few letters from you dated as follows: Mom 7 Sept., Oct. 29, 3 Nov., 6 Nov., plus one no date and a card. Dad 2 Nov."

"Thanks for passing on my congrats' to Lee, Dad."

"I'm glad that Jim is going to the U. of Minn. It is a good school and it is in a nice town."

"Thanks for the airmail stamps and pictures of Jim; they are very good."

"I'm enclosing a picture of Carothers (maintenance man and former student) and myself in our tent. The light colored cloth overhead is part of a parachute which is of no more use to the service. I'm sitting on Frost's cot (he is another fellow in the tent. Carothers is sitting at his desk." (*Carothers maintained the Section's photographic equipment.*)

"P.S. I just got back from noon chow. It was right on the ball. We had fresh Turkey, mashed potatoes and gravy, canned peas and corn, cranberry sauce, hot buns, dressing, dates, fruit cake, walnuts, pecans, almonds, and cocoa."

"If I had been home and sitting down to plates, and didn't have to stand in line, it would have been perfect. As it is I can't complain. Love, Bob

59. Tent Mates: Carothers and Watson

Three days later, Bob wrote to Jim,[337] "I received two letters from you a couple of weeks ago but waited until now to answer because of your moving. I gleaned this address[338] from several letters that Mom wrote. I hope that you get this OK. Your letters are dated 5 and 13 October."

"I certainly am glad that you can study aeronautical engineering. Don't worry about missing the action out here. You have a great opportunity and if you throw it away, I'll kick your fanny for you good and hard."

"I'll certainly take any chance of going to college that they offer me."

"Here's hoping that you get to play football at your new school, but don't let it interfere with your studies."

"We have a photographer here from Minneapolis or Minnyapopolous as we call it to kid him. He has told me a little about the town and school. And from what you've written Mom it sounds like a good place. Those luscious damsels, that you mentioned, sound very-very good."

"Our Guam picture is completed and it has been sent away to have a sound track made up. I'm now working on our film library and cutting a film on artillery."

"They are keeping us pretty busy."

About this time Captain Karl Soule wrote[339] from the Central Pacific to Bob's parents providing encouraging information about Bob's health and performance. "I had a long talk with Bob's photographic officer on the way out here, and he told me Bob had done a nice job for him, which I knew he would. Yesterday I talked to a man who saw Bob only a week ago. He reports he looks very well, and that his wound will apparently not leave a scar. It is possible that Bob may be with me before long, but I am not counting on it."

After receiving considerable mail Bob wrote,[340] "I got quite a bit of mail last night. Several letters from you, one from Turners, Bill Pillsbury, Pat, and a letter and package from Os and Max. I also received the sketch pads and clippings that you sent."

"Mom's letters are dated 11 and 13 Nov., while Zel's is dated the 12th. I got a letter from Jim the other day and he wrote me the same things that he did you."

"So you got a letter from Hdqtrs, huh?

"I think that both you and the other party got a good deal when you sold the camera. You got a good price and he didn't get gypped considering current prices."

"Our clothes dry it doesn't rain everyday. The rainy season hasn't started yet."

"I got the carton of cigarettes that you sent although they were mildewed by the time they arrived. We can get all the cigarettes that we want, including all popular brands. It is a little difficult to get Camels and Luckies (*Lucky Strikes*) at our P. X., but usually find some at another. We do alright you don't have to worry on that score."

"Over a month ago I was in the Russell Is. Group.[341] Now as you can see I'm back with the III A.C. I'm not on Peleliu."

"Ned Steele is home, now. I missed him by about seven days."

"I'm now working on a black and white film library. It certainly is monotonous work viewing and cutting film all day. I'm glad that I don't have to do it the rest of my life."

"Pat sent me some pictures of her and the family. They are very good snaps. Thanks for sending her the film."

"Can you get film in my name and then send it to her? If you can please do so."

"Closing now."

"P.S. Had a pint of fresh milk tonight it was flown in from New Zealand. It's the 1st since I left the States."

The next day Bob wrote to Zelda,[342] "Just a short note to let you know that I haven't forgotten you."

"I'm still doing the same old routine, cutting film. If I come home with film for hair and cement for saliva you'll know why."

"Tell Kilby, O'Dale, and the others Merry Christmas for me."

"I'm enclosing a make-shift card for you. I hope that it isn't too bad."

Then not to forget Jim, Bob wrote,[343] "I got your letter of the 5th a day or so ago but waited until now to answer."

"I'm very glad that you are going to Minn. U., It is a very good school. Your course sounds like a humdinger. The girls and living conditions such as laundries, cafes, stores, and libraries sound swell."

"I'm glad to hear that Bob Camp is recovering and that you were able to see him."

Bob Camp played Class B football with the author. After graduation from Vallejo High School, he joined the navy and trained to be a corpsman. He served with the Marines during the battle of Guam where he spent a harrowing twenty-four hours caring for wounded marines and lowering them down a cliff in order to get them to a field hospital. Camp was severely wounded also and after evacuation was sent to the Navy hospital at Marc Island Navy Yard.

"I'm still editing film, it's black-and-white now. I'm segregating it according to place and action that it shows, to make a stock film library."

"The work gets very monotonous at times but it isn't too bad a job. I hope that I don't have to make a living as a cutter in civilian life, though. It isn't that interesting to me."

"I'm enclosing a little nothing that I made for a Christmas Card. It isn't at all that good but the wishes are there."

"I must close now. A stack of mail came in and I haven't answered all of them yet."

Almost two weeks later Bob wrote,[344] "No I'm not on Guam. I'm on the same island that I joined the III A.C. on when I first came overseas. Now Guess." (*Of course he meant Guadalcanal.*)

"Please excuse me for not writing more often. I like to receive letters, but I'm not a good hand at replying."

"I've received my birth certificate, High School transcript, and diploma. Thank you very much."

"I've received quite a few letters from all three of you and one from Gr. Watson."

60. Christmas Card from Guadalcanal

"I'm able to buy all the necessities out here that I want. It is only the non essentials that are hard to get and I don't miss them."

"I'm glad that you like the book of verse and that you were able to get something that you wanted, Zelda."

"I'm sorry about Walt Tom and his operation."

(*Walter Tom and Jim were honorary co-captains of the Vallejo High Track team and both ran on the championship 880 Yard Relay Team. Walter was injured in a navy training exercise and one leg was amputated just below the hip. Tragically, Walter died later from post surgery complications.*)

"I'm glad to know that you are getting so much business, Mom & Dad. It must keep you hopping though."

"I don't know what Pat's favorite perfume is, but I got her a bottle of carnation (before I came out here) because it's my favorite. Now don't say 'Isn't that just like Bob?'"

"Congrats on your promotion Dad."

"Pat has a copy of every picture that I've sent you."

"Our tent decks are steel matting the same as used on airstrips."

"The last few days some of us here have been building a darkroom it is almost completed. Today and yesterday I put in some of the wiring. Yesterday afternoon two of us put in the plumbing. It is sufficient but simple."

"Franklin is here visiting us and acquiring data before joining Captain Soule"

Soule was with the Third Division on Guam, which had been ordered, along with the Fourth and Fifth Divisions, to prepare for the invasion of Iwo Jima located half way between the Marianas Islands and Tokyo. The Japanese had been reinforcing Iwo Jima, a pork chop shaped island of only 7.5 square miles, since May of 1944. The island contained two airfields and a third was under construction. Japanese fighter airplanes flying from these fields were considered a threat to American B-29 bombers flying from the Marianas. Capture of the island would eliminate the threat and provide a base for support of naval operations in Japanese waters and for fighters to escort bombers attacking the mainland. In spite of continuing American submarine and bomber attacks on Japanese reinforcement efforts, and a major attack from strafing P-38 fighters and B-24 Bombers, the Japanese succeeded in bringing 21,000 men to the island and building a labyrinth of underground defenses by the end of the year.[345]

Admirals Spruance and Turner, and General Holland Smith were designated to lead the American assault. General Harry Schmidt was in command of the invasion troops of the Fifth Amphibious Corps made up of the Fourth and Fifth Divisions with the Third in floating reserve. At the end of December the Fourth Division located at Maui, Hawaii and the Fifth Division at the big island of Hawaii received orders to join forces at Pearl Harbor. The Third Division would disembark later because it was 3000 miles closer to the target.

While preparing his photographers for the assault on Iwo Jima, Captain Soule wrote to Bob's parents,[346] "I haven't heard from Bob recently, but his officer was here last week, and he tells me Bob is doing a good job. Franklin, who was with me in Quantico and was on Palau with Bob, is here with me now, and I am expecting more of the old group soon. It is possible Bob will be with them, though I feel he deserves a good rest now."

Bob continued corresponding with the Turners,[347] "I'm back here with my original outfit the III A.C. I'm glad to be back here even though we have to stand inspections quite often. We fired carbines on the range last week. I've been cutting film and doing odd jobs. We are kept busy but not too much so."

Although Marine Photographers principle task required them to carry either still or movie cameras plus extra film, they also were armed, usually with a 45-caliber pistol or an M-1 carbine a smaller version of the Garand M-1 rifle. Photographers were usually assigned to infantry units to photograph combat action. Consequently it was imperative that photographers maintained their skill as riflemen in addition to their photographic expertise.

Two days later Bob wrote,[348] "Today we started building boxes for gear. We certainly have a lot. Last night I worked in the lab developing film and printing pictures. I worked until after taps and was a little tired when I got through."

Then with reference to a newspaper clipping of a picture taken on Peleliu, Bob added, "I spent a very short time in the ditch pictured. It was made to stop tanks, but they by-passed it."

See picture in Chapter Twelve page 170.

On Sunday Christmas Eve Bob was feeling nostalgic and homesick when he greeted his family,[349] "Merry Christmas and Happy New Year."

"Today I have had the chow relief from the fellow on watch. Tomorrow I have the watch."

"This evening we had a little party with tuna fish sandwiches, beer, rum & coke, brandy, whiskey. I left a little early and wrote Pat a letter."

"While I have been writing, wonderful programs have been and are being broadcast over the radio. Many Christmas Carols have been sung and I'm homesick: The first time in my life. I'd certainly like to be going to the midnight service with you."

"It is a silent night with half moon, bright stars and luminous clouds. The crickets and other nocturnal insects are out in full force. I was just remembering how Jim and I used to serve at Holy Communion together. Those were the good-ole days."

"May the Lord watch over thee and protect thee. Goodnight, Mom, Dad, and Zelda."

At the end of December Bob acknowledged receipt of presents from Jim,[350] "I have two letters from you, dated 12 November and 7 Dec., and a Christmas card with note inside. I also got your package of presents. The pipe is grand and is breaking in nicely. I had been debating whether to buy one or not so you settled that. I had been wanting some 'Dream-Castle' (*after shave lotion*) for quite some time and the book is being enjoyed by all of us in the section. As you can understand everything suits me to a 'T'."

"Christmas Eve we had a party, the eats & drinks consisted of tuna fish sandwiches, canned shrimp, beer, rum & coke, brandy, and whiskey. Of course everything was in fairly small quantities. Some of the fellows got to feeling good but none were too drunk."

"I went on duty at 2200 that night and continued on duty until 2200 Christmas night. I read, listened to the radio (very good programs), and wrote a couple of letters."

"I've been cutting film lately plus numerous odd jobs."

"Getting flight training in the Navy is swell. They give about the best and a flying engineer is tops. You can go to college after the war but it would cost a small fortune to get flight training equivalent to the Navy's. Be sure to finish your college and get your degree though; otherwise it will all go for naught."

"I envy you in a way. Yes I intend going to college when this is over. I found naval history interesting. Remember I wrote a composition about the 'Continental Navy' for Mrs. Baker."

"I took time out in the middle of this epistle to see the show 'Hitler's Gang'. What a sad picture."

"I must write now so I shall close. Thanks for the presents and good luck on your pre-flight." (*School*)

"P.S. I was officially transferred to the 3rd A C (*Amphibious Corps*). recently. I was here on temporary duty before."

Early in the New Year Bob commented on the Christmas presents he had received.[351] "I received four letters from you, Mom, the other day dated 16, 17, 20, 22 December and the family Xmas-card. I was very-very glad to get them."

"I opened the presents after I wrote you Christmas Eve and they are swell. The candy I opened ahead of time because it had begun to melt. The shaving-brush I like especially; we can't get them out here and the cream I like very much. The lighter is on the 'ball'. I have one that I'm using now and I'm saving yours until the time comes that I can't get fluid or I'm in combat."

Two days later Bob wrote,[352] "Lately I've been working on film, raking gravel, and other police-work. (*Cleaning the premises*) In the evenings I usually see a movie and write Pat and in the afternoons I play volley-ball sometimes."

"Tuesday I almost got to Australia. Five of us were going to shoot a story down there. We were packed and had completed the first leg of our trip when we were drawn up short. We were told that no more men were going there so we couldn't shoot the story."

61. Bob enjoying his new Shaving Brush, from 16 mm Film

"This is a jumble, but I will explain it in another letter. I certainly was disappointed."

"Tell Leta Clifford, 'Hello', for me if you please. Thanks for Mable Claire's address."

"You guessed right. The cats are doing fine. Little John has kittens now."

"I'm glad that you like Pat's present, Zel. You writing me was the first I knew of it-certainly sounds good. The whole family's presents sound swell."

"When did Bill Pillsbury get married? I didn't know anything about it. Give!"

"We had a big turkey dinner both Christmas and New Years which were very good."

"I'm glad that Doc (*Pierce*) is home, at least in the U.S."

"Write about your work, Dad. Civilian mail is not censored."

"Guam and New Caledonia are nice islands although there is nothing at either place for a married American. They have no industrial centers; consequently no cities, just towns. The scenery is nice on each, and of course they have south sea island climate. New Caledonia has no fever and Guam has very little."

62. Bob ready to leave for Australia in R4D

Preparations and training for ICEBERG, the upcoming invasion of the Ryukyus (Okinawa) continued on Guadalcanal. Bob may have been aware that a new invasion involving the Third Amphibious Corps (IIIAC) was in the offing, but he surely did not know the destination.

202

63. Photographers before Aborted Australian Flight:
L-R Calnen, Hagar, Walavich, Carothers and Watson

The Sixth Division was also training on Guadalcanal for the invasion of Okinawa as part of the IIIAC. Although seven of the nine infantry battalions of the "Striking Sixth" were combat experienced there was still a need for training as a Division with its current command structure and replacement troops. General Sheperd, commanding general, organized the training so that it "proceeded from small unit exercises through large-scale combined-arms problems employing battalion landing teams and regimental combat teams; all training culminated in an eight day division exercise in January 1945."[353]

When planning began for Operation ICEBERG, "commanders of the III Corps Artillery and the 11th and 15th Marines established liaison with one another in order to coordinate their unit training programs."[354] IIIAC Artillery consisted of the Headquarters Battery, the 2nd Provisional Field Artillery Group (scheduled to provide general support to the 6th Division) made up of the 6th 155 mm Howitzer Battalion, 8th 155 mm Gun Battalion and the 9th 155 mm Gun Battalion.[355] The 11th and 15th Regiments provided artillery support for the 1st and 6th Divisions respectively.

The principle objective was to assure "the ability to rapidly mass fires of all available guns at any critical point."[356] The training culminated in a combined problem January 11-13 involving all the Marine artillery units assigned to the Tenth Army with the exception of 12th Marines of the 2nd Division. Conditions anticipated on Okinawa were simulated, but the island population and various installations limited the firing ranges for the big guns. Aerial observers spotted the majority of the firing missions. At the end of the exercise the "Marines 'were able to have all artillery present, laid and ready to fire in an average of five minutes from the time it was reported."[357]

Bob and two others were assigned to photograph the three-day artillery training exercise with emphasis on communications. That would have included communications between forward observers and the gun crews to establish range, azimuth and elevation directions. The photo coverage may have also included movement of the howitzers, placement and firing drills. Bob concentrated on accomplishing his photographic assignment under the prevailing weather conditions as it affected lighting and his ability to obtain satisfactory composition for his intended shots, as he stated in his letter written upon his return.[358] "Last night I got in from the field. Three of us were on maneuvers for three days shooting pictures of artillery. It was interesting work, but the conditions weren't too favorable."

"Upon arriving here in camp I found a bunch of mail. Most of it was very old with one or two addressed to Quantico. Yours are dated as follows: Mom 30 April, 19 May, 21 & 24 August and a promotions congrat card; Dad 15 May; Zel 22 August. The latest one was dated 1 January 1945. One of the above included a picture of Mutt and one included a colored snap of Zel and one of Mom. Thanks for the picture of Zel at the tree with presents. Now I know what things looked like."

"I received two more sketch pads (total 5), the colored pencils, and the foot powder, thanks. There is an insured package for me at the P.O. which I shall get tomorrow."

"It has stopped raining for awhile. White billowing clouds have crawled over the dark blue mountains forming a beautiful blanket."

Two days later Bob continued to report on his activities,[359] "For the last two days I've been typing up camera report sheets (they tell about the scenes in our movie film) and technical reports about the equipment in the story. It has kept me fairly busy."

"I am enclosing a picture of myself made a few weeks ago. I do work once in a while believe it or not."

"I went to the post-office yesterday and claimed the insured package. It contained the Soretone and the indelible pencils. Thanks ever-so much

64. Proof of not Loafing

"No the ink doesn't run on the envelopes. They get out here in fairly good shape. The packages take the beating. They get banged around something terrible; especially when they take a long time getting here. All of yours have gotten here in good shape, though."

"Thanks for giving Bill and Nadine a present. I didn't know anything about their marriage until you wrote. They must not have had the date set very long in advance. They should make a fine pair. They both are swell kids."

"I am writing this on a borrowed typewriter. One of the fellows had it sent out from home. He makes good use of it and he finds it very handy. Someday after I'm a civilian again I shall get me one."

When Bob was filming the artillery maneuvers, General MacArthur waded ashore at the Lingayen landing beach while photographers recorded his triumphant return to the Philippines. The attacking forces had been hit by Kamikaze suicide bombers named after the "Heavenly Wind", a tornado that saved Japan from an invading Chinese amphibious force in the year1570. American air superiority and anti-aircraft fire was so effective that the Japanese resorted to recruiting young men eager to die for the emperor by crashing aircraft carrying bombs into American ships. The results were quite effective, but failed to stop the landings in the Philippines. However the Japanese military continued to marshal additional suicide forces that would create further devastation of U.S. naval forces in the remaining battles of the war.

Although Bob had written home twice in early January and twice again in the middle of January, his family was disappointed they had not heard from him more often and apparently complained. In response, Bob pleaded mea culpa;[360] "I received some letters from you yesterday. Zel's was dated the 5th and Mom's were dated 5th, 7th, 9th and 10th January. I also got the package containing cheese, raisins, and cigarettes. The latter were mildewed but the food was in good shape. Do not send cigarettes; I get enough out here. Thanks for the raisins & cheese."

"I agree with you; I haven't been very faithful in writing. If I write Pat and see a movie it is time for taps. I shall try to improve, though."

"Thanks for the clippings especially the one of Bill and Nadine."

"Zel, I wrote Pat about visiting you this summer but I don't like the thought of her going across country alone. I know that she can take care of herself and all that, but I'm ole-fashioned. As you can see I wasn't too encouraging."

"Excuse me for forgetting your birthday, Dad. I hope that you had a happy one."

"The other day I mailed home a package containing some souvenirs and some odds and ends. Hows about saving them for me? The book on electricity is for Dad; the necklace and bracelet is for Zel, but you'll have to get some snaps; the combs are for Mom. The natives wear the combs in their hair something like the Spanish. Just a very few wear them though. The combs originally may have been introduced by the whites for all I know. The watch got wet on Guam and can't be wound. Don't fool with it; I've tried."

"Your mail comes through OK. I'm just slow in answering. Pat's letters are very slow and uncertain though. The fellows here from N. Y. are all crabbing and I'm right there with them."

"Today I viewed some old Bouganville film. I'm going to cut it into a story. We intend making a small series of films showing the history of the III A. C. from its beginning when it was the I MAC"

"P.S. Happy Birthday, Mom."

On Saturday Bob found time to write to his brother,[361] "A while back I received a letter from you written in March and another in August. Recently I got one dated 26 November. Enclosed in one of the older letters was one to you from Pat, thanks."

"I certainly hope that you get flight training; I know how much you want it. The percentage does sound good."

"I'd like to be in some of that snow for awhile although I might not be able to take it at first. Of course I'd like to live in an enclosed and heated building not a tent as we do here."

"I'm glad that you are having dates. I know I miss the female species especially a certain little Deutch Fraulein. Tell me about some of the girls and dances so that I can get more rock-happy or 'Asiatic' as they call being crazy out here. No kidding what is the 'scoop'?"

"Last week I went out on maneuvers and shot some film on artillery communications. This week I've been viewing film exposed on Bouganville preparatory to cutting a story out of it. The cutting.... out is literally true because it is mixed up terribly."

"Closing for now; let me hear the good word."

The next letter home described movies he had seen on Guadalcanal, rehabilitation of Guam natives, and advice regarding cameras,[362] "Since I last wrote I've received several letters from you. They contained retouched prints of sailors. I also got the pictures taken at Xmas; they were enclosed with one of the letters. Thanks a lot!"

"Your retouching is very good Mom and I like your portraits, Dad. The both of you are on the ball!"

"Tomorrow we have an inspection of quarters, area, and clothes so I'm doing a little tonight in order to be ready."

"The other night we had the movie 'Naughty But Nice' starring Ann Sheridan and Dick Powell. I think that it was released in 1939. Most of our pictures are fairly recent, two years old at the most. The greatest number is from 6 months to 12 months old. Tonight we saw 'White Cliffs of Dover' starring Irene Dunne, Frank Morgan, and Alan Marshall. Last night we saw the movie 'Mrs. Skeffington' with Bette Davis and Claude Raines. They are good pictures and the latter is superb. If you see it, be sure to take along plenty of handkerchiefs. I don't mind admitting that I had a lump in my throat when I walked out at the end."

"The last few days I've been projecting film on the rehabilitation of the Guam natives for the fellows that shot it. Some of them just got back. It is quite a job covering such a large subject. All the books say the native population is appr. 25,000. In peace time the whites there were very few including the military personnel."

"Getting ready for inspection, seeing the show, and writing you I won't have time to write Pat."

"Dad, I don't know where you got such a high price quoted to you for cameras. Here are some prices of reconditioned speed-graphics Anniversary Model OAP ceiling price as of 6 April '44. 4x5 with Ektar f4.7 lens $102.00; 4x5 Bausch & Lomb Tessar f4.5 $104.00. This new speed-graphic price is taken from an advertisement by Aremac Camera Co. 1 East 43rd St., New York 17, N.Y. 4x5 graphic, lens Ektar f4.7, Graphlex shutter, built in-flash-synchronizer, Kalart Range finder, & Graflex flash unit: $206.45. Of course the shutter may not be as good as the one you had in mind but I think yours didn't have a flash unit. I guess you were right about the price though. Boy the prices are high. If you buy anything, be sure to get it new."

Bob reported about the radio program and news broadcasts he enjoyed,[363] "The other day I received Mom's letter ...Enclosed were the clippings from Zel and the Xmas pic's & Dad's birthday shot. Thanks a lot. Say Dad, were you holding something precious when the picture was taken, maybe a bottle of whiskey?"

"By the time you receive this maybe you will have gotten the package of souvenirs. A little later I sent a large envelope of Pat's letters. It went 1st class so you should receive it soon. Please save the things for me."

"On the radio Sundays we can listen to John Charles Thomas (G.E. I think), Chaplain's Hour, Hour of Charm, and other good programs. During the week the 'Melody Hour' (hillbilly & cowboy music) M. C.'s (Master of Ceremonies) are Lum & Abner, G. I. Gill (request program), Atabrine[364] Cocktail Hour (popular music), Spotlight Bands, Hit Parade, Globe Theatre (drama, mystery for service men only) etc. The programs are well rounded. The radio comes on at 0555 off at 0800; on at 1100 off at 1400, on at 1600 off at 2235. On Saturdays the morning times are the same only it stays on all afternoon. Sundays it goes on at 0155 and stays on all day. We hear full news broadcasts from the States several times a day plus headline 'hi-lites' on the hour."

In anticipation of St. Valentines Day Bob sent identical V-Mail Valentine to Zelda and Earle on February 5, 1945. On the same day he wrote,[365]

"I received your long letter of 27 January this afternoon, Mom. I certainly am glad that you are getting my letters. I've been trying to write more often."

"My work is about the same with the exception that we've been assigned cameras to take care of instead of changing from one to another as we did sometimes before. I tested, cleaned, and got all of my camera gear in shape."

"Yesterday I loafed, read and thought about Pat. She is very pleasant thinking."

"Does Marin College still have a bus service? If it does, maybe Pat can stay at our place and go to school there at Marin. I've mentioned it to her. We shall see."

"Many of these places out here are very pretty but living conditions don't promote appreciation. If there was a city here with our loved ones and were civilians with all privileges of one, it could be very enjoyable. But the way it is, no. Or if we came here of our own free will for a visit and could leave when desired, yes."

"I hope that you've recovered from being an invalid."

"Our Sr. Picnic wasn't very conservative either you know. They were going to cease all such shindigs."

"Both sets of pencils are good. Shortage of paper and such is bad. Even we don't have enough to throw away although we get along."

"P.S. In my note book that I sent home I believe there is a photograph of a camera; that is the type that I'm now using."

A few days later Bob praised hoped for improvements in Vallejo and complained about an altercation that resulted in a court martial.[366]

"The Jr. College and improvements for the Hi-School sounds grand. I certainly hope that the bill goes through. They will be a grand addition and something that the city can be proud of. A town, that size should have those things and more. People that vote against it should be sent out here for at least 2 years and made to live under the same conditions that we do."

"Your trip on the sub, sounds very interesting, Dad. (*Earle had boarded a submarine off of Hunters Point and stayed on board until arrival at Mare Island. He spoke with the ship's electrician and made notes of all the electrical items that needed repair. After arriving at the shipyard he wrote up the necessary paper work to authorize the work.*)

"We had quite a stinky week-end. A sergeant beat up a corporal that was too drunk to defend himself and is one of the best liked fellows in the outfit. We testified, all of us, for the corporal, but it was one of the most unfair court-martials ever held. The Colonel broke both of them one rank. If I had my way the corporal (original) would have made sergeant long ago and the sergeant broken to private. The only hope we have now is for the general to change things which I doubt he will do unless someone gives him the 'word'"

"Zel, did I tell you that I saw the show 'Dragon Seed'[367] out here not very long ago? You probably know that a great deal of it was filmed near Marysville."

"Did you receive the package containing Grandfather Watson's watch and the souvenirs? I sent it insured, so let me know."

"Yesterday I bought a Pierce Swiss-made wrist-watch. It is water-proof, non-magnetic, and shock resistant with numbers and hands coated with a luminous material."

"P.S. I'm enclosing a money-order for $100 to put in the bank."

In spite of the altercation Bob described in his letter, the Photo Section Marines developed considerable camaraderie and generally had a good time in their tent city. They sometimes had parties and cooked their own dinners. On one such occasion spaghetti was the main entre prepared by Walavich and several other photographers.

65. Making Spaghetti, Walavich on left

**66. Enjoying the "Sumptuous" Repast; C-W Bob, Adler 3rd, Clements
back right, Hewitt 2nd right, Walavich bottom right**

Bob had received a letter from home in which his mother described the celebration of her and Earle's thirty-third wedding anniversary and mentioned that they had joked about keeping each other rather than opting for younger mates. Bob responded.[368] "I for one am glad that you Mom & Dad have decided to keep the original model. This would be a 'helluva' time to change."

"I certainly am glad that my mail is going through to you in jig time. Pat's are coming through fairly good now. She fouled up by sending a bunch through first class instead of air mail."

"The last few days I've been sorting exposed film according to type and expiration date. It has kept me busy. In the latter part of the afternoons we play volleyball and I have quite a tan. It is a good one for me; I never do get very dark."

"I'm writing this during the noon hour. I'm in the office to answer the phone and take care of any business that comes up during the period."

"Here is something I thought to be rather cute. Maybe you'll like it too."

"A bustle is a deceitful seat full;
A girdle is a hinder binder and a
Brassiere is a flopper stopper."
"That's enough!

The same day Bob wrote to Jim about his opinion of what it would be like to be a Hollywood cameraman,[369] "In reply to your question: it is impossible to buy this photographic experience that we are getting out here. The usual procedure is to start by carrying gear, then loading film and slating, and gradually working up to a photographer. After a fellow proves himself, he is sent out to different countries to cover wars, earthquakes, famines, riots, etc. That is news. Hollywood or educational photographers start out much the same, but for my money I don't want to work in any of the Hollywood studios. The only way I'd work for them would be getting sub-contracts shooting processed backgrounds or shorts away from their hub-a-hub-a."

"It will almost certainly be a year before I get back, probably the spring of 1946."

"I'm glad you are going to Tarmac *(working on the flight line at Naval Air Station Glenview near Chicago)* and then to pre-flight *(school)*. I know that is what you want and it will be damn good experience. I'm very, very sincere in wishing you good-luck and fine weather."

"I'm glad that it's warmer there. By the time you receive this you'll be having another cold spell."

"The last few days I've been working in the cold (sorting film in a refrigerator). The temperature varies from 65° to 80° while I'm working in it. When I stepped outside it feels as though a blast-furnace were turned on me."

"I'm glad that you found a girl that you seem to like. Joyce is about the same height as Pat. She is about 5'6" stocking feet and weighs about 120 pounds. Umm! Umm! Luscious! She isn't brilliant but is very easy on the eyes and has a nice personality. I'm told that she is getting better looking all the time."

"Your boxing experience sounds very good. Just don't get any cauliflower ears, split lips, or such. We have been kept busy lately working on movie stories and gear."

Since Christmas Bob's letters contained more references to when he would be home or wanting to be home. His letter to the Turner's, was no exception,[370] "I received Jim's (*Turner*) Christmas card sent in November and your letter written 18 December. I'm sorry that I didn't write sooner. It seemed that all the mail came at once and (*I'm*) just not catching up."

"The duck hunting certainly sounded good. When I get back I'll have to try my aim and luck."

"For Christmas and New Years we had turkey and all of the trimmings. They were very good meals."

"I received many cards and presents at Xmas, thanks."

"I'm still doing the same ole things, except for editing film; I'm through with that for a while. I've been testing camera and lenses, writing dope-sheets, checking gear, and doing other odd jobs. Considering every thing I have not been getting more stagnate from lack of things to keep me occupied."

"We've been having good days of late and I've acquired a nice tan. The only trouble is if I work inside very many days I lose the bronze coloring. I would look a little strange if I were to come home in the winter with this tan. At least I'd be different."

"That's enough nonsense. I'll close now. Hope that you had a merry holiday and wish you a prosperous year."

Meanwhile back on Guam, Captain Thayer Soule had prepared his Third Division Photo Section for the invasion of Iwo Jima. Sufficient photo gear and supplies were kept for his headquarters team and the rest had been distributed to the Regimental Photo Teams. Typically the Division Photo Section reported to the headquarters Intelligence Staff Organization G-2, and the Third Division was no exception. Soule kept four photographers with him at staff and assigned 16 to the regiments, detailed to the three infantry battalions in each of the three regiments.

On D-Day February 19, 1945 the Fifth Amphibious Corps landed the Fourth and Fifth Divisions and kept the Third in reserve. The next day the 21st Marines of the 3rd Division went ashore accompanied by the assigned photo team. Being the only photo officer of nine photo teams, Captain Soule was denied permission to go ashore.

On D+3 a forty man patrol from E Company 2nd Battalion, 28th Marines Fifth Division reached the crater on top of Mount Suribachi where they were immediately engaged in battle with enemy soldiers. While the battle continued two marines raised a small flag on a pipe they found in the area. Not long afterwards, Joe Rosenthal an

Associated Press photographer, climbed to the top accompanied by Sgt. Bill Genaust, who had been in Bob's cinematography class at Quantico, and still photographer PFC Robert Campbell, both armed with weapons and cameras. The trio arrived in time to photograph the raising of a second larger flag. It was here that Rosenthal took his famous photograph for which he was awarded a Pulitzer Price and which became the basis for the Marine Corps War Memorial located outside the walls of the Arlington Cemetery. Bill Genaust, standing within a few feet of Rosenthal, recorded the event in 16 mm color on his Bell and Howell Filmo 16 mm camera. Genaust's movie film of the event was used later to prove that Rosenthal's picture was not staged as some had claimed. Genaust's film appeared in the movie "To the Shores of Iwo Jima" and numerous documentaries. Unfortunately Genaust was killed four days later in an advance against Japanese in caves and tunnels.

Karl Soule was finally given permission to hit the beach on D+5. He described the conditions as he walked up a hill,[371] "Chaos was all around us. Crippled landing craft were beached at wild angles, swamped by the sea, pounded by the surf. Trucks and tanks were upended and awash. Crates, boxes, cases, and cartons were crushed and shattered, soggy with the sea." As he reached higher ground, near the airfield, Japanese shelling startled Soule. A vehicle went up in flames, men ran in all directions, but he managed to slide under a truck. Soule saw two men blown into the air in pieces and watched a truck burn and ammunition exploding. As more shells landed and killed more men, corpsmen rushed to help the wounded.

Soule and his photo team acquitted themselves well receiving an official commendation from the Secretary of the Navy. Soule quoted it in part,[372] "All photographers in the unit demonstrated outstanding skill, devotion to duty, courage, and initiative in coverage of the action." Unfortunately they did not come out unscathed. Staff Sgt. Don Raddatz who had begged to go with Soule was killed. Galloway was wounded. Tech. Sgt. Joe Franklin, the former football player who was an instructor with Bob in Cine school, was severely wounded during a fifteen hour ordeal involving several encounters with enemy soldiers, but managed to survive after being evacuated by members of a mortar squad who carried him to safety through a hail of sniper fire.

Karl Soule was ordered back to Washington D. C in early March and the Third Division left Iwo on 27 March replaced by the 147th Infantry Regiment U.S. Army that was then responsible for mopping up and garrison duty. At that time, "Japanese killed and sealed in caves was 20,703 and 216 taken prisoner." The Marine Corps suffered officers and men KIA or died of wounds 5885; missing and presumed dead 46; WIA 17,272; combat fatigue casualties 2,648. The Navy total casualties were 2,798.[373]

By this time Bob surely knew that there was going to be another island invasion that would involve the III AC and the Sixth Division. The artillery exercise he covered was a clear message that something big was about to happen. Testing cameras, lenses, and writing dope sheets was obviously an effort to tidy up the Photo Section prior to some new event. Now as he reports in his next letter that he is working on camera gear and organizing equipment, overhauling the photo section and getting rid of unnecessary equipment had to be for a purpose other than just getting organized. Never the less his letters seemed to report only routine activities; and his Thursday evening letter gave his family no concern.[374] "Within the last three days I received three letters from you, one from Zelda dated February 3rd and two from Mom dated 6 and 11 February."

"The last few days I've been working hard on all kinds of photo-gear: film, cameras, dope-sheets, etc. I haven't been taking pictures, though."

"Stan McWilliams was just mentioned by our island-radio sportscaster. He said that he was attending the College of the Pacific, I think, and said something about him having a very high score for the season." (*Stan was an outstanding athlete at Vallejo High School and a classmate of Jim's. Stan lettered in football, basketball and baseball. While playing basketball at College of the Pacific he was the leading scorer in the nation.*)[375]

"I believed that I mentioned before about having spaghetti feed. We've had a total of three, now; one just the other night."

"Zelda if you send Pat a picture of yourself, make it 3 ¼ x 4 ¼ or so. I think that she might like it colored. Send Dick (Hutsell) a wallet-size and a 5" x 7" colored picture in a frame."

"I certainly hope that Jim can get his training in California. It would be nice being near home."

"I would have liked to have seen Jack Gavin when he was at our place." (*Jack sold his balloon-tired bicycle to Bob and Jim for $7.50 in 1940.*)

"When any of the fellows go home from here, I'll ask them to at least call you on the phone."

A few days later Bob replied to a question from home that he had been up in airplanes several times,[376] "I received a letter from you, Mom, yesterday and again today. They are dated 18 and 20 February respectively. I call that damn fast time."

"It certainly is swell that Jim can get home again, even if it is just a few days."

"Tell Lee Monroe, 'Hello', for me, please. It is nice that he can be so near home."

"Yes I've been up in planes. I've flown to the Russell Islands and back a few times and once to Bouganville and back. …. I sent some more pictures to you a while back. All or most of the pictures that I sent you I'd like to have when I get back except those that Pat has copies of and you have duplicates of. I've sent you far more pictures and other things than I did her. Don't mention it to her, though."

One of Bob's airplane trips was in the workhorse PBY.

67. PBY with flight and Maintenance Crews, Davis 3rd from right, Bob far right.

"I'm very glad that you got the money order. It certainly makes me feel good to have a little money stuck away."

216

"There is nothing you can send out except maybe a couple more bottles of Soretone about a month from now. If you send it out then I'll have probably finished what I have on hand by the time it gets here."

"The last few days we've made a complete overhaul of our section. We've turned in gear to the Q. M. (*Quartermaster*) that we've had no use for and thrown away and burnt things that they would not take. We have been collecting too many non-essential items."

The impression Bob's letters gave his family was that he was engaged in routine activities, working as a professional in the photographic business. Life was not perfect but all was well and he was settled into an almost normal routine. In actual fact he and others in the Photo Section were getting ready for participation in the upcoming invasion of Okinawa. It would not be long before he was once again filming combat in the largest amphibious operation to date and what would become the last major operation of the Pacific War.

The Sixth Marine Division also based on Guadalcanal was involved in intense preparations for a major role in the invasion. All equipment and gear was being loaded on transports, including the amtracs pictured here.

68. Sixth Division Amtracs, Photo courtesy Grant Wolfkill

14

DESTINY-OKINAWA

PROJECT ICEBERG, the attack on Okinawa in the Ryuku Islands only 350 miles south of Kyushu, the most south westerly of the four main Japanese islands, was about to begin. The largest force of the Pacific War was being assembled for the invasion of Okinawa. There would be "548,000 men of the Marine Corps, Army, and Navy together with 318 combatant and 1,139 auxiliary vessels and a profusion of strategic and tactical aircraft."[377] By comparison the landing on the coast of France on D-Day June 6, 1944 involved 3,600 landing craft of various types.

The assault would be under the command of the Navy, Admiral Chester Nimitz in charge, but the attacking troops would be under Army Lt. General Simon Bolivar Buckner, commander of the Tenth Army. His forces would include the Northern Attack Force made up of Major General Roy Geiger's III Amphibious Corps that included the First Marine Division under command of Major General Pedro A. del Valle and the Sixth Division commanded by Major General Lemuel C. Sheperd. The balance of the forces, the Southern Attack Force, would be made up of the Army XXIV Corps, commanded by Major General John R. Hodge, which included Major General Archibald V. Arnold's Seventh Infantry Division and Major General James L. Bradley's 96th Division.

The invasion would be supported by a 6000-mile supply line stretching from the West Coast of the U.S. and would include a total of eleven different ports. Initial supplies, carried by the assault troops would come from "Leyte, Guadalcanal, Espiritu Santo, Banika, Pavuvu, Saipan, Eniwetok, Oahu, and the West Coast of the U. S."[378]

Emergency reserves would be held at Saipan, Tinian, and Guam. New orders would take 120 days from requisition, procurement and shipping from the west coast to the destination. Indeed, this was to be a formidable undertaking making extraordinary demands on the logistics systems set up to support the effort.

Map 8 shows the relationship of Okinawa to the Japanese mainland and the terrain held by the American and Japanese forces.

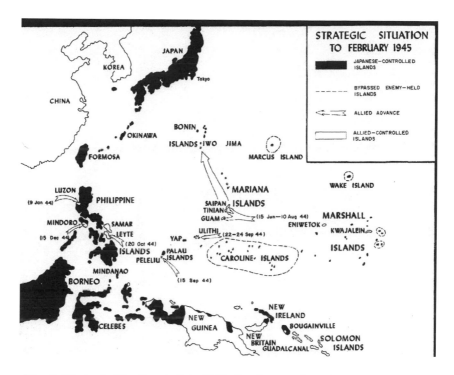

Map 8, Strategic Situation to Feb. 1945. Landmasses in white controlled by U. S. Forces. Black Landmasses controlled by Japanese.

Okinawa Is in a chain of islands known as Nansei Shoto or Ryukyu Islands, which was made up of three smaller chains of islands known as Tokara Gunto, Amani Gunto and Okinawa Gunto. The Nansei Shoto stretches 790 miles in an arc between Kyushu and Formosa. Okinawa Island is the largest of the group making up the Okinawa Gunto.

Sgt. Robert LeRoy Watson, Sgt. Hoyt Rhodes and Corporal Robert Simpson had made preparations in the III Amphibious Corps Photo Section on Guadalcanal to participate in the invasion. Subsequently they received orders to temporary duty: "On or about 15 February, 1945 you will report to the commanding officer, III Corps Signal Battalion, Corps Troops, III Amphibious Corps, for temporary duty in connection with verbal instructions. Upon completion of this temporary duty and when directed by competent authority, you will return to your regular station and resume your regular duties."

According to Hoyt Rhodes, the three photographers were transferred to the III AC Signal Battalion on February 28, 1945 to participate in the battle for Okinawa and were "assigned to work on

219

another communication story in 35mm" film.[379]

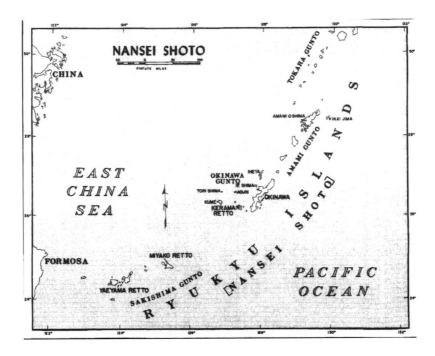

Map 9 Ryuku Islands (Nansei Shoto)

Shortly after joining the signal battalion, Bob wrote a routine letter with no indication of his new assignment, but obviously his comments about sending a package home and throwing away junk were a clue that something was changing.[380] "I received two letters from you dated 14 February; Mom & Zelda. I'm glad that you got my valentines."

"The carnations you gave Mom sound swell, Dad.

"I don't need any more reading material, although I have a couple of books in mind that you can send me later; I'll let you know what they are."

"We've been having field-days around the area lately. We threw away more junk than you can shake a stick at."

"I sent home a package 3rd class the other day that I'd appreciate you putting away until I get home. Don't fiddle with it in the meantime. I just remembered that I sent it yesterday. Watch for it and put it away. It has some personal stuff in it, so wait."

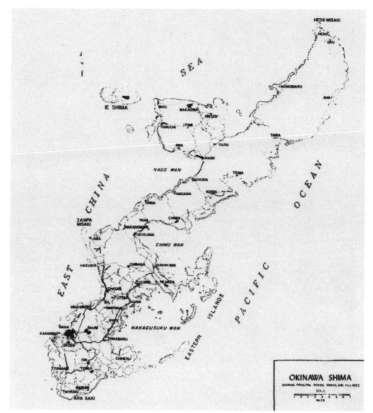

Map 10 Okinawa Shima

On the same day Bob wrote to Pat Niedert's mother and made clear his serious love for Pat, "My attentions to Pat are serious. The reason I didn't mention it before I left was because of my uncertain future."

Preparation for the Northern Attack Force departure and sailing to the Ryukyus required the commanding generals of the 1st and 6th Divisions to be responsible for loading and embarking their respective organic and attached units while the III AC had the responsibility of loading the Corps troops. Some of the Northern attack vessels had been partially combat-loaded as part of the eight day training exercise, but they "required additional time off the Guadalcanal, Banika and Pavuvu beaches to take on vital cargo and to top off water and fuel tanks."[381] "The Northern Tractor Flotilla was the first increment of TF 53 to leave the Solomons for the staging area at Ulithi. Departing on 12

March the holds and above decks of the landing ships... were solidly packed with amphibious vehicles, tanks, artillery, and various other combat gear." Many of the Marine assault troops embarked for Okinawa March 15 on fast assault transports (APA's).

Bob and Hoyt Rhodes "boarded LST 892 March 9 and left Tulagi on March 15 for Okinawa."[382] The ship, 328 feet long and 50 on the beam, was beached in Berth 17 at East Kukum Bay, Guadalcanal on Friday 9 March 1945 nearby LST 124, LST 283 and LST 20.[383] Lieutenant W.S. Miller commanded the ship with a crew of seven officers and approximately 90 enlisted men. After moving to Berth 8, LST 892 "commenced loading with combat load and 163 men and 13 officers, Marine detachments came aboard for transportation."[384] This was presumably the III Amphibious Corps Signal Battalion with attached photographers Rhodes and Watson. After a few days of difficulty the LST was able to retract from the beach at 0649 and sailed on various course until it reached Berth 12 Port Purvis, Solomon Islands and anchored at 1014. At 1231 the ship was underway for Tulagi Bay to transfer 100,000 gallons of diesel oil to YOG 41, a "gasoline barge." By 1332 Lt. Miller's ship was along the starboard side of YOG 41 where it transferred 100,000 gallons of diesel fuel, finishing two hours and eighteen minutes later. After returning to berth 12 the ship sailed on 12 March to Hutchinson Creek, Florida Island where it moored portside of USS Coronis (ARL-10), a landing craft repair ship.

No doubt alert to the ships maneuvers, relocations and anchoring in different berths and alongside other ships, Bob would have spent time observing the operations to relieve the boredom of being an inactive passenger while anticipating with some trepidation his forthcoming assignment to film the Signal Battalion during combat operations on Okinawa. The whole exercise was about to become a rare opportunity to see how the ship's crew handled routine operations as well as unexpected mishaps.

It could not have been boring for someone with Bob's curiosity. The excitement began when the ship attempted to land at Green Beach in Tulagi harbor between a Landing Craft Tank (smaller than an LST) and another Landing Ship Tank. When beaching the ship "struck LCT 146 on the starboard quarter and glanced off port bow door of LST 767. This ship immediately retracted and stood by while LCT retracted with aid of tugs."[385]

There were no personnel injuries, but there was a nine-inch hole punched on the port side two feet above the second deck and the starboard side plating was bent. After supplies were loaded on board, Bob was able to watch the ship retract from the beach, sail to Purvis Bay to anchor on the starboard side of a Delta Class repair ship, the USS Briareus AR 12 in berth 37. When the ship moored alongside AR 12, the "#6 line caught in the starboard screw because of excessive slack. The line was pulled off both ships and seized the starboard screw stopping the starboard engine."

On 14 March LST 892 sailed to anchorage 40 at Purvis Bay where it moored alongside LST 126 and LST 478 inboard at the "water hole" at Egan Bluff, Florida Island. The "water hole" had an ample supply of fresh water that enabled the Navy to supply many ships during the war in the Pacific. In this instance LST 892 took on 22,620 gallons of fresh water, bringing its total supply to 83,209 gallons.[386] At this time Lt. Miller received a top-secret movement order to proceed to Ulithi, Carolina Islands located half way between the Marianas and Okinawa as a member of Task Unit 51.11.4. At 0708 on 15 March the ship passed through the gate to the torpedo net at the entrance to Purvis Bay. Seven hours later the ship maneuvered into position in convoy 500 yards astern of LST 923 whereupon Miller exercised the crew at general quarters followed by anti-aircraft firing practice. At 1552 the ship took up its position 500 yards off "starboard beam of LST 747 as section guide of section two-composed of this ship, LST 1000, and LST 908"[387]

Sailing to Ulithi in convoy formation proved to be uneventful with occasional course changes, some zig zagging, speed changes varying between 7.5 and 10 knots, and routine general quarters exercises; the only exception was when USS Fair reported a sonar contact of a possible enemy submarine at 2000 March 19th. Depth charges were dropped, but contact was lost and never regained. With little or no naval activity to relieve their boredom, the Marines in the Signal Battalion no doubt resorted to card and dice games, reminiscences, tall tales and singing. The officers and top non-commissioned officers probably reviewed action plans for providing communications on Okinawa.

With Ulithi not too far distant, Bob took time to write home confident that his letter could now be mailed. In the short letter Post marked March 23, 1945 Bob gave no hint of his location or of the impending invasion in strict compliance with censorship rules that forbade including sensitive military information. He wrote about routine matters and as he so often had before delineated in detail what he ate at chow time. He had become skilled at revealing nothing about his personal concerns and the apprehension he no doubt felt since he was about to go into combat again.[388]

"Even though it has been some time since I last wrote, there isn't much news. The last few days I've been printing quite a few pictures.[389] It's the first time I've done this much dark room work in a long time."

69. LST 892 Underway

"We are having very good chow: fresh eggs every few days, fresh meat and vegetables and pastry at least once a day. This noon we had pork chops, mashed potatoes and gravy, canned peas, chopped cabbage with mayonnaise, cold tea, and apple pie. Umm! Umm! Not bad huh?"

"Zel-A while back I received your letter dated 21 February. Sorry about Dick, although I'm glad he told you now instead of later. I think that I know how you felt. Don't forget, every time you hit bottom and start going up you reach a higher point than before."

Bob didn't mention taking pictures, but Hoyt Rhodes spent some time operating his Filmo 35 mm movie camera.

At sometime after 0400 on 24 March, the ships radar operators reported land at a distance of 18 miles. Shortly thereafter, several emergency turns were commanded followed by a return to the base course at two-thirds speed. The flotilla arrived at Ulithi, Carolina Islands and 892 anchored in Berth 466. The transport group and tractor flotilla of Task Force 53 had arrived and anchored three days before. Bob gazed in wonder at the sight of this massive gathering of ships that included carriers, battleships, cruisers and smaller combat vessels, some enroute or returning from attacks against Japanese forces.

70. Hoyt Rhodes filming on LST 892

That afternoon the severely damaged aircraft carrier Franklin limped into the anchorage after being struck on 19 March by Kamikaze attackers whose bombs had penetrated the lower decks and in the process left the flight deck buckled and the upper rigging, aerials, and radar towers missing or completely twisted out of shape.[390] In spite of the horrendous damage the Franklin was able to sail under its own power to New York for repairs.

Troops from Task Force 53 that had been on APA's transferred to landing craft for the 1,400 mile trip to Okinawa and then were ferried ashore in small groups for organized athletics and the enjoyment of "not-too-cool cokes and beer." On 25 March these troops left Ulithi as part of the Northern Tractor Flotilla. Bob and his fellow marines no doubt enjoyed the same benefit until their departure as part of the remaining echelon. After taking on water from USS ABATAN AW-4 (a distilling ship that served landing ships) the crew was called to general quarters in response to an "air Flash Red" warning that was apparently a false alarm. On 27 March, with supplies and marines on board, preparations were made to get underway "in accordance with secret order A16-3. Destination Okinawa Shima, Japan."[391]

The flotilla formed in cruising disposition number 1 consisting of five columns of ships. LST 892 was the fourth ship in the center column with lead ship and formation guide LST 729 followed by four other LST's. Bob surely would have been impressed with the size of the fleet as he watched the maneuvers that placed four LST's and a repair ship in Column 1. Column 2 included four LST's and an LCI (Landing Craft Infantry); Column 4 contained four LST's and a tanker; and Column 5 also had four LST's and a tanker. The ships maintained station at 500-yard intervals.

Bob also had an opportunity to witness a Captain's Mast that first day underway when three seamen second class (S2c) were sentenced with penalties ranging from two days confinement with bread and water for insubordination and shirking duty and 20 hours extra duty for shirking duty. The cruise was uneventful and nothing exciting happened until 0455 the morning of 30 March when the blaring call to General Quarters was sounded to exercise the crew and anyone sleeping was rudely awakened. Up early that day, Bob took time from his daily routine of reading books and watching the aerial activity and the maneuvering of the battleships and carrier forces to compose a letter, knowing that it would be his last opportunity to write until after he landed on Okinawa.[392] "I received a number of letters from you some days ago.

"I wrote Mrs. Smart a V-mail, which I hope will make her feel good."

Bob no doubt wrote a sympathetic letter with condolences for the loss of Mr. Smart and would have added statements of admiration for him and his friendship. Mr. Smart used to pay Bob and Jim twenty-five cents for mowing his lawn.

"Thanks for taking care of Pat's letters."

"I don't know of anything for you to get me for my birthday unless it would be the book on color photography that I mentioned before. I think that it is titled 'Kodacolor & Kodachrome Photography.' It costs $6.50 or $7.50. I forget which. It's advertised in all photo mags."

"I'm very glad that Jim got to go home again. When this thing is over we'll have a big blowout."

We are on the way to invading another island. By the time you receive this it will be old news. I have a comparatively safe assignment this time, so you needn't worry."

"We are getting good chow and I'm catching up on my reading. I'm enjoying a good book named 'Elegant Journey' by John Selby."

"I didn't receive Gr. W. (*Grandmother Watson*) letter that she mentioned but I'd better write her."

As usual, Bob was nonchalant about all the excitement around him and the pending life threatening military operation, at least as he expressed himself in his letters to his parents. Not wanting to alarm them he wrote of casual subjects and assured them that his assignment was not dangerous. He partially succeeded in that his father was lulled into believing there was no danger, but his mother worried in spite of his reassurances.

In preparation for the invasion the first carrier strikes against Okinawa had been conducted on 10 October 1944 by more than 1000 planes that dropped 500 tons of bombs and fired thousands of rockets. Almost 50 ships were sunk in the harbor, ammunition dumps were blown up and thousands of bags of rice were destroyed. In February fast carrier forces that supported the Iwo Jima landings also attacked Tokyo and submarines ranging in the western Pacific took a major toll of Japanese shipping. By mid February the Japanese on Okinawa were virtually isolated with little prospect for reinforcements from Japan. The vast areas surrounding Okinawa were swept clear of mines and patrol operations by destroyers and gunboats, and radar picket ships stationed 15 to 100 miles off shore protected by carrier combat patrols further assured the isolation of Japanese forces on Okinawa. In the six days preceding the landings, minesweepers covered over 3000 square miles and destroyed 257 mines. Underwater demolitions teams cleared the beaches of obstacles in the designated landing areas for the assault forces.

During the six days prior to the landing, the Navy continuously bombarded enemy installations with as many as 27,226 rounds of 5-inch or larger caliber ammunition. By March 31 the Japanese defenders were confronted with the massive American flotilla involving 1500 ships that included 40 carriers, 18 battleships, scores of cruisers and almost 150 destroyers and destroyer escorts. The next day, Easter Sunday, designated as L-Day and referred to as Love-Day brought cloudy to clear skies, a calm sea, little surf and moderate off shore breezes with temperatures in the mid to high seventies. At 0406 hours Admiral Turner gave the order, "Land the landing force."

Elements of the Second Marine Division made a diversionary approach to the southeastern Minatoga area while the main forces headed for the Hagushi beaches. The Japanese had assumed the Minatoga area would be the main target of the landing forces and therefore concentrated defensive forces there. The feint convinced the defenders they had assumed correctly which brought some relief to the forces approaching Hagushi that began to debark ten minutes after air support arrived over the target at 0650. Ten Battleships, 9 Cruisers, 23 Destroyers, and 177 gunboats pounded the beaches before five to seven waves of hundreds of troop carrying Landing Vehicle Tracked (LVT) vehicles crossed the line of departure. Sixth Division troops landed in the north above the First Division and the Army's Seventh and 96th

Divisions landed in the South.

Troops who had experienced combat, especially on Peleliu, expected a blood bath. Fortunately the Japanese had decided to lightly defend the Hagushi beaches while concentrating their main forces in the South, as the Army would soon discover. The 22nd Marines of the Sixth Division landed at Green Beach 1 and 2 in the North just above Red Beaches 1, 2 and 3 where the Fourth Marines landed in line with Yontan Airfield. The First Marine Division Seventh Marines landed on Blue 1 and 2, while the Fifth Marines landed on Yellow 1, 2, and 3 in line with Hagushi.

Bob's good friend Grant Wolfkill landing with the Sixth Division was among those few who were wounded. He was shot in the back of his knee, but continued onto the beach and later received medical treatment. He was convinced that friendly fire had hit him, because he experienced little or no incoming rounds. The Sixth Division moved up rapidly as did the First Division against light opposition. By 1530 the majority of the III AC support troops and artillery were ashore. Within eight hours the Tenth Army had 50,000 troops on a beachhead 15,000 yards wide and 4000 to 5000 yards deep. The first day's operation for the four divisions resulted in 28 killed, 104 wounded and 27 missing.

On LST 892 still underway to Okinawa, Bob probably attended Easter Church services, conducted by the ship's chaplain, and took Holy Communion if it was offered. The day started with dawn General Quarters, but all was relatively quiet until 1717 when General Quarters was called in response to an air raid warning that was signaled all clear eleven minutes later; however another air raid alert at 1749 caused another call to GQ's that left the crew at GQ stations until 2400. During the morning hours of 2 April there were several course changes with concurrent speed changes.

After securing from another call to GQ in response to an air raid warning, the ship steered various courses in conformance with the Kerama Kaikyo anchorage in the Kerama Islands fifteen miles from Okinawa that had been seized by the Army six days before. See Map 9 on page 220. The ship passed through the submarine nets, circled Kerama Retto and finally anchored in the Kerama Passage at 1409 and responded to an air raid alert at 1839 that lasted until 1951 followed by one more at 2003 to 2012. Although used to the constant call to General Quarters and air raids that failed to materialize, Bob and his fellow Marines were no doubt on high alert with each call and experienced some anxiety especially since they were now close to their objective.

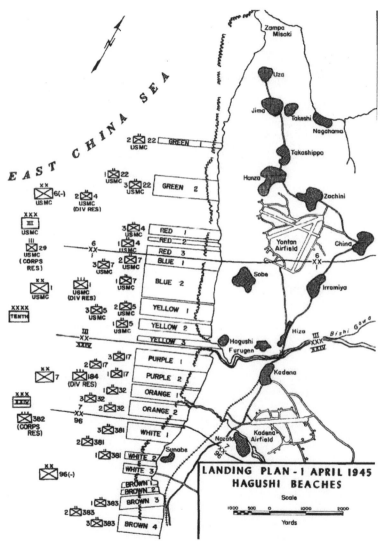

Map 11 Landing Plan Hagushi Beaches

On Monday 2 April the Marines attacking on Okinawa advanced so fast the lines were overextended causing the 7th Marines to cease attacking at 1800, one thousand yards ahead of the L+3 objective. By 4 April the Sixth Division had captured the Yontan airfield and repaired it sufficiently for emergency landings. Landing craft debarked troops not scheduled until the second or third day which caused a delay in unloading supplies. By 1600 on L+1 the 7th Marines were on a line roughly equal to the L+5 Objective.

By the third day, L+2, the 1st Division had reached the east coast, cutting the island in half, eight to thirteen days ahead of schedule. The 6th Division advancing through "heavily broken terrain honeycombed with numerous caves" had gained 3,500 to 7000 yards of ground in its area.

The Army's 7th and 96th Divisions had wheeled right on 3 April and in their drive to the south ran into heavy opposition that would prove to be the main Japanese line of defense.

On Tuesday 3 April LST 892 moved into position in response to an order from Transport Division 52 to launch LCT (Landing Craft Troops) loaded with Marines and their gear, but the order was cancelled and the ship was ordered to Yellow Beach. In preparation for going ashore, Bob and Hoyt had packed cameras, film and other essential equipment including their 45 caliber pistol.[393] The ship maneuvered into anchorage off Yellow Beach at 1458 then got underway and at 1637 beached on Yellow Beach 2, but was unable to unload troops according to the ship's log.

However, Bob and Hoyt must have gone ashore on that date as he had informed his friend Bill Pillsbury[394] and Hoyt later confirmed to Bob's Parents.[395] The two friends immediately began filming men in the Signal Battalion setting up communications.

Two days later Bob found an opportunity to write home,[396] "Here I am on Okinawa safe and sound. My schedule got fouled up, so I didn't land until the fourth day.[397] This has ruined my record."[398] "I have talked to a few civilians and they seem to be fairly peaceful, in fact, very much so. I've learned and am learning a little Japanese which is coming in handy."

"We have some new fellows in the section; they all seem to be nice guys. I knew some of them back in Quantico. In fact I taught a couple of them. The operation is running very, very smoothly so far."

"It is getting very late, so I shall close. I'll write again soon."

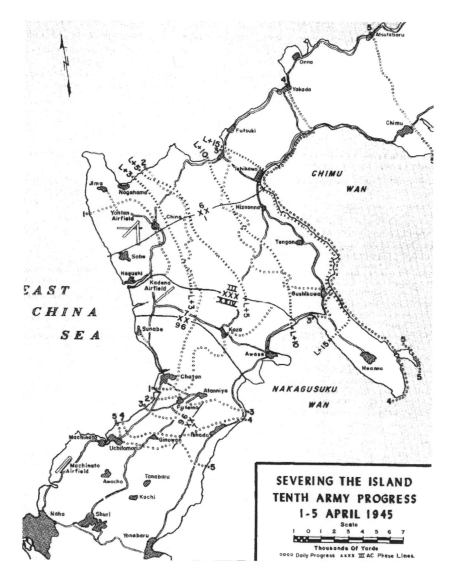

Map 12 First Division cut Island in half

Bob was happy to be with many of his fellow photographers who were either assigned to the III AC Photo Section or Regimental Photo Sections. In addition to Hoyt Rhodes and Simpson others were: Wally Walavich, his friend from Quantico; Glenn Chittenden and Walt

Spangler, still photographers from Vallejo; Chuck Miller; Mitch Plaine; Alan Gray; Bob Bailey; and Bob's good friend and fellow instructor at Quantico, Grant Wolfkill.

71. Some of Bob's Friends on Okinawa: L-R Alan Gray, Walt Spangler, Bob Bailey, & Grant Wolfkill. Photo courtesy Grant Wolfkill

While Bob and Hoyt carried out their assignment to photograph communication activities, General Buckner ordered the III AC on April 5 to explore Yabuchi Shima and to conduct aggressive reconnaissance northwards toward the Motobu Peninsula. At 0900 on the 5th, the Sixth Division started its reconnaissance to the north with infantry battalions supported by armor moving up both sides of the Isthmus. The Division made rapid progress against disorganized and light opposition. Engineering units accompanied the infantry repairing and replacing bridges, the enemy had attempted to destroy, and widened the roadways to accommodate two way traffic. By late afternoon on the April 7, the Fourth Marines set up a perimeter defense north of the village of Ora. The 29th Marines seized Nago, which had been leveled by Naval and artillery fire, on the west coast. Possession of Nago made it possible to land Marine supplies at its beaches thereby relieving the long supply line overland from Hagushi.

As the infantry regiments advanced to the base of the Mobutu Peninsula they were accompanied by artillery battalions of the 15th Regiment and also supported by naval gunfire. The advance was so rapid the artillery battalions had to move once a day on average and were forced to minimize their combat equipment and resort to radio communications rather than wire. Marine Air Groups 31 and 33 (MAG) had arrived ashore on 7 and 9 April and were supporting XXIV Corps activities in the south; but as enemy opposition stiffened on the Mobutu Peninsula Marine air units were dispatched to destroy troop concentrations, observation posts and emplacements.

Aerial reconnaissance and photo analysis confirmed that the enemy had organized its defenses to make a last stand in the mountainous terrain of the Mobutu peninsula. In response General Shepherd redeployed his troops to set up a defensive line with the 22nd Marines, across the island from Nakaoshi to Ora to provide protection of the flanks while the 29th Marines attacked to the west and the 4th Marines near Ora positioned to support the 29th Marines on the peninsula or the 22nd in the north. There was sporadic fighting during the next five days that were spent probing in the interior and to the west in an attempt to locate the main defensive bastion. Moving out on 9 April the 29th Marines ran into immediate opposition locating the main enemy forces in the area from Itomi west to Toguchi. Roadblocks, mines and demolitions now delayed American forces. From Nago westward the Japanese had destroyed bridges and set up tank traps, which prevented bypass construction, and made impassable craters in the narrow roads. Troops made frequent contact with the enemy in the rugged mountainous terrain and night counter attacks intensified, one complete with artillery was not thwarted until dawn on 11 April. Probing actions continued until the main enemy resistance was located in the Toguchi area. Now the infantry regiments were positioned to defend the terrain gained by the rapid advance, prevent enemy movements through the area of Kawada Wan-Shana Wan line, seize the northernmost tip of Okinawa, and destroy the enemy forces on the peninsula.

It is not known how much film Rhodes and Watson shot of communication activities, but some footage has been recovered from the National Archives and Marine Corps archives at Quantico. Review of those films indicates that the two cinematographers concentrated on the Signal Battalion's establishment of main lines of communication. This effort involved setting up poles, stringing lines from cable reels mounted on moving trucks, attaching the lines to the poles, stretching the lines taut and securing to the poles. Following completion of the installations the operation of radio transmitters and receivers were recorded, both in mobile vehicles and in temporary field installations. April 10, 1945 was the earliest date of the retrieved film shot by Rhodes who recorded scenes of a marine working at a radio console, a marine stringing communication lines in trees and a marine in a jeep wearing earphones and holding a microphone. The films shot by R. L. Watson were exposed on 12 April as shown below in the picture of the slate which Bob created indicating the "date, Roll Number 33, camera number 361704, III Amphibious Corps Project 5 Communication Line." It was standard procedure for a photographer to create and film a slate, often handwritten on a piece of paper, that identified the cameraman's name, organization, date, camera model number, film roll number, project number, and usually the location such as Okinawa. This information was intended to facilitate categorizing and utilizing the film after development at a location removed from the combat area, often as far away as Pearl Harbor. The Marine Corps intended to edit and incorporate the developed reels of film into historical documentaries, training films and in some cases for newsreels to be released in movie theaters. The communication films shot by Rhodes and Watson were all 35mm black and white. Four scenes captured from footage shot by Bob are shown below.

72. Slate N33 shot by Sgt. Watson　　**73. Marine working Communication Line April 12, 1945**

74.Marines reeling Line from Truck   75. Securing Line to pole

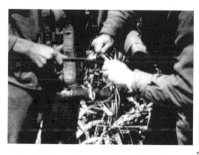

76. Splicing Communication Lines

Bob and Hoyt completed their assignment photographing the Signal Battalion activities on 12 April and reverted to the III AC Photo Section, part of G-2 Intelligence under the command of Lt. Harold Palmer. Several of Bob's friends were also under Lt. Palmer who gave them assignments either associated with Corps activities or to regiments within the Sixth Division as the situation demanded. At least by 14 April, Bob and Hoyt along with several other photographers including Mitch Plaine, Whittingham, Walavich, and Davidson were then assigned to photograph the Military Government activities designed to control and care for the civilian population. Glenn Chittenden also joined them with his Speed Graphic still camera.

Always looking at the positive side of his assignments Bob wrote,[399] "I hope that you received my last letter even if it was short."

"I'm in fine health even though the fleas are bad. They aren't harmful, but they keep us scratching.

"Rhodes, Chittenden (from Vallejo), and myself are now working on a picture of civilians. The island has a large population. So far, it's very interesting work. This is a great education in itself. We are shooting scenes of natives returning to the towns and being rehabilitated. Their fields are in good shape as are most of their homes. They'll be squared away before too long."

"Where I'm staying tonight the fellows are listening to phonograph records: Jap phonograph and records. They got the phonograph in a Jap bivouac area."

"I'll mention it again in case you didn't get my last letter. I'm on

Okinawa Shima."

"It's dark so I'll close."

In anticipation of having to cope with a large civilian population, which was one half million on Okinawa according to the 1940 census, officers who were destined to head military government teams arrived at Fort Ord California in December 1944. Many had received three months training in military government at either Princeton or Columbia Universities. These Navy and Army officers were instructed in the ICEBERG military government plan in California or at the staging areas when they joined the assault forces.[400] The plan included provisions for internment camps capable of handling up to 10,000 natives and Japanese civilians. By early May it was anticipated that as many as 306,000 civilians would need to be provided food, clothing and housing.[401] There were in fact 125,000 civilians under military government (Mil-Gov) control by the end of April.

77. Taking Break from Filming Natives, Chittenden, Watson and Rhodes

About the time Bob began filming Mil-Gov activities, the Sixth Division initiated an attack on 14 April designed to eliminate the enemy on the Mobuto Peninsula. The 4th Marines, with 3/29 attached, advanced inland to the east and the 29th Marines moved to the west and southwest from the center of the Peninsula. The attack was preceded by intense artillery, naval and aerial bombardment. By noon the Marine forces succeeded in taking a 700-foot high ridge 1200 yards inland from the west coast and then another ridge 1000 yards to the front against stiffening enemy resistance. Enemy defensive tactics employed small concealed groups that provided covering screens of the main positions as well as troops

236

hiding in concealed positions waiting for the Marines to pass without interference and would then fire on a larger group considered a prime target. This tactic enabled the enemy to kill the commander of first battalion 4th Marines in an area where there had been no firing for thirty minutes.[402] When the Marines succeeded in working up to a suspected enemy position, which they had previously raked with heavy fire, they would find little or no evidence of the enemy having been there. The attack involving 3/29 and 2/4 reached the regimental objective by 1630 hours.

The 29th Marines attacked east of Yae Take to clear the Itomi-Toguchi road to eliminate strong points previously discovered, but the attack had to be reoriented to the southwest because of intense enemy resistance. First battalion 29th Marines were able to advance 800 yards up steep slopes before being pinned down in the late afternoon. The next day the 29th Marines consolidated its defensive positions on the high ground. At 1600 hours the enemy failed to infiltrate 2/29 lines supported by heavy 20 mm fire and under cover of grenade, rifle and mortar fire.

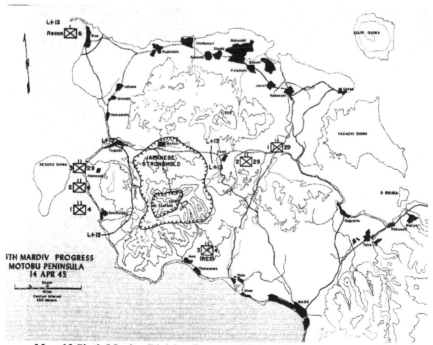

Map 13 Sixth Marine Division Progress Mobutu Peninsula 14 April 1945

At 0700 on the 15th, the Fourth Marines renewed its attack against small groups of scattered resistance. As the regiment reached half way to the day's objective it encountered more intense fire from caves and pillboxes with more effective fire on the Marines climbing the steep mountainside. Third battalion, 29th Marines advancing 900 yards to the east and south encountered heavy machine gun, mortar and artillery fire. Air strikes, artillery and naval gunfire attempted to destroy an enemy artillery piece without success that had harassed the Marines for two days. The attack ceased at 1630 with the battalions at their objectives. Supply and "evacuation of the mounting number of casualties over the tortuous terrain became more and more difficult and the troops had become very tired." Even so 1,120 dead were counted and the enemy then resorted to guerrilla operations.[403]

The Sixth Division deployed for a full scale attack and after overcoming resupply difficulties, moved out at 0900 on the 16th. Supporting artillery fire effectively kept the enemy from returning fire and the Marines succeeded in blasting the enemy from their caves. The attack also eliminated a mountain gun that had harassed the Marines for days. As the Marines reached the summit of the 1,200 foot high Mount Yae Take, the battle was waged at close quarters. Finally two companies with almost all their ammunition consumed took possession of the peak at the expense of fifty casualties. Effective 15th Marines artillery fire plus mortar and machine gun fire prevented the enemy from regrouping and initiating a counter attack. After Yae Take had been secured, 75 of the enemy launched a banzai attack at 1830 hours that was defeated by supporting artillery fire.

Heavier than usual artillery fire on the morning of April 17 proceeded the 0800 attack which resulted in the 29th Marines and the 4th Marines joining up on the Itomi-Toguchi road. The attack had to overcome supply difficulties over the rugged terrain as well as elaborately fortified enemy positions. By the end of the day the enemy "was unable to maintain his position and was, in fact, attempting to retreat in order to escape annihilation."[404] The Division had virtually eliminated the only resistance on the Motobu Peninsula so that it was then able to spend the 18th "reorganizing, resupplying and consolidating" its gains.

During the battle for the Motobu Peninsula evidence of civilian cooperation with the enemy surfaced when fires mysteriously broke out in several west coast villages during the period from 14-16 April. An enemy hit and run attack on Nakaoshi 17 April that also over ran the 6th Engineer Battalion command post appeared to have civilian collaboration. The First Division had similar experiences in its zone as early as 9 April when they discovered civilians roaming around freely at night. The First Division began rounding up civilians and put them in stockades on Katchin Peninsula. The Sixth Division was forced to await the conclusion of military activity in the north before similar action could be taken. As hostilities wound down on Motobu, the Sixth Division set up a civilian control center at Taira, and on 16 April began interning 500 to 1,500 natives daily until operations in the north ceased. Taira is located at the neck of the Motobu Peninsula on a line extending from Nago to Nakaoshi.

The civilian control centers were set up to remove the native population from the combat areas so military operations could proceed unimpeded by natives seeking refuge or possibly actively interfering with Marine troop movements. Once that was achieved, the Military Government (Mil-Gov) organization concentrated on setting up a governing system that would allow the civilians to redevelop an economy that would return the native population to self sufficiency. Mil-Gov provided emergency food and water followed by medical examinations and treatment for wounds, infections, and other infirmities. The natives were organized to cooperatively construct shelters and to resume planting and harvesting of crops using techniques and tools long familiar to them. The Third Amphibious Corps, either on its own volition or based on orders from above, considered the MIL-Gov activities so important that a significant number of photographers, both still and movie, were assigned to record the activities and the return of the civilian population to a modicum of normal life. Part of the motivation was no doubt to make a historical record, but the more important reason was probably to make it possible to evaluate the efficacy of the operation. Lessons learned could then be applied to deal with the millions of Japanese civilians during the expected invasion and defeat of the Japanese forces on the mainland islands.

While the infantry was defeating the enemy on Mount Yae Take and readying for the final drive to the northern coast of the peninsula, Bob was fortunate to have a day of leisure, probably near Taira. There he took the time to write a letter home in which he described his environment and the natives he had been photographing.[405] "We aren't doing anything today so I'm lolling on the bank of a stream writing this. It is very much like a park along the river. It is approximately 45 yds. wide and 1 ft. deep. The bank is made of stone with a grassy top and trees planted in a row along it. Next to the river are some houses and immediately in back of them are small steep hills with terraced slopes topped with Japanese pines. To my left at a bend in the stream is a bridge where a native woman is washing some vegetables and some children."

"The older people wear dark colored kimonos as do the babies. The girls wear baggy trousers and jackets."

"Some houses have straw roofs and others have tiled roofs. The walls are made of panels 1/4" thick (wood), some sliding. All yards are surrounded by trees and hedges for wind-breaks."

"The people raise wheat, rice, a type of sweet potato, cabbage, chickens, goats, and pigs."

Sketch by R. L. Watson of Stream and Bridge near Taira

"The country is very beautiful when we have time to enjoy it and the climate is wonderful. At the moment it is warm with a slight breeze blowing. The nights are good for sleep being cold."

"I certainly wish that I had a color camera here of my own."

"Rhodes, Chittenden, and I have been taking pictures of the natives the last few days. We are on our own and though we are kept busy most of the time we get some good views of the place."

The pictures below were extracted from 35 mm shots Bob made near Taira. Digital copies were made from film obtained from the National Archives.

78. Slate 39 dated April 18, 1945 shot near Taira; and Civilian tying I.D. Tag

**79. Men Constructing Camp   80. Woman with Baby Washing
       Near Taira 4/15/1945   Clothes 4/19/1945**

**81. Men in Grain Fields, Roll 62 4/22/45   82. Woman carrying Grain, roll 55
                                                    4/19/45**

The Fourth and 29th Regiments reached the north coast on 20 April after which General Geiger announced the end of organized resistance in the north. The Japanese resorted to guerrilla warfare and attempted to escape the peninsula via Taira. Garrison and sector patrols functioned while "mopping up operations continued in the rest of the IIIAC zone.[406] The fighting on the peninsula cost the Sixth Division 207 killed, 757 wounded, and six missing in action. Over 2000 dead Japanese were counted. General Oliver P. Smith commented about the progress the Sixth Division made in his personal narrative, "Troops moved rapidly over rugged terrain, repaired roads and blown bridges, successively opened new unloading points, and reached the northern tip of the island, some 55 miles from the original landing beaches, in 14 days. This was followed by a mountain campaign of 7 days' duration to clear the Motobu Peninsula."[407]

Still involved in photographing the Okinawa natives as they returned to a somewhat normal existence, Bob took the time to respond to questions he had received in a letter from his brother,[408] "I received your letter written 10 March a couple of days ago. It is very good hearing from you again."

"I'm very glad that you are finally getting your hands on planes. I certainly hope that you get to fly soon, but for gosh-sakes don't do any barnstorming."[409]

"My first job on this island was taking pictures of communications. For the last week I've been getting shots of natives. I was certainly glad to get off the comm. stuff; it was becoming most monotonous. This work is more interesting."

"The climate here is similar to Southern Calif. Most of the island is hilly and has many scenic views. I'd much rather be in a place like this than the South Pacific."

"I'll close now. I'm a little weary of writing. I just finished a nine page letter to the Folks."

83. Native Men in Military Stockade being fed; Sgt. Watson in center with camera

84. Bob caught in Sgt. Rhodes Movie Camera Lens

While the Sixth Division was rapidly advancing in the north of Okinawa and securing the Motobu Peninsula the XXIV Corps made up of the Army's Seventh and Ninety-Sixth Divisions was attacking to the south. The Army immediately encountered a series of defenses that revealed the first line of Japanese defense along the Kakazu Ridge.

The defenses were so effective it took three airstrikes, blasts from the 14-inch rifles of the Cruiser New York and support from four artillery battalions to allow one 96th infantry battalion to advance 500 yards to the northern limits of the ridge.[410] The situation was so implacable that General Hodge requested all available artillery units from Tenth Army. Marine artillery could not be employed effectively in the north so General Buckner ordered most of the IIIAC 155 mm howitzer artillery units south to support the XXIV Corps. By 12 April the Eleventh Marines 105mm howitzers and 75mm pack howitzers were also transferred to the XXIV Corps. Attacks and counter attacks continued for the next several days. Even though the Corps estimated that about 6,900 of the enemy had been killed by 14 April, the Japanese were able to continually feed replacement soldiers to the defense line. By this time Army Intelligence had learned from captured documents and maps that the enemy strength was 7000 stronger than originally estimated and was now believed to total 72,000 or even higher.

The Shuri defenses just beyond the Kakazu ridge were a labyrinth of interconnected tunnels that contained the enemy troops and sealed off gun ports; all effectively camouflaged. Full support from artillery, Tactical Air Forces, aircraft from Task Forces 51, 52, and 58, and shelling from Task Force 51 battleships, cruisers and destroyers was employed for four days against the defenses in preparation for a three division attack on 19 April.[411] In spite of the awesome barrage from 27 battalions of artillery and air attacks from as many as 375 aircraft providing close air support, the initial moderate gains ground to a halt as the Japanese defenses stiffened.

The XXIV Corps suffered heavy casualties for little gain, and although the Japanese front line units suffered heavy attrition their "sheer courage and fanatic determination" prevented the Corps from reaching its objective. For three days the attacks with artillery and naval support were confined to local strongpoints. During the night of 23-24 April the Japanese poured the "most intensive artillery fire along the XXIV Corps front yet experienced" and unknown to the Americans withdrew the forces that had held against the 96th and 7th Divisions for two weeks. When the XXIV Corps resumed a massive attack on the 24th, the Kakazu Ridge was easily taken.

On that same day Bob still involved with photographing the Military Government and native activities took time to write to neighbors and landlords Jimmie and Rita Turner. Although Bob rarely wrote about his own combat experiences, he included in the letter an understated comment,[412] "I received your Easter Card some time ago, but I've just now gotten around to replying. Thank you very much."

"As you must know by now I'm on the Island of Okinawa. When I first arrived here I took pictures for a communication story, but the last few days I've been working on a Military Government picture, which I enjoy much more. I hope that I will be able to continue in this line of work for awhile."

"At the moment I'm back at the section area. I washed clothes (the first time since I've been here) and myself."

85. Bob washing Clothes

"I too am glad that I wasn't on Iwo Jima. I had enough of that stuff on Peleliu."

"I'm very happy for the Philippine boys (*who*) are getting back home and that the people are treating them fine. They deserve all of the consideration that they are getting and more."

"Say! Where is Club 365 that you spoke of? What kind of a place is it? I hope to be on the west-coast again sometime and maybe pay the place a visit. You sound as though you enjoyed it."

Still back at the Photo Section headquarters Bob provided an update for his parents,[413] "Yesterday I came back to the Section and found a stack of mail waiting for me. Mom, yours are dated 29 Mar., and 9 & 10 Apr. Dad's is dated 4 Apr., and Zel's are dated 30, 31 Mar. and 9 April."

"So, Pat sent you a nice present, Zel? Don't worry about sending equals. She has a 'hope-chest', so here's a tip which you may accept and may not. Send her a nice small present; nothing expensive I mean. Then send her something for the chest. Make it useful. Think about that for awhile and decide."

"I'm surely glad you were able to see Karl Potter and thanks for his address. I only wish I could have been there."

"Thanks for the Soretone, papers and envelopes of clippings."

"You asked about a birthday present, the only thing that I want is the book on Kodachrome that I wrote about."

"Please send my book of trigonometry. If I remember it's blue and thin. Also send the leather binder out that I sent home. Take out

245

of it the pages that are written on and put them away. Check on the paper supply in it that is left."

"Today I had some time to myself so I washed some clothes. Boy! What a relief. Closing now."

Bob was very happy taking pictures of the natives and getting acquainted with their culture. He was with Glen Chittenden for about two weeks and they spent many hours reminiscing about their time at Vallejo High School. According to Glen, Bob befriended an Okinawa "boy whom he called his number one boy and used him to carry his camera gear."[414]

Responding to the need for fresh troops on the Shuri defense line and General Hodges order, General Geiger selected the First Marine Division as reserve for the Tenth Army. At the same time there was a discussion about using the Second Marine Division, still on Saipan, to make an amphibious landing on the southeastern coast of Okinawa in order to outflank the Japanese defenders and also to entice them to move troops to defend against the new attack. General Buckner supported by Admiral Nimitz rejected the idea and opted to continue a frontal attack with the XXIV Corps supported by the III Amphibious Corps. On 27 April the First Marine Division moved south to relieve the battered 27th Army Division that moved north to replace the Sixth Marine Division, which was then, scheduled to join the attack in the south. At the same time the Army's Ninety-Six Division continued grinding south against "counterattacks, repeated artillery and mortar barrages, and never-ending infiltration attempts."[415]

Very much in love with young Pat Niedert, Bob wrote to her frequently, probably more than to his parents. He obviously had a good relationship with Pat's parents and also wrote to them. He had no qualms about expressing himself to the Niederts and he felt free to do so. After sending them money to buy presents for Pat and themselves his intentions were thwarted and he made clear his feelings,[416] "I too was flabbergasted at all the presents that you got for Pat. I had originally intended that you take some of the money for yourself in payment for the gifts at Xmas or buy yourself something. With the rest of it you were to buy Pat something. It was alright, but after this when I send you something, use it yourself or I'll raise 'hell' when I get back, understand?"

In response to some kind words he added, "Thank you very much for the compliments. I'm sure that I have some caveman in my make-up. That helps most certainly, but understanding the female is hardest;

it's an art in itself."

Bob spent several days filming native activities in the village of Kin, then returned to the Photo Section where he was able to resume a letter he had started,[417] "I started to write this yesterday, but due to pressing business at the time I had to cease my efforts. I came back to the Section this morning to take (*care*) of a few things, get more film, send in exposed stuff."

"At Kin, where I was yesterday, some native girls are working in the galley. One of them sings 'Auld Lang Syne' and 'My Blue Heaven' in Japanese. She learned it before the war. One of the fellows there tried to teach her 'Shoo! Shoo! Baby! In English. It was quite a show and we enjoyed it very much. We, meaning Marines, enjoy kidding around with the people and learning their language."

"Wally and I took pictures of the people harvesting potatoes and their water irrigation system. Their village has very pure water. The spring is the most famous on the island."

86. Woman harvesting Potatoes   **87. Woman grinding Meal, roll 53 4/19**

"On one side of the village is a large natural cave. It runs from one edge of the village across it to the other side. At one end of the cave topside is a Buddhist temple. The architecture is the Japanese type (curved roof). Inside is beautifully hand-carved wood lacquered black; red, and gold. There are two gold lacquered statues; one is of Buddha."

"I'm out of paper so I'll close."

"P.S. I received a letter from Dad dated 17 March, another from Zel dated 18 March, and one from Mom dated 22 April today."

"On Guam I was attached to Co. G., 22nd Reg., 1st Marine Prov. Brigade. The fourth regiment was also in the Brigade. When a Marine says (4th) Marines he means a regiment but civilians and boots will use the term -----Marines and mean a division."

"4th Marines=4th Regiment. 4th Marine Division. Get the distinction? Here's the order from large to small: Army, Corps, Division, Brigade, Regiment, Battalion, Company, (or in artillery Battery), Platoon, Section, Squad, Rifle-team."

"I'm glad that you like Othello, Zel. I intend seeing some of that stuff after I get back."

The weather began to change at the beginning of May; cloudy cooler temperatures with occasional showers were the precursor to heavy rains that lead to the typhoon season from July to November. In the South the XXIV Corps including the First Marine Division attempted to gain ground against fierce opposition along the main Japanese defense line near the Asa River. Hampered by heavy rain and Japanese fire from caves at heights above the attacking battalions, the Marines' advances were limited to a few hundred yards that they were unable to hold and were often forced to withdraw to the position from which the attack commenced. The XXIV Corps made small gains with heavy losses, but the Japanese suffered more losses, which they were able to replace with fresh troops or new infantry units. The Japanese defense plan was to hold the line, giving ground grudgingly while inflicting heavy losses on the American forces in an attempt to delay the inevitable as long as possible to protect the home islands from invasion. Although the Japanese sustained substantial losses, the main forces remained intact and there became a change in attitude among many of the officers that a major effort could stop the American drive. Consequently the Japanese commander was persuaded to embark on a counter attack with the objective of destroying the XXIV Corps. The commander increased his forces with troops that had been positioned to stop an amphibious landing in the east. The attack started after dark on 3 May supported by artillery and Kamikaze air raids. There were attempted beach landings near Kuwan, and engineers tried to slip behind American lines by boat on the coast. The counter attack was thwarted by American artillery, LVT (A) crews on the alert at Kuwan, Naval anti boat screens, Navy gunfire, and bombing and strafing runs by American flyers. The Kamikaze did more damage than the Japanese infantry, but the American flyers claimed 95 Japanese aircraft.[418] The Japanese suffered a decisive defeat losing 20 or 25 percent of the original strength of army divisions and half of its artillery capability, [419]while the Marine First Division was able to make significant advances to the Asa Kawa River.

The First Division and corps artillery battalions that had been under control of the XXIV Corps reverted to General Geiger's III Amphibious Corps as the Tenth Army prepared to continue the southern attack with the XXIV Corps on the left and the III AC on the right. The Sixth Division moved up to the Asa Kawa River to the right of the First Division. Several days of heavy rain and muddy terrain delayed armor from moving into position, making progress extremely difficult. By 9 May the Sixth Engineer Battalion was able to build a footbridge across the Asa Kawa that allowed the 22nd Marines, First Division to cross over and continue the attack on the southern side.

During the time of the Sixth Division fighting for access to the Asa Kawa southern shore there is no information regarding Bob's activities or location for the period from 2 May until six days later when the troops on Okinawa learned of the defeat of Nazi Germany and Bob was able to write,[420] "I'm back at the village of Kin taking pictures again. Today it's raining so badly that nothing would turn out. Taking advantage of this free time I'm trying to catch up with my correspondence somewhat."

'A couple of days ago I received seven letters from you: Dad's 26 Feb., Mom's 5, 8, 20, March & 20, 25 April. Zel's 6 March."

"The drill and tap I found out here and sent it home thinking that by some remote chance you could make use of it, Dad."

"I'm glad that my packages arrived safely."

"It was swell that Jim could get home again before going to Tarmac. (*Duty on the flight line at Naval Air Station Glenview, Illinois*) I received a couple of letters from him since then telling about his leave and his duties at the new base. He seems to like his-set up there."

"Wolfkill is with the 6th Div. Spangler and Stillings are with the 1st Div. I haven't seen Tooliatos."

"I haven't received the purple heart."

"The day before yesterday, as we finished shooting a Chinese family invited us in to visit them. As is their custom out came the food. We had tea, a bean and rice wheat-flour cookie, sweet potato chips, and cooked ground goat meat. It all tasted good."

"They were very glad that the Americans came and wished that they could show their appreciation by giving us a banquet."

"Chow time must go."

P.S. V - E Day! Hip! Hip! Very quiet here. No one hollered and no one got drunk.

The reaction in Vallejo was also subdued. Earle Watson recorded,

"V-E Day has come and gone. Its arrival has not made any material difference in conditions here. There was very little celebrating in Vallejo so far as I have been able to find out. Some business establishments closed up for the day and all liquor dealers closed up for 2 hours. In fact most of the people here considered the war in Europe more of an incidental action as far as the war as a whole is concerned. The Pacific action is much nearer to most of us."[421]

Bob then took the time to update Jim on his activities, one more time making light of his situation,[422] "I received your letter of 18 April four or five days ago, but have just gotten around to replying."

"You asked about my assignments. On Guam I took combat pictures, so I went in with 'G' Co. 22nd Marines. On Peleliu I took combat communications pictures, so I went in with 'I' Co. 7th Marines. Here I started out taking communications in general, so I came in with the III Phib. Corps Signal Bn. For the last two weeks I've been taking pictures of the natives. They are the most interesting subjects that I've ever had. I certainly hope that I can keep in this work.

"Your work sounds very, very interesting. You certainly have gotten the breaks."

"I got the flag on Guam. Five of us went out ahead of the lines to get some pictures and I found it in a cave that the Nips had used for an aid station."

"It is raining 'cats & dogs' today, so I'm finally able to answer some of my mail."

"Some of the people here are very nice and have treated us swell. This is a wonderful experience even if there is a war going on. I have been very lucky and have missed the fighting except for a little bombing. The closest one so far has been 250 yards."

"Nothing more, so I'll close.

"P.S. What do you think of the Jap stationary?"[423]

"P.P.S. Hurray! Just got word about V-E Day, now to find some Saki."

On the same day Bob wrote to his friends Bill and Nadine Pillsbury,[424] "I received two letters from you recently. Nadine's is dated 20 March and Bill's 10 April. It certainly was good hearing from you."

"Mom sent me your letter of thanks. Someday I'll get you a real present. At the moment though being on Okinawa it is somewhat difficult."

We just received word a couple of hours ago that the war in

Europe is over. That means that this one should be finished in a year and a half."

"I'm glad that you are going to school again, Bill. Keep plugging. I'm glad to know that marriage is so wonderful. It isn't a myth after all?"

"Jim is now doing Tarmac at a field in Illinois. He should be getting flight training before too long."

"I agree with you about Texas. Louisiana and east Texas have to be better."

"I landed here the 3rd of April and made pictures of communications. Now I'm taking pictures of the Military Government set-up and the natives. It is very interesting work and I'd like to do this on every operation. Oh! What a life!"

"The people are friendly and they help us considerably. The only draw-back is that some of them are camera shy, which makes things a little difficult at times."

"Let me know how you are doing. Good luck!"

Bob certainly wrote to Pat Niedert at this time and probably more often, but he also made certain to send a letter to Pat's parents,[425] in which he discussed his love for Pat and brought up the subject of marriage. Bob mentioned that he liked the picture of his "one and only" and then added, "I still can't get over how lucky I am to have met such a wonderful and lovely girl." Then he addressed "Phil, Sr.---- I didn't say anything to you about my wanting to marry Pat because I didn't know what the future had in store for me. I still don't know but I can hope. When I get back, all arrangements can be made then. Of course I may want to rush things somewhat." Bob and Pat had discussed the possibility of marriage before he was shipped overseas, but they both wisely decided against it because of their age and more importantly the uncertainty of Bob's survival when engaged in deadly combat in the Pacific.

While the Tenth Army was engaged in bloody fighting against a tenacious foe defending from caves and fortified tunnels, the Navy forces provided aerial support when weather permitted and destroyed enemy troops and positions with naval gunfire. The Japanese were determined to inflict as much damage as possible and had elected to employ Kamikaze suicide bombers, typically making up one-third of the attacking force, simply because they were more effective than normal bombing tactics. American Destroyers and Destroyer Escorts stationed, as radar picket ships at the outer boundary of the fleet to provide advanced warning of incoming air raids were primary targets of Kamikaze attackers. On 9 May the USS Oberrender (DE-344) was singled out by a suicide pilot who managed to dive his aircraft into her starboard side, a bomb carried by the plane exploding in the forward fire room killed twenty-five sailors. Young Torpedoman George Tyrrell, whom Bob had seen on Manus Island, was blown into the water but survived to come home safely.[426]

The Kamikaze attacks took a heavy toll on the Navy ships creating a heavy workload at Mare Island Navy Yard and other shipyards in the States. As recorded by Bob's father, "The whole yard is on 7 day basis in an effort to get the ships back to you in less time. A shortage of electricians, machinists and sheet metal workers here is part of the need for more time at work per man."[427]

In anticipation of a major attack by both corps of the Tenth Army scheduled for 0700 on 11 May, combat engineers began building a Bailey bridge across the Asa Kawa at 2200 on the tenth under observed fire from artillery and small arms; even the dump where the materials were stacked was occasionally under fire delaying construction by six hours. Marine tanks were finally able to cross at 1100 on 11 May; four hours after the coordinated two corps attack began.[428] The 22nd Marines, Sixth Division led the attack and with the help of naval gun fire followed by flame throwers, demolition and tank fire succeeded in taking a hill that was a "key feature of the Asa Kawa defense system" that "contained a vast network of headquarters and supply installations within a large tunnel and cave complex."[429] When the attack was resumed on 12 May the Japanese took advantage of tombs dug in the hillsides to direct small arms fire against the advancing Marines, who never the less reached high ground overlooking the city of Naha. Here they sent patrols through the suburbs to the banks of the Asato Gawa River, and after advancing 2000 yards south of the river on the 13th, suffered 800 Marines killed and wounded. The next day the 29th Marines joined the attack left of the 22nd while the Fourth Marines held in reserve moved south to guard the Division rear. The Division succeeded in taking control of 1,100 yards along the north bank of the Asato, but the second battalion, 22nd Marines on the left flank was stopped by accurate fire from well organized defenses guarding a rectangular shaped hill that the Marines named "Sugar Loaf". Before the invasion the Japanese had sighted in lines of fire that bracketed the area so that it could be covered in the front, rear and on the flanks.

Sugar Loaf was protected by defensive positions in tunnels and caves strategically placed in Half Moon Hill and Horseshoe Hill, which together with Sugar Loaf formed a triangle that constituted the "western anchor of the Shuri defenses." In spite of being forced to stop its advance by the concentrated fire, and with a reduced combat efficiency of only 62 percent, the second battalion of the 22nd Marines was ordered to seize its objective including Sugar Loaf on the 14th. Approximately 40 Marines managed to reach the top of the hill and after digging in for the night were confronted with a Japanese counter attack which resulted in the death of all but seven survivors who were ordered off the hill at 0800 on the 15th. The 29th Marines attempted to seize Half Moon on the 15th, and were met with the same heavy resistance. Later, with support from tanks, elements of the regiment managed to occupy the northern slope of the hill; but later in the afternoon were forced to withdraw when faced with a strong counter attack in which the enemy employed machine gun, rifle, and mortar fire into the rear and exposed flanks of the Marines. Further attempts to take Sugar Loaf were also repulsed leaving the 22nd Marines without the capability to continue, so the 29th Marines were given the task.

While the attacks on Sugar Loaf and Half Moon hill were underway, Bob had been dispatched to photograph one of the supporting artillery battalions. After completing the assignment he was able to write a letter with a pencil on tissue like paper that was difficult to read,[430] "Yesterday I got back from an artillery outfit that I'd been taking colored pictures of. Upon arriving here I found waiting several letters from you."

"I believe that I told you about me taking pictures of the natives in the village of Taira and then going to Chimu (Kin). From Chimu I went to Ishikawa and made some pictures of the opening of a playground for the children. At first the people carried over quite a bit of the Jap regimentation, but that's gradually leaving them."

"I am now shooting color 16 mm film[431], which I've been hoping for ever since I got out here. Color is much more realistic and fascinating to me."

"Dad, your letters are dated 18 and 28 April, Mom, yours is dated 3 May, and Zel's were written 30 April and May 1st."

"Don't let anyone kid you; the Japanese Americans are doing invaluable work out here. We'd be lost without them. It makes me mad every time I read in an article how they are being treated on the west coast. I believe that I told you about meeting one of them from home. It certainly was good meeting him. His brother Mosai was one year behind me in school."

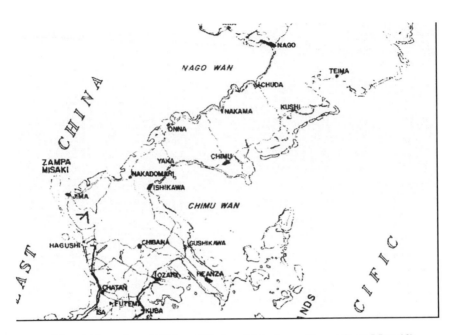

Map 14 Location of Chimu (Kim) and Ishakawa (Insert from Map 10)

"Speaking of censors, some of the damn people are like the pastor that jumped out of the burning church, missed the burro and fell in the well. Take for instance the fellow that wrote a few personal things to his wife and because the censor was so old that he could no longer enjoy the finer things of life, he cut them out. Some are just plain ordinary b------. On the other hand some are very sensible. The only subjects that are censorable are those that give 'aid or comfort' to the enemy."

"The book that I asked for is called 'Kodachrome & Kodacolor Photography' I believe. It is advertised in all photographic magazines."

"Congratulations on your promotion Dad. It certainly is swell."

"Good going on your grades, Zel; keep them up. You certainly jumped ahead of the others."

"The demonstration on Ansco color film is a great opportunity. I hope that you can attend it. I'd certainly like to be there. I understand that Ansco[432] is better than Kodachrome. A great deal of money is going to be made in the color field."

"Here I've rattled on and on about various subjects and I'm running short of paper."

"Please send Pat a nice present for me as soon as possible. The big day is very, very soon and I forgot to make arrangements with you sooner."

"Get something for Zel, too. I certainly have been neglectful. I can't get anything for them out here as you can understand.

"Don't forget that the Marines are here on this island too, and are doing a whale of a job. The Army is being shown up and won't let it be published."

"Pardon the pencil but my pen is back at the section."

In accordance with the Marine Corps policy of recording all combat action, Bob and several other III AC photographers were assigned to the Sixth Division to film the big push to Naha: Chuck Miller and Mitch Plaine were assigned to the 22nd Marines; Albert Walavich and Glen Chittenden to the 29th Marines; and Bob moved to the 4th Marines with Grant Wolfkill.

The next day, 17 May preceded by a massive bombardment from 16-inch naval guns, 8-inch howitzers, and 1,000 pound bombs, the First and Third battalions, 29th Marines launched an attack against Half Moon. Company E, Second Battalion, attacked Sugar Loaf reaching the crest each time but was unable to hold with a loss of 160 men killed or wounded. Integrated fire from Half Moon, and Sugar Loaf required the marines to capture both objectives simultaneously. With 3/29 and 1/29 150 yards short of Half Moon, Company D/29 assaulted Sugar Loaf on the 18th against fierce opposition with grenades and mortar fire employed by both protagonists, and managed to charge over the crest and destroyed emplacements on the down slope. In response to mortar and machine gun fire emanating from positions on Horseshoe ridge against the marines attacking Sugar Loaf and Half Moon, Company D was dispatched to destroy the positions, but after reaching the ridge was forced to withdraw slightly because of the entrenched enemy's heavy grenade and mortar barrage. At the end of the day the 29th Marines combat efficiency was so depleted that General Geiger released the Fourth Marines to the Division as replacement and assigned the 29th to division reserve under III AC control. Since the beginning of the Tenth Army's "major push, the 6th Marine Division had sustained 2,662 battle and 1,289 non-battle casualties, almost all in the ranks of the 22nd and 29th Marines."[433] Mitch Plaine, who had worked with Bob on making a film of the battle for Guam, and Chuck Miller were both killed photographing the combat on Sugar Loaf Hill.[434]

The relief of the 29th Marines by the 4th Marines on the morning of 19 May was hampered by a strong counter attack on Company F 2/29 forcing the company to withdraw to the northern slope of Sugar Loaf. The 4th Marines had to fight its way into the line and the 29th Marines had to fight out because of the "constant bombardment" and "opposition from isolated enemy groups that had infiltrated the lines during the night." The exchange was accomplished by 1430, but the 4th regiment suffered 70 casualties. At 1530 a Japanese counter attack was launched which was broken up after nearly two hours of fighting,[435] and this was followed by heavy and accurate artillery fire during the night. Early on the morning of the 20th two assault battalions of the 4th Marines launched an attack preceded by artillery bombardment and supported by the 6th tank battalion, the 5th Provisional Rocket Detachment and the Army 91st Chemical Mortar Company. After a 200-yard gain the attack came to a halt stymied by Japanese "machine gun and artillery fire from hidden positions in the Shuri Hill mass."[436] The marines were hit with all kinds of artillery up to an eight inch shell they dubbed "Box-Car Charlie." [437] A flanking maneuver by the reserve Rifle Company supported by armor on the left and G Company on the right succeeded in gaining the forward slopes of Half Moon and the western end of Horseshoe; and by late afternoon the Third Battalion had reached high ground overlooking the Horseshoe depression. The Japanese counter attacked at 2200 with 700 troops, who were immediately hit by the combined force of six artillery battalions plus naval gunfire. The close quarter combat, which often involved hand-to-hand fighting, was over by midnight resulting in nearly 500 Japanese dead.

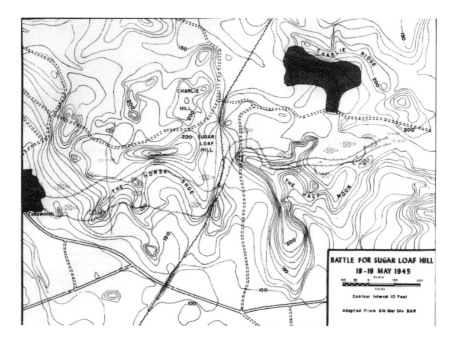

Map 15 Sugar Loaf Hill in relation to The Horseshoe, Charlie Hill and The Half Moon.

Sometime after 16 May, Bob filmed the attacking 4th Marines. On the evening of 20th he returned to the Photo Section to replenish his cartridges of exposed film and sat with his good friend Grant Wolfkill to write home.[438]

"20 May 1945 Sunday"
"Dear Folks,"

"This afternoon I received two letters from you (Mom) dated April 16th and 9 May. The first one included the pictures of the family and Grandmother W.; ….. All of you look fine. Zelda, you certainly are growing up! I shan't recognize you when I get back."

"I'm looking forward to seeing the Popular Photography (magazine) that you are sending. I'll certainly be able to use the camera. Thanks for sending it

"I certainly am glad that you saw the Agfa demonstration. At our former base we listened to a radio program, which broadcast from a different 'nite-spot' each time. Once it was from the Claremont

Hotel.[439] I have heard quite a bit about (it) and now from you. It must be alreet!"

"Wolfkill is here sitting next to me. We are with the 4th Marines, now. It is a crack outfit and deserves the good reputation that it has."

I'm shooting color film as I've been wanting to do. It's been so long though that I have to think more than once about my exposure. I'm catching on fast, though."

"Pardon the pencil; I left my pen back at the section."

"It's getting late, so I'll close.. Love Bob" "P.S. I received Zel's letter written 6 May the other day. Tell Marna hello."

"Sgt. R. L. Watson 490975"

Grant also wrote to his parents and mentioned that he was with Bob.[440]

The next morning they went out together then split up as Bob joined the marines attempting to gain a foothold on the Asato River. When they separated Grant told Bob, "Be careful, it's dangerous where you are going. The fighting is really intense."[441]

The Fourth Marines led the attack to capture a position along a line adjacent to the Asato River backed by the 22nd Marines' supporting fire. In spite of heavy rain that turned shell torn slopes into "slick mud-chutes" and strong enemy defenses, Third Battalion, Fourth Marines preceded by demolition and flamethrower teams managed to establish a defense line that reached halfway between Horseshoe and the Asato River. In order to overcome the devastating artillery fire from Shuri, that was outside the zone of action of the Sixth Division, which had impeded the advance of the Fourth Marines in the Half Moon area, the First Marine Division was redeployed to neutralize the Shuri bastion. As a result of that effort the 4th Marines were able to gain the northern bank of the Asato and send patrols across the shallow river 200 yards into the outskirts of Naha on 22 May. The troops dug in on the northern bank of the river while subjected to sporadic heavy artillery and mortar fire. Despite the continuing rain during the night, scouts from the 6th Reconnaissance Company were able to cross the river at will and determined "that the river was fordable at low tide" and "no occupied positions had been found."[442]

Because of the success of the patrols during the previous night, General Sheperd ordered the Fourth Marines to increase patrol activity across the river and to be prepared to cross in force if resistance proved to be light. From dawn until 1000 the marines "received long range machine gun and rifle fire from the high ground near Machisi," the immediate objective. Two assault battalions were able to wade across in shallow water and reach a ridge line near Machisi where reverse slope mortar emplacements and fire from fortified Okinawan tombs forced the advance to stop 100 yards short of the objective.

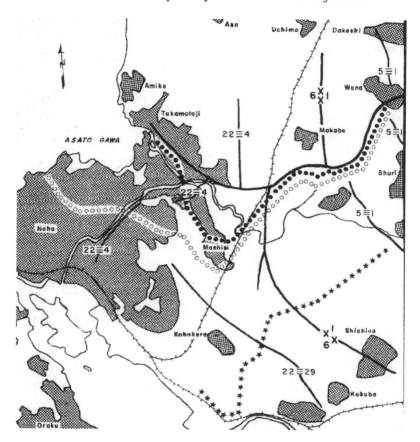

Map 16 Showing Objective Machisi across Asato River

Steady rain turned the once benign Asato into a "chest high raging torrent" forcing the marines to stand in the water for hours passing supplies by hand to troops on the other side while under heavy enemy fire. During the afternoon the 6th Engineer Battalion attempted to haul parts across the Asato in order to have sufficient material to build a Bailey bridge on the morning of the 24th. The convoy was forced to fall back because of unusually accurate enemy artillery fire, which severely wounded the Division Engineer and a bridging officer. The engineers then attempted to build a bridge using scuttled Amtracs as a base in the stream on which they intended to lay timbers. The plan was abandoned when anti-tank mines blew up two of the Amtracs. The engineers then resorted to laying two foot bridges 50-feet long across the river enabling troops to cross into Naha on the morning of the 24th.[443]

In order to adequately supply the troops advancing into Naha and to Machisi and to give armor support it became imperative that a bridge capable of carrying heavy equipment be constructed across the river. After the mines that destroyed the amtracs were swept from the area, the engineers began constructing an 80 foot long Bailey bridge at dawn on the 24th and worked all morning and part of the afternoon under "the most adverse terrain and weather conditions, and in the face of accurate enemy artillery shelling." [444] In order to have a record of the bridge construction, Sgt. Robert Watson was ordered there with his 16mm movie camera to film the activity in color. One more time Bob was on assignment, alone, by himself, in a chaotic situation, not with any of his friends, armed with his camera to film fellow Marines, brothers under arms who were unknown to him

Just one month shy of his twenty-first birthday, Bob filmed the construction effort from the ground, then moved onto the bridge for a different view of the activity. At 1410 the 6th Engineers sent a message to the 6th Division, "Bailey bridge in 1400 X Will require 45 minutes to doze approaches X Enemy bracketing it with Arty X Fire coming from east X."[445] A shell landed near the bridge spraying shrapnel that killed Bob and three other marines instantly. An engineer told Nugent, a cameraman also on the front line, that a photographer had been killed on the bridge. Nugent went there immediately and although Bob's identification disc and pocketbook disappeared during the mayhem, his damaged camera was beside him. When Nugent "saw the body he knew it was Bob, since he and Bob had been good friends back in Quantico."[446]

Glen Chittenden and Albert Walavich had been assigned to the 29th Marines and had returned to the Sixth Division Photo Section after Chittenden had been hit by a Japanese grenade. Two days later Captain Freulich head of the Photo Section told them of Bob's death.

88. Bailey Bridge across Asato River, photo by Hendrickson Marine Photographer

Esteemed by his friends in the photo section and highly regarded by his officers, the news of his death was devastating to the entire group. After official identification was complete, Bob was buried as soon as possible.. in "Grave #400, Row # 16, Plot B"[447], Sixth Marine Division Cemetery near Yontan Airfield.

89. Sixth Marine Division Cemetery   90. Grave 400, Row 16. Plot B

Lt. Harold Palmer and Bob's friends in the Photo Section paid their respects on Memorial Day at a service conducted by Chaplain D. Mayberry, an Episcopal minister.[448] The pall bearers were Lt. Harold Palmer, Pfc. Franklin K. Adler, Pfc. Frank A. Cannistraci, Sgt. Hoyt Rhodes, Corp. Albert R. Walavich and Corp. John Whittingham.

**91. Memorial Service for Sgt. Robert LeRoy Watson: Paul Bearers CCW:
Pfc. Franklin K. Adler, Pfc. Frank A. Cannistraci, Corp. John Whittingham,
Corp. Alfred R. Walavich, Lt. Harold Palmer, and Sgt. Hoyt Rhodes**

92. Grant Wolfkill says goodbye to a Good Friend; picture courtesy G. Wolfkill

15

AFTERMATH

Friday, the first day of June 1945 Bertha went to work as usual at Corbin's Photo Store in Vallejo where she was happy waiting on customers, but she especially enjoyed developing film and printing or enlarging photographs in the darkroom. There was nothing unusual about the day; Earle was at work on Mare Island Navy Yard and Zelda was in school at Vallejo Senior High School. Early in the afternoon an envelope was handed to Bertha that was covered with big bold letters declaring "Western Union Telegram." Through a cellophane window she could see that it was addressed to Mr. and Mrs. Earle L. Watson (Parents). Bertha was not expecting a telegram from anyone, certainly not at the photo store. Fearing for the safety of her oldest son Robert, a sudden rush of adrenalin made her nauseous as she stared at the ominous missive. Struggling with shaking hands she tore open the seal, pulled out a yellow form with narrow strips of paper pasted on it containing words sent by teletype that she was afraid to read. Forcing herself to focus on the dreaded document, quickly bypassing the salutation, she read,

"DEEPLY REGRET TO INFORM YOU THAT YOUR SON SERGEANT ROBERT L WATSON USMCR WAS KILLED IN ACTION 24 MAY 1945 AT OKINAWA ISLAND RYUKYU ISLANDS IN THE PERFORMANCE OF HIS DUTY AND SERVICE OF HIS COUNTRY"

Crying hysterically, the grieving young mother forced herself to continue reading the obligatory boilerplate language.

"WHEN INFORMATION IS RECEIVED REGARDING BURIAL YOU WILL BE NOTIFIED. TO PREVENT POSSIBLE AID TO OUR ENEMIES DO NOT DIVULGE THE NAME OF HIS SHIP OR STATION. PLEASE ACCEPT MY HEARTFELT SYMPATHY= A A VANDEGRIFT GENERAL USMC COMMANDANT OF THE MARINE CORPS"

AFTERMATH

By this time Bertha could hardly stand; Mr. and Mrs. Corbin rushed to her side, helped her sit down and tried their best to comfort the poor distraught mother who felt as if her very own life had been ripped from her. Reconciled to the devastating news Bertha forced herself to deal with the situation and managed to telephone Earle who immediately left work and headed home. A call was soon made to the Officer of the Day at the Navy Pre-Flight School, St. Mary's College located in the Moraga Valley, near San Francisco to inform Naval Cadet James Watson. Bertha also telephoned the sad news to Rita Turner, her landlady and friend, and asked her to keep an eye out for Zelda when she came home from school and to make sure she was not left alone. Zelda arrived home around 4 P.M. and Rita came over to be near her. When Bertha arrived she told Zelda who immediately burst into tears. Mother and daughter hugged each other, crying profusely while Rita tried to comfort them.

When Lt. Jake Miller, commander of the Eighth Battalion, received the information from the O.D. (officer of the day) he immediately called Jim out of the daily three hour Field and Track athletic session; took him aside and started telling him, "War is very dangerous and we have to expect that bad things can happen." Jim interrupted Miller and said, "You are going to tell me my brother was killed. Aren't you?" Lt. Miller confirmed Jim's worst fears and said he could have leave immediately to be with his parents. "You can go for the weekend or you can have two weeks leave, but in that case you will have to drop back a class." Jim replied firmly that he would just take the weekend, so he would not get behind his class and delay his completion of the course.

Jim was consoled by an older class mate who had been an air crewman flying off an aircraft carrier in the Pacific before entering Pre-Flight School. Talking to a combat veteran somehow made it easier for him to deal with the loss of his older brother. After a tearful shower he donned his dress uniform, took a Greyhound bus to Vallejo and walked toward his home. Feeling the need to talk to someone before facing his family, he stopped at a local department store where a good friend was working. Jim told her about his brother being killed, and after a consoling conversation continued on home.

When Jim walked in the door at 642 Louisiana Street he was immediately greeted with hugs from Bertha, Zelda and Earle. Everyone was crying and holding each other trying to come to terms with the terrible news. Earle, sobbing uncontrollably, asked Jim, "Was

I a good enough father?" Unhesitatingly he gave the answer his father wanted to hear, "Yes of course you were."

The anguished parents held out hope that it was a mistake because previously Captain Thayer Soule had told them that Bob had been reported killed once before, but the erroneous information was withdrawn and corrected before his family was notified. Sometime during this sad reunion Bertha managed to call Pat Niedert to tell her the devastating news. Naturally Pat burst into tears and could hardly talk; she was so distraught. The family spent the weekend sobbing, commiserating with each other and struggling to deal with the unreal, unbelievable reality that Bob was gone and they would never see him again. They tried to gain some comfort by attending Holy Communion and a memorial service in a small chapel at the Episcopal Church on Sunday. But the pain was magnified because Bertha and Earle were under the impression that Bob had been selected to attend officer's training, and if only his orders had come through earlier transferring him back to the states.

So many families had lost loved ones during this terrible war, fathers, brothers, sons and daughters and the end of hostilities was not in sight. The war in Europe was over, but plans were being made for the invasion of the Japanese home islands; there was still a long struggle ahead and more lives would be lost. The Watsons maintained their resolve and returned to their obligations: Jim bussed to St. Mary's Sunday night, Earle got up at his usual early hour Monday and caught the 6:30 Jitney to Mare Island, Bertha reported for work at Corbin's, and Zelda attended her first Monday morning class. Life went on; the family followed the normal routines with heavy heart and determination to see it through. One of the two blue service stars hanging in the window was replaced with a gold one. Bertha was now a "Gold Star Mother" joining the ranks of the thousands of other mothers who had lost sons in the world conflict.

When Zelda returned to school she was standing near a group of friends who were consoling Ann, a friend who had told them she had received a telegram informing her that her husband, a sailor, was missing in action. Unable to cope with the situation because of her own loss, Zelda started to walk away from the group and "was criticized for not "being sympathetic; "one of the girls told me I was being a snob." Zelda explained to her friends, "I'm sorry, but my brother was killed on Okinawa and I don't want to talk about it and I don't want to detract from Ann's attention." Such Incidents made it even harder for the family to deal with their grief.

Pat Niedert wrote to Bob's parents the day after she received the heart breaking news and informed them that she had received a letter from Bob the day before dated May 18, 1945. In that letter Bob "talked of coming home, and wanted to know where I'd like to go to spend a honeymoon. It wasn't very long—he said he wrote it so that I'd know he thought of me every second and so I wouldn't get lonely."

Pat's mother, Madge, also wrote with condolences and praise of Bob, "I can sincerely say that your son, Bob was a grand boy. He was considerate, full of fun, quiet and sincere in all his actions. We will never forget him; his memory will always be with us."[449]

"Your son, Bob, never figured on anything happening to him and always wrote to Pat with extreme faith in the future. He always quoted poetry and made up the nicest verses. He always seemed to be meeting her on a 'Grassy Hill' high above the clouds. He never wrote about the war and she received letters until the last, a cheerful and romantic letter."[450]

In early June General Vandegrift wrote a sympathetic letter[451] as a follow up to his earlier telegram. "It is a source of profound regret to me and to his comrades in the Marine Corps that your son, Sergeant Robert LeRoy Watson, United States Marine Corps Reserve, lost his life in action against the enemies of his country and I wish to express my deepest sympathy to you and members of your family in your great loss."

"There is little I can say to lessen your grief but it is my earnest hope that the knowledge of your son's splendid record in the service and the thought that he nobly gave his life in the performance of his duty may in some measure comfort you in this sad hour." Signed, A. A. Vandegrift.

On Okinawa 3000-4000 enemy forces attempted to abandon the Shuri bastion on 26 May, but were caught in the open and bombarded with naval gunfire that "blasted Japanese troops with their tanks, vehicles, and artillery pieces" killing an "estimated 500."[452].
Relentless harassing fire from all available sources was heaped on the enemy to keep him disorganized and to take advantage of the withdrawal. Unfortunately continuing rain and muddy terrain prevented the American forces from making a full-scale attack. By the 27th the Marines succeeded in crossing the Asato River and moved on into Naha. By 29 May elements of the First Marine Division were able to capture Shuri Castle "once the seat of the rulers of Okinawa" that

had served as the Japanese "center for controlling the defense of the island."[453] The Japanese were forced to withdraw eleven miles south of Shuri where they established new headquarters outside of Mabuni deep within a cave. The new position enabled the Japanese to slow the American advance while organizing the defense of the Kiyamu Peninsula. By the end of May the Tenth Army had overrun the Shuri redoubt and had seized all but eight square miles of the island; in the process "General Buckner's forces had killed an estimated 62,548 Japanese soldiers and captured 465 others in 61 days of the bloody endeavor."[454] On June 1 the operations at Hagushi Beach were changed from landing assault forces and equipment to garrison forces in anticipation of the occupation phase of Operation Iceberg.

During the first days of June the First Marine Division took up positions held by the Sixth Division, which prepared to invade the Oroku Peninsula and the Army's Seventh Division succeeded in reaching the east coast and closing off the Chinen Peninsula completely. On 4 June the Fourth Marines landed in LVT's on a 600-yard long beach divided into Red 1 and 2 while the 29th and 22nd Marines attacked from the North. Against stiff opposition from enemy forces ensconced in caves and tunnels the three Marine regiments of the Sixth Division succeeded in compressing the Japanese garrison on Oroku into a small pocket by 9 June. The Marines prevailed in spite of enemy artillery fire, counter attacks, mud that made use of tanks difficult, blown roads and bridges, small arms and automatic weapons fire, and grenade launcher barrages. The determined Japanese defenders initiated a series of local counter attacks against the marines during the night of 10-11 June; in response, General Sheperd "launched an all-out armor-supported attack, committing the greater portion of eight infantry battalions to destroy the enemy."[455] At 1750 on June 12, General Sheperd reported to General Geiger that all organized resistance on the peninsula had ended and after taking the nearby island of Senaga Shima on 14 June the ten-day battle for the. Oroku peninsula ended

Fighting continued with all elements of the Tenth Army participating to secure the entire island until 21 June when the official announcement of the end of all organized resistance was made. In an attempt to delay the American invasion of the Japanese home islands the futile defense of Okinawa cost the Japanese 107,539 dead and an additional 23,764 assumed sealed in caves or buried by the Japanese; approximately 42,000 of the total were assumed to be civilians who were unfortunately in the vicinity of Japanese troops who were killed by naval and artillery bombardments. The Tenth Army paid a high price for the conquest: 7,374 killed or died of wounds, 31,807 wounded or injured in combat, and 26,221 non-combat casualties. The British and American naval forces also suffered while supporting the Tenth Army during 82 days of ground operations: 34 ships and other vessels were sunk and 368 damaged; 763 carrier based aircraft were lost to all causes; 4,907 navy personnel were killed or missing in action; and 4,824 were wounded. American forces claimed the destruction of 7,830 Japanese aircraft and 16 combatant ships.[456]

Although leaders in the Navy and Army Air Force believed Japan's ultimate surrender could be achieved by blockade and aerial bombardment the Army argued for a full invasion of the industrial heartland. Plans were made for the necessary military action and conquests that would lead to the invasion of the home islands in March 1946. These plans were set aside after atomic bombs were dropped on Hiroshima 6 August and Nagasaki 9 August and the Japanese government sued for peace on 10 August. The Japanese government agreed to comply with terms established in the Potsdam declaration issued on July 26 as a result of a meeting attended by President Harry S. Truman, British Prime Minister Winston Churchill, and Soviet leader Joseph Stalin.

As the battle for Okinawa concluded and Japan unconditionally surrendered, the Watson family began to receive consoling letters from Bob's friends in the Marine Corps. Captain Soule now in Honolulu after the battle for Iwo Jima wrote, "I know there is nothing I can say to ease your sorrow, and I myself feel that I have lost a true and loyal friend. There is, I think, one thing you should fully realize. Bob was doing an exceptional job, a job of building in a world where most men were tearing down. Through his pictures he not only was recording history but helping, through training films, to save lives, when most men around him were taking them."

"There is little information that I can give as to details. He spent a lot of time at the front, and one day during a particularly, heavy fight, was hit by mortar fire. I have assurance from those who were there that the end was instantaneous."

"No doubt you will receive more letters, for Bob had many friends. I am, as you can see, very poor at writing letters-particularly of this type. I do want you to know, however, that even though someone else may express his thoughts more fully, I feel that I have lost a true and loyal friend He is not the first to go, nor will he, unfortunately be the last. He, like so many others who have done so much, cannot live to see the goal for which he fought.   For the moment, at least, he has gone ahead to that goal and beyond, to the ultimate good toward which we are all striving. We who must go slowly on will reach it too, and there he will be, with all the others who have gone ahead."[457]

Kolon Kilby, esteemed football coach at Vallejo High, paid tribute to Bob in his weekly newspaper column,[458] "We now know of more than 25 former Vallejo High School students who have paid the supreme sacrifice in the present world conflict. The last to be added to the long list was Robert LeRoy Watson, the kid with the pleasing smile. We not only recall Bob as the fellow with the winning smile, but we remember him most as a 'crack' end on the 1941 N.B.L. championship squad. Bob was one of those fellows possessed with a lot of courage. He was known in football as a 'crashing' end. That, my good ones, is a flank man who throws his body headlong under all of the interference that comes his way.   Yes, sir, it takes courage, nerve, and stamina, to become a crashing end and that, my friends, is what Bob was all wrapped up in one. We know that he was that kind of soldier on Okinawa. It's a tough assignment to put down in words our thoughts concerning the 'scrappy' fellow who was so well liked about the Apache campus. His younger brother, Jim, former Apache football captain in 1943, expressed his sentiments better than I could ever do, 'Bob is everything in kindness and personality that I could ever hope to be. I was and am as proud of him as anyone in this world. I guess certain things have to be the way they are; I only hope there is some mistake.' Our condolences go out to the whole Watson family, who will get some satisfaction from knowing that they had a hero son, loved by all that knew him. Good bye, Bob."

Lt. Harold Palmer, Bob's commanding officer in the III AC Photo Section, wrote "Bob was held in high esteem by all hands of this section. I cannot explain my feelings, regarding your loss, but Bob was a fine man, we thought the world of him."[459]

Bob's good friend Hoyt Rhodes that he had served with through three battles wrote, "For what comfort it is worth to you, I do know that Bob suffered no pain. He was killed instantly by a shell at the northern edge of Naha. He was photographing the erection of a bridge which was to be used by the 22nd Marines to cross a river into Naha. He died carrying out orders in his usual cheerful & efficient manner as a true marine." "As you might already know, Bob & I worked together on Guam, Peleliu & Okinawa. I don't know of anybody that I thought more of or would rather be with. His fine character & personality showed the result of a good home & careful upbringing. I am sure that there was nobody in the Photo Section that was better liked than Bob." "I am sure that Bob's loss was also felt greatly by Pat, as they were deeply in love, & would have made a fine couple."[460]

By direction of the Commandant of the Marines Corps, Colonel A. E. O'Neil informed Mr. and Mrs. Watson[461] "that you are entitled to the Purple Heart with gold star and the inclosed Purple Heart certificate posthumously awarded your son, the late Sergeant Robert LeR. Watson, U. S. Marine Corps Reserve, in the name of the President of the United States and by direction of the Secretary of the Navy."

Captain Soule wrote again,[462] "During the past few days I have seen several of the men who were with Bob, and all of them have told me repeatedly how much they miss him. It was a real shock to all of them, and I know you would be very proud if you could hear the fine things they say about him."

Grant Wolfkill wrote,[463] "Losing Bob was a terrible shock to all of us so I can appreciate your feelings at his leaving us. He was a wonderful friend and everything the Marine Corps looks for in a man--clean, honest, brave, and ambitious. We were staying together at the time with the Fourth Marines. As you say he would never have mentioned that he was in danger—he wasn't the type. We both wrote home that night—both mentioned being together, then went out together that next morning. We split up and that was that. I didn't see him again until it was all over. He went quickly, mercifully, without ever knowing that anything had happened. He went doing his duty. I am proud at having known Bob and will never forget him."

Lt Palmer and Grant were now together as they each wrote letters and Palmer replied to a letter from Bertha,[464] In addition to Nugent's identification confirmed by Glenn Chittenden, Palmer stated, "Bob's body was identified by Sgt. Hoyt Rhodes, it definitely was Bob. The identification disc and pocket book were lost, but his damaged camera was beside him, and Rhodes, being a very close friend, knew Bob very well. As much as I wish that I could pass a thread of hope on, that your boy may still be alive, I am sorry but he has definitely been identified."

"I know how this must have unnerved you, and I appreciate you writing to me for it makes me feel better to know that the Watson family is holding up after their loss. Yes. Everyone thought quite a bit of your boy. All Bob's personal articles should have reached you by now. In order to be sure that his personal effects did not go astray, I personally mailed them to you. I don't remember whether he had his wrist watch on or not, but if he was wearing it at the time he was in action the concussion might have thrown it off his arm."

'I am proud to know you folks, and to see how you are standing up under the loss. I showed your letter to Karl Soule, he was Bob's officer at Quantico. I tried to read your last paragraph out loud to him, but my voice cracked, I guess I'm not so brave."

"About Bob's school transcript-Well, Bob was very well liked by both officers and men. There was a letter of instruction about going to College, and I talked to Bob about going. I thought he would make a good officer, and the government would pay his way to college. It was the V-12. I explained he'd have to set Pat aside until he was commissioned, that was why he sent for his transcripts. By the time the records arrived, the program was completed and Bob's opportunity for college had fallen through."

In early Fall Zelda enrolled in San Jose State College and moved to a dormitory to begin her college studies. Earl began thinking about resigning his job at Mare Island so he could re-establish his electrical contracting business in Colusa. In October, after being given the choice of remaining in the Navy and completing the flight training program or being separated from the service in the inactive reserve, Jim elected the latter and made plans to enroll in the School of Engineering at the University of Washington to earn a degree in Aeronautical Engineering.

Thayer Soule, aka Karl, was getting out of the Marine Corps and making plans to return to his earlier profession of filming Travelogues. He informed the Watson's[465] "In a couple of weeks, Bob Van Derveer and I plan to leave for Mexico, driving down to make a movie for Holmes[466]. This is a project I have planned for several years, and now it is actually coming true----except for one detail. I had hoped that the last name of my companion would be Watson. Of course I can have no idea of how parents feel, but losing Bob was the worst thing in the whole war for me. (*Soule had hoped to hire Bob to work with him on the travelogue movie.*)

Sgt. Hoyt Rhodes was also honorably discharged and reunited with his wife in San Jose, California where he was employed in a large commercial bank. Zelda was able to meet him and learn more about her brother's experiences in the Pacific War. Hoyt maintained contact with the Watson's for many years.

A short time after Jim started classes at the University of Washington, Earle left Mare Island and he and Bertha moved back to Colusa. Earle restarted his electrical contracting business and Bertha opened a Photo studio. Although small, their businesses were successful and they quickly settled back into the community social life. Zelda finished a semester at San Jose State and returned to Colusa to seek employment. In May Madge Niedert informed them that Pat had met and fallen in love with a sailor stationed on the USS Franklin; they married and had an accident on a motorcycle coming home from their honeymoon. Although thrown from the bike and knocked unconscious, Pat was not seriously hurt but suffered from shock. Her new groom's arm, leg and side were injured, but also recovered. Everyone in the Watson family was supportive of Pat's decision to marry; she too needed to get on with her life.

Zelda soon responded to the charms of a young suitor and married Byron Harbison on September 1, 1946. They moved to a small house on the Harbison family farm where Byron had been working ever since his discharge from the Army.

Thanks to the effort of Doctor Edwin Pierce, in December 1946, the family received notification that "Members of the Vallejo 20-30 club presented to the Scouts of Troop 9, Boy Scouts of America, a collection of merit badge pamphlets which established the Robert L. Watson Memorial Library for the troop which they sponsor. The library is being established by the 20-30 Club in memory of Robert L. Watson who was killed in action in World War II on Okinawa while serving with the United States Marines. Watson was prominent in scouting, being a Life Scout and at the time of his entry into the Marine Corps, and second mate of Sea Scout Ship 99 which at that time was sponsored by the 20-30 Club."[467]

An official letter arrived in July 1945 informing the grieving parents that "you are entitled to the Purple Heart with gold star and the inclosed Certificate Posthumously awarded to your son....." "You are also entitled to the Asiatic-Pacific Campaign Medal...." A second letter denied entitlement to the "Navy Unit Commendation awarded the First Provisional Marine Brigade" for service in the recapture of Guam because the III Amphibious Corps Photo Section was not included in the commendation. Even though Bob was assigned to the Brigade, the bureaucracy could not recognize his service. Another letter in October

1946 added the American Campaign medal and the Victory Medal World War II, and also the "Presidential Unit citation with ribbon bar and two stars awarded the First Marine Division, reinforced, for service on Peleliu and Ngesebus, Palau Islands, and Okinawa, Ryuku Islands." Although Bob did not serve with the First Division on Okinawa, he was entitled to the commendation. Conversely even though he served on Okinawa with the Headquarters Signal Battalion and the Sixth Division of the III Amphibious Corps he was not awarded the unit commendations.

General Shepherd, Commanding General, Sixth Division, wrote a letter of appreciation to the Division Photo Section, Copy Captain Freulich, in which he wrote, "It is my desire to express to the personnel of the Photographic Section my admiration and sincere appreciation for their wholehearted cooperation and untiring effort and for their excellent work accomplished during the Okinawa operation." He also mentioned that the section of approximately thirty-eight men "suffered a total of fourteen casualties, of which four were killed in action." These numbers do not include the photographers assigned to the First Division or the III AC Corps Photo Sections. All of the citations are included in Appendix 4.

While still grieving, especially Bertha who would burst into tears whenever she thought of Bob, the family was reminded again of their loss when Earle received a letter from the new Commandant of the Marine Corps, General C.B. Gates. The letter informed him that "The return of American dead of World War II from overseas cemeteries has been provided for by the Congress. The records of this office indicate that you are the person authorized to direct the final disposition of the remains of the late Sergeant Robert L. Watson, U. S. Marine Corps."[468]Earle, with Bertha's approval, rejected the option of burial at the National Cemetery, Honolulu, Territory of Hawaii or the Philippine Islands. They decided against burial in any National Cemetery, and elected to have their son's remains buried in the Colusa Cemetery.

A year later, after multiple exchanges of correspondence, notification of shipment of remains accompanied by a military escort, and bill of lading for a headstone, a sealed casket was shipped from Okinawa to California and eventually arrived in Colusa consigned to J. D. McNary's Mortuary. The funeral was scheduled for Saturday April 9, 1949 to allow time for out of town friends and relatives, including Jim in Seattle, to arrive. The week turned into a very sad and difficult time especially for Bertha: Her father, Hiter Capito, died on Tuesday, the same day his brother Leonidas, aka Dassy, was buried. An Episcopal funeral service was held for Bob at 11 A. M. and a service was held for Hiter at 2 P.M. in a church of another denomination: Graveside services were held separately.

A tent was set up at Bob's gravesite to accommodate the family and close relatives. There was a substantial attendance including several of the thirteen-member Colusa County Marine Corps League organized by Ned Steele, who had played football with Bob and served with the First Division on Guadalcanal, Gloucester and Peleliu. There was a brief Episcopal graveyard service followed by the Marine escort's presentation of the American flag with 48 stars to Bertha. The casket was sprinkled with flowers and dirt and prepared for lowering into the pit. After considerable crying and offering of condolences the family returned home for refreshments and consolations from friends.

Ned Steele and members of the Marine Corps League retired to a local bar where they held an all night wake. The former Marines offered toast after toast to their departed friend, interspersed with choruses of the Marines Hymn sung at least a hundred times. "From the halls of Montezuma to the shores of Tripoli......We are proud to claim the title of United States Marines." Memories of Bob were recounted followed by praises for his courage, character and friendship. As the night wore on the singing became more raucous, the voices hoarse and the wake more celebratory. When dawn sneaked up on the revelers they were a motley bunch of soused Marines, proud of their service and proud of their lost comrade who gave his life for the Corps and his country.

EPILOGUE

E arle reestablished his business relationship with Jack Burton, owner of a Colusa hardware store, and successfully operated a modest electrical contracting business until his retirement in 1965. With his own labor, he built a 1,200 square foot house plus a separate photo studio, shop and garage. Earle always enjoyed a round of golf, and after retirement typically played 36 holes several days a week. As he grew older the number was reduced to 27 then 18, and finally quit when his legs hurt after 16. Death came at the age of 88 after a long bout with emphysema.

Bertha established a successful photography business operated from the studio Earle had built. She specialized in portraits, but was often hired by the local sheriff to photograph automobile accidents and crime scenes. Her most interesting job was photographing flooded farmland from a two seat light aircraft. Bertha passed away at the age of 86 after suffering a stroke.

Zelda and her husband Byron raised two boys and a girl. After farming for a few years Byron worked in various building trades until retirement. Zelda was employed in the Colusa County Library System for twenty-nine years until her retirement in 1989. After being widowed in 1997, she became active in the Episcopal Church and continues to serve as a lay preacher. Zelda dotes on her five grandchildren and four Great grandchildren.

Ned Steele returned to Colusa after the war and took over his father's movie theater business. He eventually operated five theaters and a freight business hauling movie films up and down the west coast of the United States. Ned joined his brother in Oregon raising cattle until his retirement. The old warrior died in 2012 a few months after his 89th birthday.

Lt. Colonel Karl Soule pursued an active travelogue photo business until his retirement in 1995. After completing each film he traveled the country presenting the films and narrating in theaters. Karl wrote two books: "Shooting the Pacific War", a narrative of his years in the Marine Corps; and "On the Road with Travelogues" that related his years in the photo travelogue business. Karl and his wife retired to Arizona. He maintained correspondence with Earle and Bertha until their deaths. Karle died in January 2004.

Hoyt Rhodes lived and worked in San Jose until his retirement, after which he and his wife moved to Lake Almanor, California where he continued to pursue his photographic interests.

Glenn Chittenden was sent to China after the battle for Okinawa and returned to California after discharge from the Corps in 1946. As of 2009, Glenn was living in northern California.

Grant Wolfkill worked for Karl Soule for a few years then became a BBC and then an NBC field producer. Grant was captured in Laos after a helicopter crash May1961 along with the pilot and a crewman. They were imprisoned and shackled for fifteen months by the communist Pathet Lao. Grant's determined fortitude helped his fellow prisoners survive for which President John F. Kennedy awarded him the Freedom Medal in 1962. He wrote his story, "Reported to be Alive" with Jerry Rose. Leading a very energetic life, Grant won second place driving a Porsche Spyder in the 1960 Macau Grand Prix. He continued to work as a photojournalist for a number of years until he was appointed vice president of public information for a pharmaceutical company. Married with two successful children; he is now retired and lives in the State of Washington.

Lt. Harold Tiger Palmer became owner of a successful real estate business in Glendale, California. In 2008 at the age of 92 he went to the office twice a week and had kidney dialysis three times a week.

Akiji Yoshumira returned to Colusa and managed his in-laws dry cleaning business until his retirement. He and his wife traveled to Washington D.C. to visit the Smithsonian Museum to view the display of Merrill's raiders and photographs of him as a Lt. in the Burma campaign. Unfortunately he died of an aneurism before he was able to see the display.

James Watson graduated from the University of Washington with Bachelor of Science degrees in Aeronautical and Mechanical engineering. He had a successful 37-year career in the Defense Aerospace Industry. In 2008 James was given the Distinguished Alumnus award by the Aeronautics and Astronautics Department of the University of Washington School of Engineering. He married Diane Rebard and together they had three children and four grandchildren. In 2008 James and Diane sailed on a "World War II" Cruise to the Pacific visiting many of the islands prominent during the war including Guadalcanal, Guam and Okinawa. They visited the Peace Memorial constructed on the southern part of Okinawa where they located Robert LeRoy Watson's name among the names of all those who died on the Island.

93. Prefectural Peace Memorial, Photo by James Watson

94. Prefectural Peace Memorial Name Display, Photo by James Watson

95. James Watson standing by R L Watson's Name, photo by Diane Watson

96. Close up of Robert LeRoy Watson's Name, Photo by James Watson

APPENDIX 1

"This Is My Rifle"
The Creed of a US Marine

This is my rifle. There are many like it, but this one is mine.

My rifle is my best friend. It is my life. I must master it as I must master my life.

My rifle, without me, is useless. Without my rifle, I am useless. I must fire my rifle true. I must shoot straighter than my enemy who is trying to kill me. I must shoot him before he shoots me. I WILL...

My rifle and myself know that what counts in this war is not the rounds we fire, the noise of our burst, nor the smoke we make. We know that it is the hits that count. WE WILL HIT...

My rifle is human, even as I, because it is my life. Thus, I will learn it as a brother. I will learn its weaknesses, its strength, its parts, its accessories, its sights and its barrel. I will ever guard it against the ravages of weather and damage as I will ever guard my legs, my arms, my eyes and my heart against damage. I will keep my rifle clean and ready. We will become part of each other. WE WILL...

Before God, I swear this creed. My rifle and myself are the defenders of my country. We are the masters of our enemy. WE ARE THE SAVIORS OF MY LIFE.

So be it, until victory is America's and there is no enemy, but peace!

APPENDIX 2

ORDERS

1990-100-35-fc   MARINE CORPS SCHOOLS
       MARINE BARRACKS, QUANTICO, VIRGINIA.

                         16 March 1944.

MARINE CORPS SCHOOLS)
            :   Transfer
TRANSFER ORDER #190-44)

References: (a) MC Serial #21)29, dated 13 March 1944.
              (b) CMC ltr 1990- to AN-321-ac to Comdt., MCS,
                  dated 10 September 1942.

    1.   In accordance with instructions contained in
reference (a), the following transfer is hereby ordered effective
17 March 1944:

    FROM: Marine Corps Schools Detachment (Photographic
                 Section), Marine Corps Schools.
    TO: Headquarters, Fleet Marine Force, San Diego Area,
                 Camp Elliott, Linda Vista, California.

WATSON, Robert L., Corporal (EPR)   (490976)   (SSN-043)

    2.   Corporal Robert L. WATSON, #490975, will proceed
via rail to Headquarters, Fleet Marine Force, San Diego Area,
Camp Elliott, Linda Vista, California, leaving this post on
17 March 1944, whereupon arrival he will report to the Commanding
General, thereat, for further transfer to the First Marine Amphibious Corps, for duty, with the Photographic Section of that Corps.

    3.   Staff returns will be forwarded by mail.

    4.   Corporal WATSON is authorized to delay fifteen (15)
days in reporting to Camp Elliott, Linda Vista, California, and
has given his address while on delay as: 642 Louisiana Street,
Vallejo, California.

    5.   Corporal WATSON is directed to maintain proper
decorum at all times while traveling on trains and other conveyances
and is warned not to discuss matters pertaining to naval policies
or administration with persons outside of the U. S. Naval Service.
Violation of these orders will result in disciplinary action.

    6.   The Post Quartermaster will furnish the necessary
transportation and subsistence for the travel involved. All un-
used transportation requests, railroad tickets or portions thereof
will be immediately turned over to the Post Quartermaster upon
arrival at destination.

    7.   The travel herein enjoined is necessary in the
public service.

        BY COMMAND OF BRIGADIER GENERAL C. B. CATES:

                                F. L. ANDERSON,
                                2dLt, USMCWR,
                        Assistant Adjutant-Secretary.

Copy to: CMC.   CG, FMF, Camp Elliott, Calif.
            CG, Post.   CG, 1st Marine Amphibious Corps.
            PM, HQMC.   OIC, Photo Section.
            QM, HQMC.   CO, MCSDetachment.
            Post PM.   Personnel Clerk, MCS.
            Schools QM.   F I L E.
            Post QM.   Corporal WATSON.

Orders for Corporal Watson to First Amphibious Corps

2445-30
7/49-gwl
Serial 3521

HEADQUARTERS, III AMPHIBIOUS CORPS
c/o Fleet Post Office
San Francisco

14 February, 1945.

From: The Commanding General,
To :   Sergeant Hoyt RHODES, (456199), U. S. Marine Corps
          Reserve.
          Sergeant Robert L. WATSON, (490975), U. S. Marine
          Corps Reserve.
          Corporal Robert SIMPSON, (284493), U. S. Marine Corps
          Reserve.
Via :   The Commanding Officer, Headquarters and Service
          Battalion, Corps Troops, III Amphibious Corps.

Subject: Orders to temporary duty.

     1.   On or about 15 February, 1945, you will report to the
Commanding Officer, III Corps Signal Battalion, Corps Troops, III
Amphibious Corps, for temporary duty in connection with verbal in-
structions.

     2.   Upon completion of this temporary duty and when di-
rected by competent authority, you will return to your regular
station and resume your regular duties.

     3.   There is no expense to the government involved in
the execution of these orders and none is authorized.

                              E. YALOWITZ,
                              By direction.
- -
Copy to: CG, FMF, Pac
             C-1, III PhibCor
             C-2, III PhibCor
             PhotoO, III PhibCor
             CO, SoPacEch, FMF, Pac
             CO, CorTrs, III PhibCor
             CO, III CorSigBn, CorTrs, III PhibCor
             CO, Hq&ServBn, CorTrs, III PhibCor (2)
             Each man (10)
             F I L E
- -

Orders for Sgt. Watson to III Corps Signal Battalion

APPENDIX 3

NOTIFICATION OF WIA AND KIA

IN REPLYING ADDRESS
COMMANDANT OF THE MARINE CORPS
WASHINGTON 25, D. C.
AND REFER TO

SERIAL 490975
DGU-296-pm

HEADQUARTERS U. S. MARINE CORPS
WASHINGTON

7 November, 1944.

My dear Mr. and Mrs. Watson:

     Delayed information has just reached this Headquarters that your son, Sergeant Robert L. Watson, U. S. Marine Corps Reserve, was wounded in action in the Palau Islands. The report further states that his injury responded to medical treatment and he was discharged from the hospital on 26 September, 1944.

     Doubtless your son has communicated with you since that time, informing you of his welfare. However, should any further reports regarding him be received, you will be informed promptly. Please notify this Headquarters immediately of any change in your address.

     Sincerely yours,

     D. ROUTH,
     Major, U. S. Marine Corps.

Mr. and Mrs. Earle L. Watson,
  642 Louisiana Street,
    Vallejo, California.

Notification of Wounded in Action on Peleliu

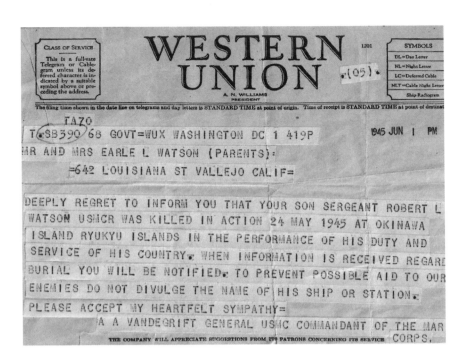

DEEPLY REGRET TELEGRAM

US MARINE CORPS CASUALTY REPORT KIA OKINAWA

APPENDIX 4

AWARDS AND COMMENDATIONS

IN REPLYING ADDRESS
COMMANDANT OF THE MARINE CORPS
WASHINGTON 25, D. C.
AND REFER TO

SERIAL 490975
DGP-cag

HEADQUARTERS U. S. MARINE CORPS

WASHINGTON

JUL 2 4 1945

My dear Mr. and Mrs. Watson:

    I am directed by the Commandant of the Marine Corps to inform you that you are entitled to the Purple Heart with gold star and the inclosed Purple Heart Certificate posthumously awarded your son, the late Sergeant Robert LeR. Watson, U. S. Marine Corps Reserve, in the name of the President of the United States and by direction of the Secretary of the Navy. The Purple Heart which is being engraved will be forwarded to you within the next two months.

    You are also entitled to the Asiatic-Pacific Campaign Medal for your son's service in the Asiatic-Pacific Area. The medal will not be ready for issuance until six months after the war, and it is requested that you make application to this office for the award at that time.

Sincerely yours,

A. E. O'NEIL,
Colonel, U. S. Marine Corps.

Inclosure: 1.

Mr. and Mrs. Earle L. Watson,
   642 Louisiana St.,
     Vallejo, Calif.

Notice of Entitlement to Purple Heart with Gold Star

IN REPLYING ADDRESS
COMMANDANT OF THE MARINE CORPS
WASHINGTON 25, D. C.
AND REFER TO

SERIAL 490975
DGF-gjf

HEADQUARTERS U. S. MARINE CORPS
WASHINGTON

JUN 18 1946

My dear Mr. and Mrs. Watson:

In reply to your letter of recent date, information is furnished that in addition to the awards mentioned in our letter to you dated 24 July 1945, as next of kin of the late Sergeant Robert LeR. Watson, U. S. Marine Corps Reserve, you are also entitled to the American Campaign Medal for your son's service in the United States during World War II and the Victory Medal for his service during World War II. The medals will be forwarded to you as soon as they are available. In the event you change your address, please notify this office.

You are not entitled to the Navy Unit Commendation awarded the First Provisional Marine Brigade for service in action against the enemy on Guam, Marianas Islands, inasmuch as the organization with which your son served, was not included in the Commendation.

Sincerely yours,

A. E. O'Neil,
Colonel, U. S. Marine Corps.

Mr. and Mrs. Earle L. Watson,
P. O. Box #137,
Colusa, California.

Entitlement of American Campaign Medal, and Victory Medal; Declination of Navy Unit Commendation awarded the First Provisional Brigade for Service in action against the enemy on Guam

The failure to recognize Corporal Watson's entitlement to the Navy Unit Commendation awarded the First Provisional Brigade was undoubtedly the result of a bureaucratic error. Clearly his service with the 22nd Marines on Guam entitled him to the commendation.

THE SECRETARY OF THE NAVY
WASHINGTON

The Secretary of the Navy takes pleasure in commending the
FIRST PROVISIONAL MARINE BRIGADE

for service as follows:

"For outstanding heroism in action against enemy Japanese forces during the invasion of Guam, Marianas Islands, from July 21 to August 10, 1944. Functioning as a combat unit for the first time, the First Provisional Marine Brigade forced a landing against strong hostile defenses and well camouflaged positions, steadily advancing inland under the relentless fury of the enemy's heavy artillery, mortar and small arms fire to secure a firm beachhead by nightfall. Executing a difficult turning movement to the north, this daring and courageous unit fought its way ahead yard by yard through mangrove swamps, dense jungles and over cliffs and, although terrifically reduced in strength under the enemy's fanatical counterattacks, hunted the Japanese in caves, pillboxes and foxholes and exterminated them. By their individual acts of gallantry and their indomitable fighting teamwork throughout this bitter and costly struggle, the men of the First Provisional Marine Brigade aided immeasurably in the restoration of Guam to our sovereignty."

James Forrestal

JAMES FORRESTAL,
Secretary of the Navy.

All personnel serving in the First Provisional Marine Brigade, comprised of: Headquarters Company; Brigade Signal Company; Brigade Military Police Company, 4th Marines, Reinforced; 22nd Marines, Reinforced, Naval Construction Battalion Maintenance Unit 515; and 4th Platoon, 2nd Marine Ammunition Company, during the above mentioned period are hereby authorized to wear the NAVY UNIT COMMENDATION Ribbon.

Navy Unit Commendation for First Provisional Brigade

Another error was made with regard to the Presidential Unit Citation awarded the First Marine Division for service on Peleliu and Okinawa. Corporal Watson served with the Seventh Marines on Peleliu and was therefore entitle to the first award. The second star for service on Okinawa was misdirected because he did not serve there with the First Division, but did serve with the Sixth Division.

Presidential Unit Citation Awarded the First Marine Division for Service on Peleliu and Okinawa

Because Sgt. Watson served with the Fourth Marines Sixth
Division on Okinawa he should have also received posthumously
the Presidential Unit Citation for that organization.

THE SECRETARY OF THE NAVY,
Washington.

The President of the United States takes pleasure in presenting the PRESIDENTIAL
UNIT CITATION to the

SIXTH MARINE DIVISION, REINFORCED

consisting of
The Sixth Marine Division; First Marine War Dog Platoon; Fifth Provisional Rocket
Detachment; Third Platoon, First Bomb Disposal Company; Marine Observation Squad-
ron Six; Sixth Joint Assault Signal Company; First Armored Amphibian Battalion;
Fourth Amphibian Tractor Battalion; Ninth Amphibian Tractor Battalion; First
Section, Second Platoon, First Bomb Disposal Company; 708th Amphibian Tank Bat-
talion, U. S. Army; Third Armored Amphibian Battalion (less 4 platoons); 91st
Chemical Mortar Company (Separate), U. S. Army; First Platoon, Company B, 713th
Armored Flame-Thrower Battalion, U. S. Army,
for service as set forth in the following

CITATION:
"For extraordinary heroism in action against enemy Japanese forces during the
assault and capture of Okinawa, April 1 to June 21, 1945. Seizing Yontan Airfield in
its initial operation, the SIXTH Marine Division, Reinforced, smashed through organized resistance to capture Ishikawa Isthmus, the town of Nago and heavily fortified
Motobu Peninsula in 13 days. Later committed to the southern front, units of the
Division withstood overwhelming artillery and mortar barrages, repulsed furious
counterattacks and staunchly pushed over the rocky terrain to reduce almost impreg-
nable defenses and capture Sugar Loaf Hill. Turning southeast, they took the capital
city of Naha and executed surprise shore-to-shore landings on Oroku Peninsula, securing the area with its prized Naha Airfield and Harbor after nine days of fierce fighting. Reentering the lines in the south, SIXTH Division Marines sought out enemy
forces entrenched in a series of rocky ridges extending to the southern tip of the
island, advancing relentlessly and rendering decisive support until the last remnants
of enemy opposition were exterminated and the island secured. By their valor and
tenacity, the officers and men of the SIXTH Marine Division, Reinforced contributed
materially to the conquest of Okinawa, and their gallantry in overcoming a fanatic
enemy in the face of extraordinary danger and difficulty adds new luster to Marine
Corps history, and to the traditions of the United States Naval Service."
For the President.

JAMES FORRESTAL,
Secretary of the Navy.

Sixth Marine Division Presidential Unit Citation

Had he survived, Sgt. Watson surely would have received a copy of the letter of appreciation from General Lemuel C. Shepherd Jr. to the Photographic Section, Sixth Marine Division

```
1355                      HEADQUARTERS
043/163              SIXTH MARINE DIVISION
                         IN THE FIELD

                                      5 June, 1945.
     Serial:


     From:       The Commanding General.
     To  :       The Photographic Section, Sixth Marine Division.

     Subject:    Letter of Appreciation.

          1.         It is my desire to express to the personnel of
     the Photographic Section my admiration and sincere apprecia-
     tion for their wholehearted cooperation and untiring efforts
     and for their excellent work accomplished during the OKINAWA
     operation.

          2.         Within a period of two months, your section of
     approximately thirty-eight men suffered a total of fourteen
     casualties, of which four were killed in action.  Despite
     these heavy casualties, photographers remained constantly
     with the most forward elements, risking their lives in order
     to obtain the best possible combat pictures.

          3.         You have set and maintained an enviable record
     for processing pictures in the field.  Your work has pro-
     vided unit commanders with valuable information prior to their
     advances into enemy territory, and they have stated on various
     occasions that time and lives have been saved by your efforts.

          4.         The courage, determination, and efficiency of
     the Sixth Marine Division Photographic Section have been at
     all times in keeping with the highest traditions of the
     Naval Service.

                              [signature] Lemuel C Shepherd
                              LEMUEL C. SHEPHERD, Jr.
     - - - - - - - - - - - - - - - - - - - - - - - - - - - - - - -
     Copy to:      Captain Freulich
                   SRB each man concerned.
     - - - - - - - - - - - - - - - - - - - - - - - - - - - - - - -
```

**Letter of Appreciation from General Shepherd to Sixth Marine Division
Photographic Section**

END NOTES

PROLOGUE

[1] The Donner Party led by George Donner and James F. Reed traveled from Missouri to California Sierra Mountains via a so-called short cut that in fact delayed their arrival until October 1846. The Party made up of several families became trapped in the Sierras because of heavy snows. Almost half the party died before they were rescued. The passage they took became known as the Donner Pass.

[2] Encyclopedia.com source: The Columbia Encyclopedia Sixth Edition, Selective Service Training Act

[3] From American Legion Youth Programs

CHAPTER 1

[4] Bertha Watson's diary

[5] The base was commissioned as the Marine Advanced Expeditionary Base, San Diego, California on December 1, 1921. It was also the headquarters of the 5th Marine Brigade. The West Coast Marine Recruit Depot located at Mare Island Navy Shipyard in Vallejo, California moved to the new base in August 1923. On January 1, 1948 it was officially designated as the Marine Corps Recruit Depot, San Diego.

[6] Post card dated January 11, 1943

[7] Letter postmarked January 11, 1943

[8] Letter postmarked January 11, 1943

[9] Ibid

[10] Lyrics found in Bob's effects.

[11] Letter dated January 17, 1943

[12] Ibid

[13] Letter dated January 22, 1943. This would have been Bob's last paycheck from his job as an electrician's helper.

[14] Ibid

[15] To the Shores of Tripoli released in 1942 featured John Payne as a wealthy son of an officer whose cocky attitude was modified by his sergeant played by Randolph Scott. The movie earned an Oscar nomination for Best Color Cinematography.

[16] Letter dated January 26, 1943

[17] Ibid

CHAPTER 2

[18] Letter dated January 30, 1943

[19] Camp Matthews was closed August 21, 1964. The University of California at La Jolla is now located on the former site of the camp

[20] Conversation with Captain Jerry Conover, retired. Conover marched his platoon from the recruit depot to Camp Mathews when he was a drill instructor during the Korean War.

[21] Letter dated February 2, 1943

[22] Letter dated February 6, 1943

[23] Ibid

[24] Bill Pillsbury was a fellow member of the DeMolay and also a fellow sea scout.

[25] His mother's thirty-eighth birthday was January 30, 1943 as was his parents' twenty-first wedding anniversary.

[26] Letter dated February 6, 1943

[27] Letter dated February 9, 1943

[28] Letter also dated February 9, 1943

[29] Tyrone Power was in the 3rd Platoon and eventually qualified. He enlisted in August 1942 as a private in spite of his studio's offer to get him an officer's commission. Before Power could start Boot Camp he was sent back to 20th Century Fox at the request of the studio to film the movie "Crash Dive". It was a patriotic film and credits included Tyrone Power, U.S.M.C.R. After finishing boot camp, he went to officer's candidate school in Quantico, Virginia and was commissioned a 2nd Lieutenant. Because Power had already flown substantial hours as a civilian private pilot he was processed through a short intensive flight training program at Corpus Christi, Texas. He earned his Naval Aviator's gold wings and was promoted to First Lieutenant. Power served in the Pacific theater with VMR-352 delivering supplies to Iwo Jima while flying an R5C military transport.

[30] Letter dated February 16, 1943

[31] Letter dated February 18, 1943

CHAPTER 3

[32] Letter to Jim dated February 20, 1943

[33] Letter dated February 20, 1943

[34] Letter dated February 22, 1943

[35] Letter dated February 25, 1943

[36] Lee Scott was a cornet player and leader of a big band in Vallejo. He asked Jim to audition with the band when it played for a dance. After half hour of playing, Lee hired Jim to play whenever the second trumpet player, a fireman, was on duty at the firehouse. The pay was two dollars an hour.

[37] Letter dated March 1, 1943

[38] Letter dated March 4, 1943

[39] Letter dated March 6, 1943

[40] Letter dated March 7, 1943

[41] Standby For Action was a typical wartime movie. Bosley Crowther in a review published March 12, 1943 wrote, "It centers about another of those impudent whelps who must learn a service code." Robert Taylor stars as "a

sneering, smart-cracking society naval officer, and Brian Donlevy" stars as "the hard-way commander of an old line destroyer" who shapes up Taylor with the help of Walter Brennan "the ancient Mariner, and Charles Laughton, who "plays Old Iron Pants, the admiral."

[42] Four stacker destroyers entered service with the U.S. Navy at the end of World War I. They were obsolete before World War II, but fifty were transferred to the British Royal and the Canadian Navies as part of the lend lease program. Some saw front line service with the U.S. Navy at the beginning of the war, but were later relegated to convoy service and fast transport. Most of the ships were altered in numerous ways and few remained with four stacks. Many had one or two of the four boilers removed to increase the range or provide more accommodations. Some modified, as high-speed transports were equipped with four landing craft with room for 200 marines and were used during the Pacific campaign. Bob worked on some of these ships as an electrician's helper on Mare Island. It would be ironic if he worked on the fast transports later used by the marines in the pacific.

[43] From the web page of the California State Military Department, The California State Military Museum, Preserving California's Military Heritage, San Diego Metropolitan Area during World War II.

[44] Ryan Aeronautical Company later developed the X-13 Verti-Jet, the vertical take-off and landing tail sitter. The author was the group flight test engineer for the project from 1953 to 1956.

[45] Letter dated March 9, 1943

[46] Letter dated March 10, 1943

[47] Karl Thayer Soule, Shooting the Pacific War: Marine Corps Combat Photography in WW II (Lexington, Kentucky: The University Press of Kentucky), pp. 11-17.

[48] Letter dated March 10, 1943

[49] Letter dated March 12, 1943

[50] From extant copies of tax returns

[51] Letter dated March 13, 1943

[52] Letter dated March 15, 1943

[53] Horace Heidt was one of the most successful bandleaders during the late 1930s and early 1940s. He had the ability to find and recruit good talent. Performing constantly on the radio, he and his orchestra had more than 50 hit records. Many future successful jazz players, including pianist Frankie Carle and guitarist Alvino Rey, played in Heidt's orchestra before becoming famous themselves. One of his vocal groups was Donna and her Don Juans, led by Donna Woods. Gordon Mac Rae was featured in the group at times as was Art Carney who became famous in the television show "The Honeymooners"

[54] Fred Lowery, blinded by scarlet fever when he was two years old, became the most successful professional whistler during the 1940s and 1950s. He practiced whistling seriously when his fellow students at the Texas School for the Blind in Austin encouraged him. Whistling was considered a novelty musical act at that time and Lowery found success. His whistling was more than a novelty and he had no trouble finding work. He was perhaps best

known for his rendition of "Indian Love Call" a popular song from the film Rose Marie starring Jeannette MacDonald and Nelson Eddy

[55] Letter dated March 17, 1943

[56] Letter dated March 19, 1943

[57] Letter dated March 25, 1943

[58] Letter date April 1, 1943

[59] The Marine Corps Base located near Quantico, Virginia was an important facility during World War II where the Officer Candidate and Photo Section Schools were established early in the war. The First Marine Aircraft Wing was also developed there

[60] John C. Fremont High School in Los Angeles had the United States' first high school photography class founded by Clarence A. Bach. One hundred forty-six combat photographers were graduates of Fremont High School.

CHAPTER 4

[61] Letter dated April 5, 1943

[62] Bob's uncle Raymond Capito who was now in the Army

[63] Letter dated April 5, 1943

[64] Letter dated April 5, 1943 from Leta Clifford to Bertha

[65] Bertha's diary March 31, 1943

[66] Letter date April 11, 1943

[67] Ibid

[68] From a second letter dated April 11, 1943

[69] Letter dated April 13, 1943

[70] Letter dated April 14, 1943

[71] Letter to Jim dated April 14, 1943

[72] Letter dated April 16, 1943

[73] Letter dated April 19, 1943

[74] Ibid

[75] Glenn Miller was a trombone player and a famous bandleader in the 1940s. At the age of 38, too old to be drafted, Miller persuaded the Army to let him enlist and lead an Air Force Band. He broadcast a radio propaganda program to Germany in which he discussed the war effort in the German language. On December 15, 1944, Major Miller was flying from London to Paris to perform for the soldiers that had just liberated Paris when his small plane went down in the English Channel. Neither he nor any of the crew was ever found.

[76] Letter dated April 20, 1943

[77] Letter to Jim and Zelda dated April 20, 1943

[78] From letter dated April 26, 1943

[79] Letter to Zelda dated April 26, 1943

CHAPTER 5

[80] Letter dated May 4, 1943

[81] Floyd Capito was the youngest brother of Hiter Capito, Bertha's father. Floyd was a long time merchant in New Franklin, Mo who sold many items over the years including horse whips, the first radios and refrigerators,

Studebaker cars, and in his later year's furniture. He was known to have the first gravity feed fuel pump in the area.

[82] The 4x5 speed graphic was a very popular press camera built around a rugged composite wood steel and aluminum box weighing five pounds when fully equipped. In addition to a front leaf shutter, the camera has a rear focal plane shutter capable of exposures as short as 1/1000 of a second for action shots.

[83] Last page of letter dated May 4, 1943, but dated May 6, 1943

[84] Letter dated May 8, 1943

[85] Letter dated May 8, 1943

[86] Adolph Hitler was born April 20, 1889.

[87] Letter dated May 8, 1943

[88] The farmers in Colusa County that had orchards hired Mexican workers to harvest the fruit. One story shed like structures were usually provided for the workers' sleeping quarters. The sheds had two or three electric lights hanging from knob and tube electrical wiring that was strung across the open ceiling under the ridgepole of the roof. A single switch attached to the wall near the door operated the lights.

[89] Letter dated May 12, 1943

[90] Letter dated May 13, 1943

[91] The toaster was a simple manual design that held two slices of bread, one on each side, within a panel door hinged at the bottom. When the bread that was next to an electrical heating element was toasted, the operator who had to have been watching carefully was then required to open the door, turn the bread over and reclose the door to toast the other side. This device was a big improvement over toasting bread by placing it under a broiler in an electric stove. Automatic pops up toasters were not generally available at this time.

[92] Second letter dated May 13, 1943

[93] Although the Marine Corps established a photo section at Quantico in the fall of 1941, it had no photography school within the Corps. Until the school was established at Quantico, all Marine photographers were trained at civilian or U.S. Navy schools. Even after the establishment of the school at Quantico some students were still sent to other schools.

[94] Bleus was killed over Rabaul in a B-25, Genaust was killed on Iwo Jima, Schultz KIA, Watson killed on Okinawa,

[95] Letter dated May 20, 1943

[96] Second letter dated May 20, 1943

[97] Grant Wolfkill whom Bob met on the train from San Diego to Quantico was one of the three that remained at Quantico. Interview of Wolfkill by the author in 2008.

CHAPTER 6

[98] Letter dated May 26, 1943

[99] Letter dated May 29, 1943

[100] Letter dated May 31, 1943

[101] Letter dated June 3, 1943

[102] Letter to Jim dated June 3, 1943

[103] Grover Klemmer set the world record in the 400 meter race with a time of 46.0 seconds and ran 440 yards in a time of 46.4 seconds in 1941. Harold 'Hal' Davis tied Jesse Owens' world record 0f 10.2 seconds for the 100 meter dash in 1941. He won the AAU 100 yard title three times and the 220 two times. While still in high school Davis ran 100 yards in 9.7 seconds. Cornelius 'Dutch' Warmerdam was the first man in the world to pole vault the 'impossible' height of 15 feet in 1940 using a bamboo pole. Warmerdam was at the meet and Jim witnessed him pole-vaulting over 15 feet.

[104] Letter dated June 9, 1943

[105] Letter dated June 15, 1943

[106] Letter dated June 21, 1943

[107] Letter dated June 21, 1943

[108] Letter dated June 30, 1943 Tuesday

[109] Bertha's diary July 10, 1943

CHAPTER 7

[110] Letter dated July 18, 1943

[111] Harpers Ferry located at the confluence of the Potomac and Shenandoah Rivers in Jefferson County West Virginia was the site John Brown's raid on the Armory in 1859. John Brown was a revolutionary abolitionist who practiced armed resurrection in an attempt to eliminate slavery. Brown was subsequently tried for treason against the state of Virginia and hanged.

[112] Letter dated July 20, 1943

[113] A bill to establish the Women's Army Auxiliary Corps, H.R. 4906 was passed May 15 1942. The women in the organization were neither civilians nor military until it was reorganized and converted to full military status as the Women's Army Corps in late summer 1943.

[114]When President Roosevelt signed a law July 30, 1942 establishing the WAVES., Women who enlisted as WAVES were given full military status . The first-ever female commissioned officer Lt. Cdr. Mildred McAfee was the Director of the organization.

[115] Letter dated July 22, 1943

[116] Letter dated July 24, 1943

[117] Letter dated July 29, 1943

[118] The March of Time was a newsreel series shown in movie theaters from 1935 to 1951. Roy Edward Larsen, a Time Inc. executive, created it.

[119] Letter dated August 5, 1943

[120] Letter dated August 8, 1943

[121] Letter dated August 13, 1943

[122] Letter dated August 16, 1953

[123] Letter dated August 20, 1943

[124] Thayer Soule page 27

[125] Ibid page 146

[126] Ibid page 146

[127] Zorita was a stripper who featured a twenty-minute dance with a Boa Constrictor and a Python.

[128] Letter dated August 28, 1943

CHAPTER 8

[129] Letter dated September 1, 1943

[130] Thayer Soule page 147

[131] Letter dated September 5, 1943

[132] Letter dated September 9, 1943

[133] William H. Genaust eventually became a Sgt. and filmed the raising of the flag on top of Mount Suribachi on Iwo Jima. His movie film was shot from the same angle as Joe Rosenthal's famous picture and provided proof that Rosenthal's picture was not staged as some had claimed.

[134] Letter dated September 11, 1943

[135] Thayer Soule page 148

[136] Letter dated September 12, 1943

[137] Letter dated September 13 & 20, 1943

[138] Letter dated September 23. 1943

[139] Grant Wolfkill became one of Bob's best friends. Grant told the author they met on the train from San Diego to Quantico, although this is the first time Bob mentioned Grant.

[140] Walter Spangler, from Vallejo, worked as a photographer for one of the local newspapers. Bob knew him there.

[141] Ted Gephardt, an All American from the University of Oregon, was the new assistant coach under Kolin Kilby. The old formation was a modified short punt formation with unbalance right or left, but with spaces between left guard and end and also between the right guard, each of the tackles and the right end.

[142] Letter dated September 25, 1943

[143] Letter dated September 30, 1943

[144] Letter dated October 1, 1943

[145] Letter dated October 2, 1943

[146] Letter dated October 4, 1943

[147] Letter dated October 7, 1943

[148] Letter dated October 11, 1943

[149] Letter dated October 12, 1943

[150] Letter dated October 14, 1943

[151] Letter dated October 17, 1943

CHAPTER 9

[152] Letter dated October 20, 1943

[153] Letter dated October 27,1943

[154] Letter dated October 30, 1943

[155] Letter dated November 8, 1943

[156] Letter dated November 10, 1943

[157] Letter dated November 13 & 16, 1943

[158] Letter dated November 20, 1943

[159] Letter dated November 26, 1943

[160] Letter dated November 29, 1943

[161] Thayer Soule, page 149

[162] Letter dated December 2, 1943

[163] Letter dated December 7, 1943

[164] Father Richard R. Houssell was the former priest at the St. Steven's Episcopal Church in Colusa where Bob served as an acolyte.

[165] Letter dated December 9, 1943

[166] Letter dated December 13, 1943

[167] Letter dated December 15, 1943

[168] Letter dated December 18, 1943

[169] Thayer Soule, page 148

[170] Letter dated December 21, 1943

[171] Letter dated December 26, 1943

[172] The ultimate objective was Rabaul, but the Joint Chiefs of Staff ordered Mac Arthur to bypass Rabaul and instead occupy Kavieng in New Ireland and Manus in the Admiralties.

[173] Video interview of Ned Steele made for veteran's project

[174] The battle for Cape Gloucester officially ended on April 22nd with a loss of 310 marines killed and 1,083 wounded.

[175] Letter dated February 21, 1944

[176] Letter dated December 28, 1943

[177] Letter dated December 30, 1943

[178] Letter dated January 4, 1944

[179] Bob picked up on the old journalism method of indicating the end of a story. It started in the 19th century when three XXXs were used to indicate the end of a telegraph message. The Roman numeral for 30 is XXX.

[180] Letter dated January 7, 1944

[181] Letter dated January 10, 1944

[182] Letter dated January 16, 1944

[183] Letter dated January 19, 1944

[184] Letter dated January 24, 1944

[185] E-mail from Norm Hatch to the author in 2008

[186] Letter dated January 27, 1944

[187] Letter dated January 30, 1944

[188] In his book, "Shooting the Pacific War", Soule wrote, "As the weeks slid by, I seldom left the post. Quantico suited my mood perfectly."

[189] Letter dated February 1, 1944

[190] Letter dated February 2, 1944

[191] Letter dated August 16, 1944 from Pat Niedert to Zelda

[192] Letter dated February 4, 1944

[193] Samuel Elliot Morison, The Two Ocean War A short History of the United States Navy in the Second World War (Boston: Little, Brown and Company 1963) page 310

[194] Letter dated February 8, 1944

[195] Letter dated February 13, 1944

[196] Telegram dated February 15, 1944

[197] Letter dated February 15, 1944

[198] Letter dated February 16, 1944

[199] Letter dated February 22, 1944

[200] Letter dated February 26, 1944

[201] Letter dated March 1, 1944

[202] Jim took a bus to San Francisco February 29, 1944 accompanied by his mother; he took the train to Flagstaff, Arizona and reported for duty as an Apprentice Seaman in the Navy V-12a (V-5) Program.

[203] Letter dated March 8, 1944 to Jim who was by then in Co. C. Platoon 3, Navy V-12 Unit ASTC, Flagstaff, Arizona

[204] Letter dated March 9, 1944

[205] Letter dated March 12, 1944

[206] Bob had sent Jim a telegram telling him he would be coming through Flagstaff and suggested that he get a pass so they could see each other. The executive officer of the V-12 unit denied Jim's request. Although Jim had come to appreciate the wisdom of the decision he had an underlying disappointment for years at not being given the chance to see his brother. It wasn't until writing this biography and reading the 12 March letter that he learned Bob did not go through Flagstaff.

[207] Letter dated March 14, 1944

CHAPTER 10

[208] Letter dated March 15, 1944

[209] Letter dated March 5, 1944

[210] E-mail from Zelda in 2009

[211] Ibid

[212] Letter dated April 5, 1944

[213] Letter to Jim dated April 5, 1944

[214] Letter dated April 9, 1944

[215] Letter dated April 10, 1944

[216] Letter dated April 12, 1944

[217] Letter dated April 14, 1944

[218] Letter dated April 17, 1944

[219] Letter to Zelda dated April 17, 1944

[220] Letter to Jim dated April 18, 1944

[221] Jim and Zelda both had Scarlet Fever when they were nine and eight years old respectively. The officers in charge of the V-12 contingent at Arizona State Teachers College at Flagstaff, Arizona in their wisdom sent a detail to clean up the sickbay filled with measles and scarlet fever patients. Jim was in the detail. The consequence was an epidemic of the two diseases that affected at least a third of the contingent.

[222] Long distance telephone service at that time was not efficient. Calls had to be placed with a long distance operator who would wait for clearance to make

the connection. When access was obtained the operator would call the party placing the call and would complete the connection to the party being called.
[223] Letter dated May 4, 1944
[224] V-Mail dated May 14, 1944. Victory Mail was usually a single page about 3 X 4 inches on a side using a process similar to a photocopy.
[225] Letter dated May 18, 1944
[226] Telephone conversation with Harold "Tiger" Palmer in November 2008. Former Lt. Palmer was 92 years old at the time.
[227] Letter dated February 26, 1945
[228] Letter dated May 20, 1944
[229] Theron was a cousin of Bertha Watson and nephew of Ella Capito. Bob used to listen to the University of California football games on the radio. Theron was a lineman on the team and his name was mentioned often.
[230] Raymond Clapper went out with naval striking forces on a mission to bring awareness of the Pacific War to the people at home so that they would know "how much our men are doing and in what a living hell they must sometimes do it." The article that referred to Maj. McDaniel was sent by wireless from Munda, Solomon Islands. Clapper was onboard a naval aircraft when he was killed. His article states in part, "I have just spent an evening in barracks with pilots of the most famous Marine torpedo-plane squadrons in the South Pacific. It is the second oldest in the Marine Corps, and was the first squadron on Henderson Field at Guadalcanal, where it brought down 15 Jap planes in the first ten days."
[231] V-mail dated May 22, 1944
[232] V-mail dated May 29, 1944
[233] V-mail dated May 31, 1944

CHAPTER 11

[234] Henry L. Shaw, Jr., Bernard C. Nalty, Edwin D. Turnbladh, Central Pacific Drive History of the Marine Corps Operations in World War II, Volume III, (Department of the Navy Historical Branch, G-3 Division, Headquarters, U. S. Marine Corps, 1966), Page 455
[235] Letter to Jim dated 8 May 1945 "On Guam I took combat pictures, so I went in with "G" Company 22nd Marines."
[236] Letter dated February 7, 1946 from Hoyt Rhodes, former Sergeant in the Photo Section.
[237] Page 10 of Log Book of the U.S.S. LST 270 9 June 1944
[238] Shaw, Jr., Vol. III, page 455
[239] Log Book of U.S.S. LST 270 page 15 June 15, 1944
[240] V-Mail dated July 2, 1944
[241] Shaw, Jr., Vol. III page 278
[242] Ibid page 299
[243] An island in the Caroline Islands. It is located in the Yap State of the Federated States of Micronesia.

[244] Shaw, Jr., Vol. III, page 292 and Samuel Eliot Morison, <u>New Guinea and the Marianas March 1944-August 1944 History of United States Naval Operations in World War II</u> (Urbana, Il: University of Illinois Press, First Illinois paperback, 2002), page 207.

[245] Conversation with Grant Wolfkill on May 2, 2008.

[246] V-mail dated July 2, 1944 written on board ship about the time Bob arrived at Eniwetok for a chance to go ashore while the forces replenished supplies.

[247] Most of the first sentence was censored, but with the help of modern scanners and computers to decipher the censored words, it is most certain that the italicized words are 90 % correct as confirmed by his later letters.

[248] V-mail dated 14 July

[249] Letter dated July 14, 1944 written on Navy stationery while on board ship. Bob crossed out the United States Navy emblem at the top of the page. He had no Marine Corp stationery.

[250] Henry L. Shaw, et al, page 448

[251] Ibid. Page 448. From 8 July until W day (21 July) a total of 836 rounds of 16 inch, 5,422 14 inch, 3,862 8 inch, 2,430 6 inch, and 16,214 5 inch shells were slammed onto the island.

[252] Henry L. Shaw Jr., et al, Page 458

[253] Ibid

[254] Ibid Page 461

[255] Ibid Page 472

[256] Ibid Page 473

[257] Conversation with Grant Wolfkill May 2, 2008

[258] F-stop or focal or focal ratio, a dimensionless number, determined the quantitative measure of lens speed or the amount of light exposure necessary to properly expose the film.

[259] Henry L. Shaw Jr. et al, Page 473

[260] Ibid Page 475

[261] Ibid Page 483

[262] Ibid Page 494

[263] Ibid Page 496

[264] It is not known for certain that Bob was still with Company G, but based on subsequent letters, the author assumed he was still attached.

[265] V-mail dated July 27, 1944 written on Guam

[266] Shaw Jr. Henry L. et al page 523

[267] V-mail dated July 30, 1944

[268] Peter Maslowski, <u>Armed With Cameras, The American Military Photographers of World War II</u>. (New York: The Free Press, 1993), pp. 228-230. "Ten cameramen made *The First Provisional Brigade on Guam*". "Claude Winkler died filming a dog platoon in action, Martin McEvilly lost his life photographing infantrymen at the front. Howard Foss was moving alongside the lead tank attacking Guam's airfield when a fatal bullet struck him." Maslowski also wrote in detail about Hal Watkins who was wounded three times before he was evacuated.

[269] Letter dated July 31, 1944

[270] In a letter dated August 31, 1944 Bob wrote, "I have a picture of a group of us on Guam. It was made at the Marine Barracks on Orote Peninsula."

[271] Letter dated August 2, 1944

[272] Letter dated August 3, 1944

[273] Telephone conversation with Harold "Tiger" Palmer November 2008

[274] Letter dated August 31, 1944 when Bob was with the 1st Marine Division.

[275] Letter dated August 12, 1944

[276] Letter dated October 15, 1944

[277] MS Weltevreden served Allied supply and troop transport duty in the Pacific during WW II. She was one of 105 foreign flagged merchant ships obtained through the ship Requisition Act of 1941 that operated under the US War Shipping Administration.

CHAPTER 12

[278] George W. Garand and Truman R. Strobridge Western Pacific Operations History of US Marine Corps Operations in World War II Volume IV (Historical Division, Headquarters, U. S. Marine Corps 1971) page 58.

[279] Letter dated 31 August 1944

[280] Letter from Karl Soule dated 3 September 1944 posted in Quantico, VA

[281] Major Halpern was in charge of the III Amphibious Corps Photo Section on Guadalcanal during the battle for Guam.

[282] Soule, page 165

[283] Conversation with Grant Wolfkill May 2, 2008

[284] Communication film assignment, addressed to all photographers, from the III Amphibious Corps Headquarters, from detailed instructions extant in Bob's effects.

[285] Max Hastings, Retribution The Battle for Japan, 1944-45 (New York: Alfred A. Knopf, 2008), page 113

[286] LST 734 Deck Log- Remarks Sheet Friday 15 September 1944

[287] Garand and Strobridge Page 108

[288] Gunfire directed from either flank along the length of a column or line of troops.

[289] From a video taped interview of Ned Steele who was a Sgt. assigned to First Division Headquarters Company Intelligence unit during the battle for Peleliu.

[290] Henry Berry Semper Fi, Mac Living Memories of U. S. Marines in World War II (New York: William Morrow) page 72

[291] Staff Sergeant Norman Hatch shot some of the earliest Marine Corps combat movie footage of WW II during the amphibious assault on Tarawa. The resulting film 'With the Marines on Tarawa" won the 1944 Academy Award for Most Outstanding Documentary Short Subject. Hatch made the only known shot of enemy forces and American troops in the same frame. He was awarded the Navy Commendation Medal for his outstanding work.

[292] Garand and Strobridge Page 119

293 Ibid, Page 120

294 Ibid, Page 131

295 Ibid Page 132

296 Ibid Page 145

297 Ibid Page 145

298 Conversation with Grant Wolfkill May 2, 2008

299 Ibid

300 Letter to Jimmie and Rita Turner dated October 19 1944

301 Bob's Service Record recorded the following: "Sep 44 WIA & evac."

302 Letter to Jim dated 15 October 1944, "I landed with the 2nd wave and was evacuated the 6th day because of a slight cheek wound."

303 Mable Tyrrell wrote to Bob's parents on October 7, 1944 telling about the encounter, "We received an 'Air Mail' letter from Georgie this noon from somewhere in the South Pacific telling us he had seen Bob for a few minutes. Bob was in on the last engagement but came out O.K. You can figure that out. We think that means Peleliu. He was leaving for another destination and said he hadn't had time to write home." Bob also mentioned the visit in two letters dated 15 October 1944.

304 Transcribed in a letter from Dorothy Silverthorne to Bertha Watson dated October 13, 1944

305 Letter dated 24 September 1944 from Captain Karl Soule posted in Quantico, VA

306 Letter dated September 27, 1944

307 Letter dated October 8, 1944 addressed to "Dear Folks"

308 Letter dated October 15. 1944 addressed to "Dear Folks"

309 Letter dated October 17, 1944

310 Letter dated February 7, 1946 written to Mr. Earle Watson and mailed from San Jose, California. On the other hand, Bob's service record states that he returned to Guadalcanal on 26 September 1944.

311 Letter dated October 19, 1944 addressed to the Rita and Jimmie Turner, neighbors and landlords of the family flat in Vallejo.

312 Ira, an engineer working at Mare Island Navy Yard, rented a room from the Turners.

313 Lew Lehr was a comedian that we watched on Fox Movie Tone News. He often ended his segment with the catchphrase, "Monkeys is the cwaziest peoples."

314 From video taped interview of Ned Steele.

315 Jim Moran and Gordon Rottman, Peleliu 1944 The forgotten corner of hell.(New York Osprey Publishing Ltd., 2002) Page 89.

CHAPTER 13

316 Bill Sloan, The Ultimate Battle Okinawa 1945-The Last Epic Struggle of World War II, (New York Simon & Shuster) page 12

317 Max Hastings, Retribution The Battle for Japan 1944-45 (New York Alfred A. Knopf 2008), page 97

318 Ibid page 95

[319] Ibid page 96

[320] Richard Wheeler <u>A Special Valor The U.S. Marines and the Pacific War</u> <u>(New York: Harper and Row 1983)</u> page 311

[321] Samuel Eliot Morison, <u>The Two Ocean War A Short History of the United States Navy in the Second World War</u> (Boston : Little, Brown and Company 1963), page 435

[322] Ibid Page 436

[323] Letter dated 25 October 1944 from Hq. Co. Hq. Bn. 1st Marine Division.

[324] Visit of Captain Soule on October 15 mentioned in Chapter Eleven. The different time zone may have accounted for the discrepancy in the date of the visit.

[325] A $25 war bond sold for $18.75 and was worth the face value at maturity. Bob made three monthly payments of $6.25 to buy each bond.

[326] Letter dated 28 October 1944

[327] A podiatrist in Vallejo and also skipper of the Vallejo Sea Scouts, but now in the Army.

[328] Letter dated October 30, 1944

[329] Henry Berry page 97

[330] Letter dated November 1, 1944

[331] Letter dated November 8, 1944

[332] Letter dated November 10, 1944

[333] Letter dated November 14, 1944

[334] George Tyrrell confirmed to the author in 2008 that he had seen Bob on Manus Island

[335] Letter to Turners dated November 14, 1944

[336] Letter dated November 16, 1944

[337] Letter dated November 26, 1944

[338] Pioneer Hall Navy V-12 Unit, Univ. of Minn. Minneapolis, Minn.

[339] Letter dated November 19, 1944

[340] Letter dated November 30, 1944

[341] Island of Pavuvu in the Russell's with the First Division after leaving Peleliu

[342] Letter dated December 1, 1944

[343] Letter dated December 1, 1944

[344] Letter dated December 12, 1944

[345] Richard Wheeler, page 319

[346] Letter dated December 31, 1944

[347] From letter dated December 19, 1944

[348] Letter date December 21, 1944

[349] Letter dated December 24, 1944

[350] Letter dated December 30, 1944

[351] Letter dated January 4, 1945

[352] Letter dated January 6, 1945

[353] Benis M. Frank and Henry L. Shaw Jr., <u>Victory and Occupation History of U.S. Marine Corps in World War II Volume V,</u> (Historical Branch, G-3 Division, Headquarters, U. S. Marine Corps, 1968), pp. 88-90

[354] Ibid

[355] Gordon L. Rottman, <u>U.S. Marine Corps WW II Oder of Battle: Ground and Air Units in the Pacific War 1939-1945,</u> (Westport, CT: Greenwood Publishing Group Incorporated, 2002) page 358

[356] Benis M. Frank and Henry Shaw Jr., pp. 88-90

[357] Ibid page 89

[358] Letter dated January 14, 1945

[359] Letter dated January 16, 1945

[360] Letter dated January 19, 1945

[361] Letter dated January 20, 1945

[362] Letter dated January 26, 1945

[363] Letter dated February 1, 1945

[364] Atabrine, a synthetic drug used to combat malaria as a replacement for quinine, was distributed to American troops stationed on the South Pacific islands. Complaints against the yellow pills became common. Atabrine was bitter, appeared to impart its own sickly hue to the skin. Some of its side effects were headaches, nausea, and vomiting, and in a few cases it produced a temporary psychosis. Source: http://home.att.net/~steinert/wwii.htm The radio show took its name from the Atabrine pill.

[365] Letter dated February 5, 1945

[366] Letter dated February 12, 1945

[367] The movie, made in 1944, was based on a Pearl S. Buck story about a band of local villagers who fight back against Japanese occupiers in the years before World War II. The villagers are led by an outspoken Jade Tan, played by Katherine Hepburn.

[368] Letter dated February 15, 1945

[369] Letter dated February 15, 1945

[370] Letter dated February 17, 1945

[371] Thayer Soule, pp. 190-191

[372] Ibid page 210

[373] Samuel Eliot Morison <u>The Two Ocean War</u>, page 524

[374] Letter dated February 22, 1945

[375] Stan McWilliams served in the Army from February 1945 for 22 months. He returned to C.O.P. where he excelled in baseball and basketball. After graduation in 1950, the Boston Red Sox drafted him as a pitcher. Stan played seven years in the minor league system and in 1951 was named the top pitcher in the California league with a 23-10 record and a 2.55 ERA for San Jose. McWilliams coached successfully at Vallejo Junior College (now Solano Community College): baseball for 29 years and basketball for 22 years. Stan died April 7, 2008.

[376] Letter dated February 26, 1945

CHAPTER 14

[377] Benis. M. Frank and Henry L. Shaw Jr., page 60

[378] Ibid, page 70

[379] Letter from Hoyt Rhodes to Mr. (Earle) Watson dated February 7, 1946

[380] Letter dated March 1, 1945

[381] Benis M. Frank and Henry L. Shaw Jr., page 93

[382] Letter from Hoyt Rhodes to Mr. (Earle) Watson dated February 7, 1946. Bob's service record, obtained from the National Personnel Records Center, states, "15 Mar 45 sailed from Guadalcanal, S. I. via USS Circle. 1 Apr arr Okinawa, R.I." The USS Circle, AKA-25 was actually named Circe after the asteroid 34 Circe. According to HyperWar: World War II on the World Wide Web, Circe sailed from Honolulu on January 23, 1945 for Guadalcanal with Marine reinforcements and ammunition, ferried troops in the area through February, then after practice landings at Savo Sound staged at Ulithi and sailed for Okinawa on 21 March. The log of LST 892, a record of the ships activities during that period, is consistent with time lines based on Rhode's and Bob's letters. The service record has to be in error.

[383] LST 892 Deck Log-Remarks Sheet page 15 Friday 9 March 1945

[384] Ibid page 17

[385] Ibid page 23

[386] Ibid page 26

[387] Ibid page 27

[388] Letter dated March 23, 1945

[389] This begs the question: Where was the dark room? Did he and Rhodes manage to set up a temporary facility on the LST?

[390] Benis M. Frank and Henry L. Shaw Jr., page 94

[391] Deck Log LST-892 Tuesday 27 March 1945

[392] From letter dated March 30, 1945

[393] M1911 single-action, semi-automatic, magazine fed, and recoil operated 45 caliber hand gun

[394] Letter dated May 8, 1945

[395] Letter dated February 7, 1946

[396] From letter dated April 5, 1945

[397] Hoyt Rhode wrote in a letter dated February 7, 1946 that they landed on April 3, 1945. Bob wrote April 3 in one letter and April 4 in an other.

[398] Bob had landed with the second wave on Guam and Peleliu and expected to do the same on Okinawa.

[399] Letter dated April 13, 1945

[400] Frank M. Benis, and Henry L. Shaw Jr., page 92

[401] Ibid Page 77

[402] Ibid page 145

[403] Ibid page 148

[404] Ibid page 154

[405] From letter dated April 18, 1945

[406] Benis M. Frank and Shaw Jr., Henry I. page 155

[407] Ibid page 155, Smith Personal Narrative page 82

[408] Letter to Jim dated April 21, 1945

[409] Jim was stationed at Naval Air Station Glenview outside Chicago, IL waiting for assignment to Navy Pre-flight School. He was called a "Tarmac" and his principal duties were to crank the inertial starter on Stearman

Biplanes, so flying cadets could start the engine, directing the parking of the airplanes using hand signals and washing the airplanes. Barnstorming refers to the acrobatic flying done at low altitudes by pilots after WW I, typically using the Jenny training aircraft.

[410] Benis M. Frank and Henry L. Shaw Jr., page 188

[411] Ibid page 192

[412] Letter to Rita and Jimmy Turner dated April 24, 1945

[413] Letter dated April 24, 1945

[414] Glen Chittenden letter to Mr. & Mrs. Watson dated June 19, 1945

[415] Benis M. Frank and Henry L. Shaw Jr., page 197

[416] Letter dated April 30, 1945 to Mr. and Mrs. Phil Niedert

[417] From letter dated May 2, 1945

[418] Benis M. Frank and Henry L. Shaw Jr., page 209

[419] Ibid page 213

[420] Letter dated May 8, 1945

[421] Letter to Bob dated May 9, 1945; Bob never received the letter.

[422] Letter to Jim dated May 8, 1945

[423] The Japanese stationery was similar to tissue paper with a red border outlining the writing area that was divided by red horizontal lines. There was Japanese writing in the center right section of each page.

[424] Letter dated May 8, 1945

[425] From letter dated May 8, 1945 addressed to Mr. and Mrs. Niedert

[426] Telephone conversation with George Tyrrell 2008

[427] Letter dated May 24, 1945, a letter to Bob that he never received. Earle was assigned to Planning for submarine repair. At the time of the letter he was assigned two submarines with a third coming in.

[428] Benis M. Frank and Henry L. Shaw Jr., page 223: General Shepherd, Commanding General Sixth Division, called the bridge building a splendid feat of combat engineering.

[429] Ibid page 231

[430] Letter date May 16, 1945

[431] Bob had been shooting black and white 35mm film using the larger and heavier Bell and Howell Eyemo camera. Captain Soule had been promoting the use of the smaller and lighter 16mm camera using color film, which was now becoming the standard.

[432] The U. S. Government seized Agfa Ansco a German company operating in the United States during the war and Treasury agents supervised operations of the company. The user could process Ansco color film whereas Kodachrome had to be processed in a factory, which required weeks. All Ansco film produced during the war was requisitioned by the military.

[433] Benis M. Frank and Henry Shaw Jr., page 252

[434] Letter from Glenn Chittenden to Mr. and Mrs. Watson dated June 19, 1945

[435] Benis M. Frank and Henry L. Shaw Jr., page 252

[436] Ibid page 253

[437] Annex A to Sixth Marine Division Special Action Report Phase III Okinawa Operation 4th Marines

[438] Letter dated May 20, 1945; postmarked 27 May 1945

[439] The Claremont Hotel established in 1915 was located in the Berkeley Hills near San Francisco. A radio broadcast of a big band dance was featured regularly on the radio during WW II.

[440] Letter to Mr. and Mrs. Watson dated August 7, 1945

[441] Interview with Grant Wolfkill in 2008

[442] Benis M. Frank M. and Henry L. Shaw Jr., page 273

[443] Annex F to Sixth Marine Division Special Action Report Phase III Okinawa Operation 6t Engineer Battalion page III-3

[444] Sixth Marine Division Special Action Report Okinawa Operation Report Phase III 30 June 1945 page III-12

[445] Sixth Marines in the Field Journal From: 0001 24 May 45 To: 2400 24 May 45, page 4

[446] Letter dated June 19, 1945 from Glen Chittenden to Mr. and Mrs. Watson

[447] USMC Casualty Report 31 May45, Casualty No. 048305.

[448] The Muster Rolls May 1945 U. S. Marine Corps that included the III Amphibious Corps for the period 1May to 31 May 1945 lists Sgt. Watson, Robert L (Photo) Died, Headquarters Company, See Addendum "E". Addendum E reads "1-23 (May) Forward Echelon, Okinawa, Ryuku Islands; 24 (May) KIA; not misconduct; char Exc; 24, remains interred in 6th Mar Div Cemetery, Row #16, Grave #400, Plot "B." Apparently someone keeping records lost track of Bob and thought he was not accounted for and wrote a misconduct report that was corrected when the true situation was determined.

CHAPTER 15

[449] Letter dated June 2, 1945

[450] Letter dated December 7, 1945

[451] Letter dated June 5, 1945 from A. A. Vandergrift General, U.S.M.C. Commandant of the Marine Corps

[452] Benis M. Frank and Shaw Jr., Henry I. page 278

[453] Ibid page 284

[454] Ibid page 298

[455] Ibid page 320

[456] Ibid page 369

[457] Letter dated June 16, 1945

[458] Kolon Kilby's Comments, Sports Section Vallejo Times Herald Friday, June 15, 1945

[459] Letter dated June 25, 1945

[460] Letter dated June 18, 1945

[461] Letter dated July 24, 1945

[462] Letter dated July 25, 1945

[463] Letter dated August 7, 1945

[464] Letter dated August 7, 1945

[465] Letter dated January 23, 1946

[466] Burton Holmes, famous before the war as a producer of travelogues

[467] Vallejo Times Herald of December 2, 1946

[468] Letter from Commandant of the Marine Corps dated March 25, 1948

GLOSSARY-SHIP CONFIGURATIONS

1. Troop Transport, APA

    A typical APA had a length of 475 feet, beam of 61 feet and a speed of 15 knots. The crew consisted of 37 officers and 416 enlisted men. It had accommodations for troops that totaled 37 officers and 917 enlisted men. Typical armament included two single six inch gun mounts, two twin 40 mm anti-aircraft gun mounts, or in some configurations four single three inch/50 caliber dual purpose gun mounts instead of the fore and aft six inch gun mounts.

2. Landing Ship Tank, LST

    A Landing Ship Tank was 328 feet long, beam of 56 feet and a forward draft of 8 feet 2 inches and 14 feet 1 inch aft. Maximum speed was only 9 knots or 10.4 miles per hour when fully loaded, providing a range of 6000 miles. A maximum of 2100 tons could be carried in the tank deck well, along with cargo carried on the weather deck. The tank deck was 258 feet long and 30 feet wide enabling it to carry tanks and trucks loaded side by side or in single rows. LSTs were fitted with boat davits fitted to handle embarked Landing Craft Vehicle, Personnel (LCVP) or Landing Craft Personnel (LCP). Normal armament consisted of two 40 mm Bofors cannon twin mounts, four 40 mm single mounts, 12 20mm Oerlikon canon single mounts, and .30 caliber and .50 caliber machine guns for increased anti aircraft protection.

3. Landing Craft, Vehicle, Personnel

    An LCVP (Higgins Boat) was 35 feet 9 inches long and 10 feet 6 inches in the beam. Maximum speed was 12 knots lightly loaded and nine knots with a full load of 26,600 pounds. The crew normally consisted of a coxswain, a mechanic and a crew hand. When equipped, armament included two .30 or .50 caliber machine guns. An LCV could carry a single one-ton truck and 36 fully armed troops. The LCP, the approximate size of the LCV, had a speed of nine knots and carried 25 fully loaded .30 and one .50 caliber machine gun with a crew of three, the LVT carried 24 troops.

3. Landing Craft Mechanized

An LCM (3) was 50 feet long and 14 feet in the beam. Maximum speed was rated   at 8 knots when fully loaded. The displacement was 104,000 fully loaded and 52,000 pounds light. Its range was 140 miles fully loaded at maximum speed. The maximum range was 850 miles cruising at six knots. The crew consisted of   a coxswain and two gunners manning .50 caliber Browning machine guns. The LCM with a cargo well 31 feet long and 10 feet wide was designed to carry and land a 30 ton tank or motor vehicles on the beach. An adaptation fitted with rocket racks was designated Landing Craft Mechanized (Rocket).

5. Landing Craft Tank

The LCT was 114 feet 2 inches long and 32 feet in the beam. The displacement was 283 tons fully loaded and 133 tons light. The LCT cargo deck was 90 feet long and had the capacity to carry five 30 ton tanks, four 40 tons, three 50 ton or nine trucks. The maximum speed was 8 knots with a range of 1200 nautical miles. The crew consisted of one officer and 11 sailors. Armament included two single barrel Oerlikon dual purpose anti aircraft and anti surface cannon.

6. Landing Vehicle Tracked (Amphtrack)

The LVT was 26 feet long and 10 feet 8 inches in the beam. Speed on land was 20 mph and 8.6 knots on water. The LVT carried a crew of three and 30 troops and was able to land on the beach and proceed in land. The main armament was two .50 caliber Browning machine guns supplemented by two .30-06 Browning machine guns. After the Battle for Tarawa, LVT's were armored and another version known as gun-armed "Amtanks" or LVT (A) carried a 75-millimeter howitzer.

BIBLIOGAPHY

Adcock, Al WW II US Landing Craft in Action Squadron/Signal Publications, Inc. 2003

Annex A to Sixth Marine Division Special Action Report, Phase III Okinawa Operation. 4th Marines. 30 June 1945

Berry, Henry Semper Fi, Mac Living Memories of the U.S. Marines in World War II Quill William Morrow New York 1982

Bix, Herbert P. Hirohito and the Making of Modern Japan Harper Collins 2000

Frank, Benis M. and Shaw Jr., Henry I. Victory and Occupation History of U.S. Marine Corps Operations WW II Volume V Historical Branch, G-3 Division Headquarters, U.S. Marine Corps 1968

Garand, George W. and Strobridge, Truman R. Western Pacific Operations History of U. S. Marine Corps Operations in World War II Volume IV Historical Division, Headquarters, U.S. Marine Corps 1971

Hallas, James H. Devil's Anvil The Assault on Peleliu Praeger Publishers 1994

Hallas, James H. Killing Ground on Okinawa "The Battle for Sugar Loaf Hill" Prager Publishers 1966

Hastings, Max Retribution The Battle for Japan, 1944-45 Alfred A. Knopf New York 2008

Hosokawa, William Kumpai Nisei: The Quiet Americans University Press of Colorado 1969

Jersey, Stanley Coleman Hell's Islands The Untold Story of Guadalcanal Texas A&M Press 2008

Kennedy, David M. Freedom From Fear The American People in Depression and War 1929-1945 Oxford University Press 1999

Korda, Michael With Wings Like Eagles The Untold Story of the Battle of Britain Success Research Corporation 2009, hard cover by Harper Collins

Lodge, O. R. Major, USMC The Recapture of Guam, Historical

Branch G-3 Division Headquarters U.S. Marine Corps 1954

Miller, Edward S. Bankrupting the Enemy, The U.S. Financial Siege of Japan Before Pearl Harbor, Naval Institute Press, Annapolis, Maryland

Miller, Thomas G. The Cactus Air Force, Harper & Row, Publishers 1969

Morison, Samuel Eliot, The Two Ocean War, A Short History of the United States Navy in the Second World War, Atlantic Little, Brown, 1963

Morison, Samuel Eliot, History of United States Naval Operations in World War II Volume Eight New Guinea and the Marianas March 1944-August 1944 University of Illinois Press 1953, Paper Back 2002

Muster Rolls U. S. Marine Corps Vol. 13 Fleet Marine Force No. 7, III Amphibious Corps, AAA Battalions, Defense Battalions May 1945

Shaw, Jr. Henry I. Central Pacific Drive History of U.S. Marine Corps Operations in World War II Volume III, Historical Branch, G-3 Division Headquarters, U. S. Marine Corps 1966

Shock, James R. The U.S. Army Barrage Balloon Program Military Monograph 315, Merriam Press, 2006

Sixth Marine Division in the Field Journal From 0001 23 May to 2400 May 1945

Sledge, E. B. With The Old Breed at Peleliu and Okinawa Oxford University Press 1981 by Presidio Press

Sloan, Bill Brotherhood of Heroes The Marines at Peleliu, 1944-The Bloodiest Battle of the Pacific War Simon & Schuster Paperbacks, 2005

Soule, Thayer Shooting The Pacific War Marine Corps Combat Photography in WW II The University Press of Kentucky 2000

Wheeler, Richard A special Valor The U.S. Marines and the Pacific War, Naval Institute Press, Annapolis, Maryland 1983, First Blue Jacket Books Edition 2006.

Wukovits, John One Square Mile of Hell The Battle for Tarawa, New American Library a Division of Penguin Books 2006